WICKED GOOD YEAR

HOW THE **RED SOX**, **PATRIOTS** & **CELTICS** TURNED THE HUB OF THE UNIVERSE INTO THE CAPITAL OF SPORTS

STEVE BUCKLEY

itbooks

AN IMPRINT OF HARPERCOLLINS*PUBLISHERS*

HarperCollins books may be purchased for educational, business, or sales promotional use. For information please write: Special Markets Department, HarperCollins Publishers, 10 East 53rd Street, New York, NY 10022.

FIRST EDITION

Designed by Ashley Halsey

Library of Congress Cataloging-in-Publication Data has been applied for.

ISBN 978-0-06-178738-6

09 10 11 12 13   OV/RRD   10 9 8 7 6 5 4 3 2 1

In memory of my big brother, Paul Buckley.
And in celebration of the birth of his beautiful granddaughter,
Ella Josephine Buckley.

CONTENTS

1

DUCK BOATS

Used to be it wasn't a parade in this town if it didn't include a collection of politicians—various Kennedys and Curleys, Fitzgeralds and Flynns—cheerfully waving to the crowd as the procession made its way through town.

But that all changed with the championships—lots and lots of championships, thus inspiring lots and lots of parades. Only now they were being called "rolling rallies," a trendy term dreamt up by someone down at City Hall, mere "parades" being so twentieth-century. And while the politicians could be counted on to be somewhere in the middle of these modern-day victory marches, smiling, waving, desperately looking for the cameras, the real draws, the only draws, were the athletes: the ace pitcher with the bloodied sock who vowed to win a championship . . . and did; the star quarterback who had yet to reach his thirtieth birthday but already was being compared with Hall of Famer Joe Montana; the power forward so . . . well, so powerful that the day he arrived in town was the day the preseason prognosticators were inspired to upgrade his team from also-ran to championship *contendah*.

But the ace pitcher with the bloodied sock had had his rolling rally. Two of them. The star quarterback, too, had been down these urban roads—three times in five seasons. Now it was time for the powerful power forward and *his* team to get a rolling rally.

And as he held the championship trophy of the National Basketball Association high over his head on this sunny, mid-June morning in

2008, the powerful power forward, Kevin Garnett, could not stop think-ing about his coach, Doc Rivers: a modern man, yes, yet a modern man whose motivational techniques were more in keeping with cornball stuff taken directly from the 1930s radio serials.

Doc Rivers had not merely *talked about* a rolling rally back on Sep-tember 25, 2007, which was when the Celtics swung open the training-camp doors. No, talking would have been too easy. Instead, Rivers held a damned dress rehearsal, actually took his top players down to Rolling Rally Central and said, "Let me show you."

Garnett had no idea what was going on that morning, back when Rivers, beginning his fourth season as head coach of the Boston Celtics, invited him over to his apartment for a "meeting." Okay, so maybe Gar-nett *said* he understood, back then, if only because he was new in town, having only recently been obtained by the Celtics in a blockbuster trade with the Minnesota Timberwolves. But, really, he had to see it, feel it.

And now, nine months later, on this bright, celebratory morning, Garnett turned around and looked behind him—the first time he had looked back since joining the Celtics. And what he saw became a snap-shot of the mind he will carry with him for the rest of his days: A sea of green, he said to himself. Thousands of people, all of them in green, all of them cheering, all together. Many more vehicles trailed behind him, eighteen in all, carrying other members of the world champion Boston Celtics, along with the owners, the front-office folks, various hangers-on, and, of course, the politicians. All being mobbed, all being cheered.

Sea of green, Garnett said to himself again, and then he laughed.

Yes, this was it.

This was what Doc had in mind.

Had Garnett been able to see through all the green confetti that was exploding from a collection of sideline gizmos and blanketing the streets as the rolling rally moved along, he might have been able to lock eyes with Ray Allen.

No chance. Garnett was near the front, and Ray Allen, well, Ray Allen was back there, somewhere, amid all the green, riding atop one of the other vehicles.

And he was thinking about Carnegie Hall, Ray Allen was, as the rolling rally continued its slow, steady, two-mile march from Causeway Street to Copley Square.

"How do you get to Carnegie Hall?" the old joke begins.

"Practice, practice," the old joke ends.

Only to Ray Allen, it's not a joke. A child of the military—his father, Walt, was an Air Force mechanic—Ray Allen lived in California and Oklahoma, Germany and Great Britain, before the family settled in South Carolina. And at every stop along the way, his mother, Flora, nudged him toward piano lessons, forever making with the grand, hopeful speech about how it would all lead to Carnegie Hall.

But you have to practice, practice, Flora always told him. You have to sacrifice. Nothing comes easy.

Years later, Ray Allen listened to an updated, retooled-for-basketball version of the speech about practice, about sacrifice. Only now he was a professional basketball player, newly acquired by the Celtics from the Seattle Sonics. And now he was standing in the lobby of an apartment building as Doc Rivers, armed with his plot line from the 1930s radio serial, made the speech.

And then Doc Rivers said, "Come on, let's go for a ride."

Now, on this sunny June morning, nine months later, Ray Allen was taking that same ride again.

He had made it, he told himself.

Carnegie Hall.

Before Kevin Garnett had figured it out, before Ray Allen had figured it out, Paul Pierce was able to put the pieces together.

He, too, had made the trip to Doc Rivers's apartment that morning nine months earlier, having been told he had to be there for a "meeting." He, too, had wondered what the fuss was all about.

But Kevin Garnett and Ray Allen, for all their collective worldly experience as National Basketball Association superstars, were new in town. Not so with Pierce. On the cusp of beginning his tenth season in the NBA, he had spent his entire career in Boston—which is to say, he understood the city's many rites and traditions, some of them quaint, some of them quirky, some of them so off the charts it was doubtful he'd ever attempted to explain them to his friends back home in Inglewood, California.

This "meeting" he had figured out. Though not at first. When Doc Rivers's administrative assistant, Annmarie Loffin, called Pierce and asked if he could join the head coach of the Boston Celtics at his apartment for this . . . this . . . meeting, and when she added that, oh, by the way, the newly acquired tandem of Kevin Garnett and Ray Allen had also been instructed to attend, he assumed it would be a bull session, lots of X's and O's jotted down on napkins at the kitchen table, routine stuff, nothing more.

That morning, as they stood in the lobby of Doc Rivers's apartment building on Huntington Avenue in Boston's Back Bay, across from the Prudential Tower, the coach pointed to an odd-looking vehicle idling out on the street, and that's when Paul Pierce laughed. He had it figured out.

"I want you to know what happens when you win a championship in this town," Rivers said to three basketball players who had amassed lots of personal glory and lots of money over the years but who had never come close to winning a championship.

"Get on," he said. "We're going for a ride."

When the Allies invaded Normandy on June 6, 1944, more than two thousand specially designed amphibious vehicles, nicknamed "Ducks" by American GIs, were used to transport troops and supplies to shore. After France was liberated, British prime minister Winston Churchill, King George VI, and French general Charles DeGaulle were all brought to shore on Ducks.[1]

These blocky, homely looking vehicles had served their country with honor and distinction. When the war was over, they were not unlike the soldiers they had carried to shore on the beaches of Normandy: they returned home looking for a job. As near as anybody can figure, the civilian Ducks were first used for tourism purposes in Wisconsin Dells, Wisconsin, to take passengers on wilderness trails and then down the Wisconsin River to the beach at Lake Delton. The company, still in business, is called the Original Wisconsin Ducks.

The Ducks came to Boston in 1994, when their owners began selling sightseeing trips throughout the city, including a "splashdown" and cruise along the Charles River that offered views of both the Boston and Cambridge skylines. The people at what is now Boston Duck Tours don't much like it when their vehicles are called Duck Boats—"They're Ducks," corrects Cindy Brown, who runs the company—but the masses have ruled otherwise. Folks just call them the Duck Boats.

However one chooses to address these heroic if unheralded veterans of World War II, they are wildly popular in Boston. Each Duck Boat has a given name that either is cleverly alliterative or plays off some facet of Boston history—*Commonwealth Curley, Olga Ironsides,* and *Copley Squire* are but a few—and each has a driver, or "con-duck-tor," whose own name is just as goofy: Major Tom Foolery . . . Paul Reverse . . . Ace Bandage.

After a young quarterback named Tom Brady led the Patriots to a 20–17 victory over the St. Louis Rams in Super Bowl XXXVI, the Duck Boats were deployed on the morning of February 5, 2002, for a joyous victory procession through the Back Bay. The Pats used the Duck Boats for their next two Super Bowl celebrations, and the Red Sox climbed aboard after winning the 2004 World Series—the team's first championship since 1918.

Doc Rivers caught part of the 2004 rolling rally for the Red Sox from his apartment. He stood there, looking out his window, watching the parade pass him by.

Three years later, looking for a motivational edge as the rebuilt 2007–2008 Boston Celtics were beginning training camp, he paid $750 out of his own pocket to charter a Duck Boat. The man had a plan.

At precisely eight o'clock that September morning, longtime Boston Duck Tours con-duck-tor Charlie Perry, or Admiral Amnesia when he's on the clock, knowing only that he was to pick up a private party for a tour of the city, pulled up in front of Rivers's apartment in the only Duck Boat he'll drive, a battleship-gray World War II relic now being addressed in polite society as *Haymarket Hannah.*

A lifelong Boston sports fan who grew up on Cape Cod—when he was a kid, his father took him to Game 3 of the 1986 World Series at Fenway Park—Perry immediately recognized Paul Pierce when the four men came out of the building.

Rivers did the talking, explaining that he wanted Perry to take them on a ride through the city, including some of the streets on which the Patriots and Red Sox had traveled during their various championship celebrations. Perry, stepping into his Admiral Amnesia character, explained that he had a policy he absolutely had to enforce before allowing anyone to step aboard *Haymarket Hannah*.

"You have to quack like a duck," Admiral Amnesia said. "Three times."

It was going on twenty-two years since the Celtics last won a championship. Nothing else had worked. What the hell.

"Quack, quack, quack," they all said, going along for the ride before going along for the ride.

Admiral Amnesia started the motor.

The good admiral didn't say much. Though asked to point out a landmark here and there—the State House, Boston Common, King's Chapel Burial Ground—he otherwise refrained from diving into the touristy spiel he'd been delivering for twelve years.

Garnett, forming a bond with *Haymarket Hannah* and sounding a lot like Will Smith as he piloted the aliens' spaceship in *Independence Day*, said, "I have got to get me one of these!"

"Well, then go out and buy one," said Pierce.

"I don't have any place to keep it," he said.

"With all the money you make," said Pierce, "just build a garage for it."

Showing his passengers what *Haymarket Hannah* was capable of, Admiral Amnesia did a splashdown in the Charles River before returning to the Back Bay.

Finally, he asked Doc Rivers if he could speak. Sure, Rivers said. Admiral Amnesia explained to the group that his father-in-law, Don Rice, who had played basketball at Colby College in Waterville, Maine, back in the fifties and later coached the high school team in tiny Bucksport, Maine, and at Greenfield Community College in western Massachusetts, adhered to a long-held opinion that a team must have two key ingredients if it has any hope of being successful.

Nobody said anything.

"Fundamentals and execution," Admiral Amnesia said anyway, quoting the legendary Don Rice. "That's what it takes. Fundamentals and execution."

Pierce, Allen, and Garnett laughed, the joke being that three top-of-the-line professional basketball players, due to earn a combined $56 million in the coming season, were getting advice on what it takes to win from a tour bus driver who called himself Admiral Amnesia.

The only one not laughing was Doc Rivers.

"When good advice is given," Rivers would later say, "it doesn't make much difference where it comes from. I'll listen to anybody if they're making sense."

When the trip ended and *Haymarket Hannah* came to a stop back at Huntington Avenue, Rivers opened up his wallet, pulled out every last piece of folding money he had, and gave the wad to Admiral Amnesia.

2

ESCAPE FROM LOSERVILLE

L oserville.

It was not a place but a state of mind. And it had become Boston's newest and meanest nickname, an unflattering billboard at the edge of town warning ye sports fans to abandon all hope who enter here.

Popularized by *Boston Herald* sports columnist and WEEI talk-show host Gerry Callahan to describe the state of affairs with Boston's sports teams, Loserville was short, catchy, and unflatteringly, embarrassingly perfect.

"Boston has become the skid row of professional sports, a sad, squalid place where playoff pipe dreams go to die," Callahan wrote in an October 18, 2000, column. "Here we sit in Loserville, USA, wallowing in regret and misery, wishing someday we might find out what it's like to be Oakland, Seattle or even St. Louis."[1]

The beginnings of Loserville trace back to October 1999, with the Red Sox taking on their forever rivals from New York, the Yankees, in the American League Championship Series (ALCS). It was a series trumpeted as the first-ever postseason showdown between the Red Sox and Yankees, the 1978 American League East playoff game between the two teams having technically gone into the books as a regular-season affair. In 1999 the Yankees made it to the ALCS after completing what had become a sort of postseason limbering-up exercise for them in recent years, which is to say they beat the Texas Rangers in the

Division Series, with former Red Sox ace Roger Clemens submitting seven shutout innings in the finale.

For the Red Sox, getting to the ALCS was not so easy. They received four shutout innings from *their* ace pitcher, Pedro Martinez, in the opener of their Division Series against the Cleveland Indians, and it was a good sign: everybody agreed that the team's World Series hopes depended on their Dominican Dandy, whose 23–4 record during the regular season remains one of the best in modern baseball history.

But Martinez suffered a back sprain while throwing a pitch in the fourth inning, and then aggravated his injury while covering first base on a grounder hit by the Indians' David Justice to end the inning. He came out of the game. The Red Sox lost 3–2.

As the *Herald* put it, "Now the superhuman Martinez is idled by a malady that's so very human: He's got a sore back."[2] Martinez was out, for how long nobody knew, and Boston's playoff prospects were further dampened when the Indians rolled to an 11–1 victory in Game 2. Even if the Red Sox could climb back and tie the series, a report in the *Herald* looked at the big picture: "While Martinez was initially listed as day-to-day, Sox hopes for their first World Series title since 1918 will obviously be dealt a severe [fatal?] blow if he is lost for any length of time."[3]

But the Sox rallied for two straight victories, including a 23–7 steamrolling of the Tribe in Game 4 on a gray, overcast Sunday night at Fenway Park, sending the series back to Cleveland for a Monday night Game 5.

What happened that night at Jacobs Field remains one of the most riveting events in Red Sox history. The game had been a slugfest for three innings, the Indians racking Sox starter Bret Saberhagen and reliever Derek Lowe, the Red Sox doing likewise with Cleveland starter Charles Nagy. But when the game moved into the bottom of the fourth inning, all eyes were directed to right field, to the visiting team's bullpen. The door swung open, and out stepped Martinez. Earlier that afternoon he had been seen loosening up in the outfield, his status for Game 5 still officially listed as uncertain, but the Sox were hoping that if they kept the score close they might be able to get some innings out of their ailing ace. Now Martinez trotted in from right field, and it was not unlike the scene in the film *A Bronx Tale* when a collection of rowdy bikers tries to take over Sonny's Bar: as soon as Chazz Palminteri locks the front door and says, "Now youse can't leave," those bikers know they're screwed.

The Indians were screwed. His back still bothering him, his fastball crossing the plate at no better than ninety-one miles per hour, Martinez found a way to reinvent himself for this one night. Relying on a repertoire of changeups and curves, Martinez dazzled the Indians with six no-hit innings; he faced twenty-one batters, retiring eighteen of them. And when Boston left fielder Troy O'Leary hit a three-run homer in the seventh inning—earlier in the game he hit a grand slam off Nagy— the Red Sox were headed for their showdown with the Yankees in the American League Championship Series.

"I saw Pedro two days ago in Boston, and he couldn't even throw a baseball," said Saberhagen. "It just blows my mind what he did."[4]

Sox third baseman John Valentin, who hit three home runs and drove in twelve runs during the series, was now standing in the middle of the Boston clubhouse, soaked with champagne, offering a commentary on the Red Sox' upcoming meeting with the Yankees in the ALCS.

"They better sweep us," he yelled, repeating a line that had initially been uttered by manager Jimy Williams and that the Red Sox were hoping would be the ongoing theme of their postseason.

"They better sweep us," Valentin said again. "That's all I can say."[5]

Summing it up for the shocked Indians, Bud Shaw of the *Cleveland Plain Dealer* concluded it was just as well it was the Red Sox who were moving on to the ALCS. "With their pitching," wrote Shaw of the Indians, "they didn't belong in the same ring as New York."[6]

As the series unfolded, neither did the Red Sox. What had been hyped as a grand showdown between two historic rivals turned out to be merely another road stop for this latest Yankee dynasty, which would produce four World Series championships between 1996 and 2000. The problem was that the Red Sox didn't have much in the way of pitching after Martinez; their starters in Games 1 and 2 of the ALCS were left-hander Kent Mercker, who had made five regular-season starts after being acquired in August for a pair of minor leaguers, and right-hander Ramon Martinez, Pedro's older brother, a onetime star with the Los Angeles Dodgers whose shoulder had been rebuilt and who was now trying to rebuild his career.

Mercker allowed two runs in four workmanlike innings, and the game was tied 3–3 after nine. Second baseman Jose Offerman led off the tenth with a single off Yankees closer Mariano Rivera, but he was cut down at second base by a horrendous call by umpire Rick Reed, who failed to rule that the Yankees' Chuck Knoblauch had dropped the ball on a force play. Reed admitted his mistake after the game—that is, after Yankees center fielder Bernie Williams won it with a home run off Red Sox reliever Rod Beck in the bottom of the tenth.

Ramon Martinez did his job in Game 2 in that he gave the Red Sox a chance to win, allowing three runs in six and two-thirds innings. But Yankees starter David Cone was a little better, allowing only two runs in seven innings. The Yankees won 3–2.

Game 3, played at Fenway Park on Saturday, October 16, 1999, had added significance on several levels. Pedro Martinez was back on the mound for Boston, five days after putting the Indians to bed in Game 5 of the Division Series, and the Yankees' starter was Roger Clemens, a beloved figure during his days with the Red Sox and now a despised turncoat from New York. It was a happy, festive day for Red Sox Nation, what with Clemens being hit so hard he was lifted just one batter into the third inning, and with Martinez, the fire having returned to his fastball, mowing down the Yankees with seven shutout innings, striking out twelve.

After completing a 13–1 victory, the Red Sox were right back in the series. As Peter Botte put it in the *New York Daily News*: "Perhaps most embarrassing to the bottled Rocket, he also allowed his former team to get off the mat and back into the AL Championship Series with a Game 3 rout."[7]

Wrote David Lennon in *Newsday*, "The Yankees unraveled against Pedro Martinez yesterday, and in doing so, they exposed a handful of flaws that could haunt them later in this series."[8]

Nobody could have known it at the time, but Game 3 was not a beginning but an end. The Yankees bounced back with a 9–2 victory in Game 4, scoring six runs in the top of the ninth to turn a nail-biter into a blowout. It didn't help any that for the second time in the series the umpiring crew blew a call involving Knoblauch. In the bottom of the eighth, when it was still a one-run game, the Yankee second baseman fielded a grounder by Valentin and tagged out the runner advancing from first, Jose Offerman. Problem was, Knoblauch had clearly missed Offerman. But umpire Tim Tschida, out of position, made the wrong call. And for the second time in the series, an umpire admitted as much afterward.

Things got ugly. Jimy Williams was ejected. Fans threw debris on the field. A Fenway Park security officer got into a shouting match with Yankees pitcher Jeff Nelson. Crew chief Al Clark briefly cleared the field. After the game, Yankees owner George Steinbrenner accused Williams of "inciting" the Fenway masses. The Boston manager offered a biting rebuttal, saying, "When Georgie-Porgie speaks, I don't listen. I didn't incite the fans. The situation incited the fans."[9]

Game 5 came and went. The Sox were trailing 4–0 when they came to bat in the bottom of the eighth, having managed only three hits off Yankees starter Orlando Hernandez. Suddenly, there was hope: Jason Varitek led off the eighth with a home run, and Nomar Garciaparra followed with a double to left. But the New York bullpen finished off the inning without allowing another run, and in the top of the ninth the Yankees' Jorge Posada busted open the game with a two-run homer off Sox reliever Tom Gordon.

Final score: Yankees 6, Red Sox 1.

And Boston sports fans entered Loserville.

It would be two years, three months, and one day before a Boston-based professional sports team participated in another postseason game. Seasons would come, seasons would go, but never would the postseason bunting be taken out of storage and sent to the dry cleaners with an urgent message tacked on that the order had to be back in time for Game 1. Playoff battles were being waged in such far-flung places as Detroit and Dallas, Phoenix and Philly, San Diego and even San Jose; Boston fans could read and they could watch, but they could not touch. That's the way it is when you're locked behind the walls of Loserville. For all the whining and caterwauling about how the Red Sox hadn't won a World Series since 1918, here was a crisis that didn't involve silly curses or the last wishes of dying grandparents. Never mind championships. Boston fans just wanted a damned playoff game.

The climate changed, dramatically, historically, on January 19, 2002, when the Patriots emerged with a snowy 16–13 overtime victory over the Oakland Raiders in an American Football Conference (AFC) wild-card showdown. The game became famous for an official's fourth-quarter call that saved Tom Brady from a fumble and set the stage for Adam Vinatieri's game-tying and game-winning field goals, thus adding the terms "tuck rule" and "snow game" to local sports lore. It was the last game ever played at Foxboro Stadium, a gritty, no-frills joint located twenty-six miles south of Boston that had served the Patriots well for thirty-one seasons, and the first playoff victory by a Boston sports team since Pedro Martinez mastered the Yankees back in October of '99. Not to mention the Patriots' first big step on their improbable march to victory in Super Bowl XXXVI.

Yet upon reflection, and with the unfolding of events as our guidepost, the game that changed Boston sports history, the game that began the busting-down of those walls surrounding Loserville, took place a few months earlier, on October 23, 2001. In the fourth quarter of what would be a 10–3 loss to the New York Jets, veteran Patriots quarterback Drew Bledsoe was forced out of the game after taking a hellacious hit from Jets linebacker Mo Lewis, whereupon Pats coach Bill Belichick unleashed Brady, a sixth-round pick from the 2000 draft, the 199th player chosen overall.

Already there had been speculation that Belichick was going to make a quarterback switch, choosing the younger Brady over the aging, faltering Bledsoe. Yet Brady had remained a mystery to anyone outside the Patriots' inner circle; when the team drafted him out of the University of Michigan, on April 16, 2000, most reporters covering the team reacted with a journalistic shrugging of shoulders. Michael Felger, weighing in for the *Herald*, wrote that Brady was a "curious selection, given the presence of [backup quarterbacks] Michael Bishop and John Friesz on the roster."[10] The *Globe*'s Nick Cafardo said the Patriots "passed on the athletic Joe Hamilton of Georgia Tech to go for Tom Brady," but assured readers that the selection "should not affect backup quarterbacks John Friesz or Michael Bishop."[11] Noting that the Patriots had surrendered their first-round pick in the 2000 draft to the New York Jets in order to bring Belichick to New England, the *San Diego Union-Tribune* graded the team thusly: "How can you give any team that surrenders a first-round draft pick for Bill Belichick anything better than a 'D'?"[12]

Nearly a decade later, it is not a question of whether Brady and Belichick will be inducted into the Pro Football Hall of Fame, but when. Together, they ushered the Boston sports market into its greatest period of prosperity. When Brady emerged as MVP of Super Bowl XXXVI, he and his team offered Boston sports fans their first opportunity to celebrate a championship since the '86 Celtics.

Loserville? The Patriots came back two seasons later and won Super Bowl XXXVIII. In 2004 the Red Sox shocked the world by rebounding from a 0–3 deficit to the Yankees in the ALCS and went on to sweep the St. Louis Cardinals for their first World Series championship in eighty-six years. Three months later, the Patriots defeated the Philadelphia Eagles in Super Bowl XXXIX for their third championship in four seasons.

Loserville? Boston sports fans were getting fat and happy, and the rest of the country wasn't much liking it.

But there was still more to come for Boston sports fans.

Was there ever.

From October 28, 2007, to June 17, 2008, a period of seven months and twenty days, three of Boston's professional sports teams stood on the grand stage of their respective leagues, vying for championships. It was the greatest period of prosperity not just in Boston sports history but in *any* city's sports history. The golden age began with the Red Sox winning their second World Series in four years and ended seven months and twenty days later with the Celtics winning their first NBA championship in twenty-two years. In between, the New England Patriots roared through their 2007 regular season, emerging as the first team in the era of the sixteen-game schedule to go undefeated. In Super Bowl XLII at University of Phoenix Stadium in Glendale, Arizona, they faced off against the New York Giants, a team dismissed by many as no more than a collection of gridiron drones whose sole responsibility was to please stay out of the picture as the Patriots took their rightful place as the Greatest Team in Football History.

Instead, both teams made history as they participated in the Greatest Super Bowl Ever Played. But there can be only one winning team . . . and it was the Giants, whose shocking 17–14 victory ended New England's bid to become the first NFL team to post a wire-to-wire season without a loss since the 1972 Miami Dolphins.

The game would be talked about for weeks, months. True, the rebuilt Celtics were 36–8 on the day of Super Bowl XLII, en route to posting the best regular-season record in the NBA, their winter exploits providing a tonic for ailing Boston sports fans. As Ray Allen told the *Herald*'s Mark Murphy, "I played in two football environments before I came here. Milwaukee has always had its heart with the Packers, and then Seattle was in the Super Bowl two years ago. There is always disappointment when a team loses, and then they turn to you."[13]

Turn to them they did. But in toppling the Los Angeles Lakers in the 2007–2008 NBA Finals, the Celtics did more than capture their first championship in twenty-two years. If those seven months and twenty days could be looked upon as a Broadway musical, then the Celtics' rolling rally was the dazzling eleven o'clock number, every cast member up on the stage, belting out a tune that would stay in your head for years.

Three teams, three different sports. And in their respective championship runs, they had one thing in common: having determined they needed fresh new players, they went out and got them.

3

"A SCOUTING/PLAYER DEVELOPMENT MACHINE"

The Ale House, located near the intersection of Colonial Boulevard and Metro Parkway in Fort Myers, Florida, is a spring training hangout for Red Sox minor leaguers. A lively, informal, have-one-on-me franchise joint, this particular Ale House has more than thirty different kinds of beer on tap and as many flat-screen monitors on the walls, all of them tuned in to whatever televised sporting events happen to be going on at the moment, and the menu features zingers—breaded chicken tenders—that management proclaims to be "world famous."

But rarely do world-famous ballplayers step into the Ale House. The fat-cat big league stars have moved on because their generous paychecks and endorsement deals have landed them their own spring training condos, and anyway, with wives and kids along for the spring training ride, they don't hang out with teammates as often as they did during their minor league days; when they do, the hanging takes place at upscale places that are beyond a busher's means. But many of them passed through the Ale House back in the day, investing their modest minor league per diems in plates of zingers and mugs filled with cold Miller Lite while talking a lot of smack about what'll happen when *they* get to the Show.

"Just wait," say all the minor league hopefuls who frequent the Ale House. Speaking these words to themselves, mostly.

This is where a twenty-three-year-old kid named Jonathan Papelbon, quaffing beers, watched the Red Sox take on the St. Louis Cardinals in the 2004 World Series. Sent to Fort Myers to participate in an old-timey baseball ritual called the Fall Instructional League, which is a sort of summer school in autumn for top-tier minor leaguers in need of a new pitch, or a better stance, or maybe just an improved outlook, Papelbon sat there at the Ale House on those October nights in '04, mapping out his future. And to him, the future looked good.

A fourth-round pick in the 2003 amateur draft, Papelbon was on the fast track to the big leagues. A six-foot-four, 225-pound right-hander with short-cropped blond hair and eyes as big and wide as pie plates, he was coming off a season at Single-A Sarasota in which he was 12–7 with a 2.64 ERA, with a fastball that was routinely clocked at ninety-five miles per hour, and with movement. He projected to be at Double-A Portland at the beginning of the 2005 season; the way Papelbon looked at it, he'd be in Boston by the end of the summer.

On the night of October 26, 2004, as he and some of his minor league teammates and a few coaches watched Pedro Martinez pitch seven shutout innings to lead the Red Sox to a 4–1 victory in Game 3 of the World Series, Papelbon was impressed. To a degree.

This guy ain't got shit on me, he told himself as he watched Martinez dazzle the Cardinals. *I can do this.*

By the spring of 2005, just four months after his private Ale House boast, he was in big league camp for the first time, unknown to many of the veterans beyond all the talk that he was the goods. And then he showed them. In the bottom of the fourth inning of a March 24 Grapefruit League game against the Baltimore Orioles in Fort Lauderdale, Papelbon, making his first spring training appearance with the big club, exploded a fastball in on Sammy Sosa, forcing the aging slugger off the plate. In the top of the inning, Orioles pitcher Daniel Cabrera had twice thrown inside on Red Sox reserve outfielder Jay Payton, hitting him on the hand with the second pitch, and here now was the rookie Papelbon, in the home half of the inning, brushing back Sosa, one of the game's celebrated players.

Nobody had taken Papelbon aside and told him to go after Sosa. He just *knew*—knew that if the Red Sox wanted to get the attention of the Orioles, then the way to do it was to buzz Sosa.

"He handled himself real well," Red Sox pitching coach Dave Wallace said after the game. "He was very focused. He had his game face on."[1]

"Remember the name, folks," wrote the *Herald*'s Tony Massarotti of Papelbon. "And not just because it sounds like some shi-shi restaurant in the trendy South End."[2]

The *Globe*'s Chris Snow called it "what could be one of those seminal moments in a prospect's career."[3]

Papelbon opened the season at Portland. In July, after undergoing some finishing school at Triple-A Pawtucket, he was promoted to Boston. Getting a start against the Minnesota Twins in his debut, he struck out the first two batters he faced. He allowed three runs in five and a third innings, getting a no-decision in Boston's 4–3 victory over the Twins, after which he was sent back to Pawtucket for a couple of weeks. When he returned to the big leagues, it was for good.

The team he rejoined was flawed and ailing. Matt Clement, a big off-season free-agent signing, was 10–2 with a 3.85 ERA before the All-Star break, but 3–4 with a 5.72 ERA after the break, part of the problem being that he had been conked on the side of the head by a line drive off the bat of the Tampa Bay Devil Rays' Carl Crawford in late July. Curt Schilling, whose heroic pitching in the 2004 postseason had become the stuff of legend, paid a price in 2005: he spent seventy-six days on the disabled list and made just eleven starts. Reliever Keith Foulke, who had saved thirty-two games in 2004 and was on the mound for the last out of the World Series, hobbled through most of the 2005 season on bad knees. He missed fifty games; when he did pitch, he struggled. The Sox were so desperate for bullpen help that Schilling, trying to pitch his way back to health, volunteered to pitch out of the bullpen and made twenty-one relief appearances.

But the Red Sox could still hit. Man, could they hit. Designated hitter David Ortiz, on his way to finishing second in the American League Most Valuable Player balloting to the Yankees' Alex Rodriguez, hit .300 with 47 home runs and 148 RBI. Left fielder Manny Ramirez hit .292 with 45 homers and 144 RBI. Center fielder Johnny Damon, poised for free agency, chose a good time to have a great season: a .316 batting average, 10 home runs, 75 RBI, and a .366 on-base percentage.

The Red Sox made it into the playoffs, securing the American League's wild-card berth on the last day of the season. But it was a Pyrrhic victory: not knowing their fate going into the regular-season finale against the Yankees, the Red Sox needed to start Schilling, who was becoming his old self again. He allowed one run in six innings in the Sox' 10–1 victory, but the price Boston paid was that the man who had already become the best postseason pitcher of his generation wouldn't be sufficiently rested until Game 4 of the best-of-five Division Series matchup against the Chicago White Sox. The series never got that far: the White Sox won the series in three straight games and, as the Red Sox had done a year earlier, ended decades of futility by going on to win the World Series. Schilling, known as a meticulous game-planner, was reduced to sitting in the dugout, preparing for a Game 4 that never happened.

But the Red Sox had found their closer of the future. Just one year removed from the Instructional League (*This guy ain't got shit on me—I can do this*), Papelbon was now backing up his bravado. Appearing in seventeen games, all but three of them in relief, he was 3–1 with a 2.65 ERA. He made two relief appearances in the Division Series, working four shutout innings. It was his first postseason rodeo. It would not be his last.

What nobody could have predicted was how quickly the future arrived. Understand, first, that the Red Sox, going into the 2006 season, believed they had improved their roster and were prepared to make a run for the World Series. Despite a terrific off-season soap opera in which boy genius general manager Theo Epstein had briefly quit the club over a clash with president/CEO Larry Lucchino—including a now-famous Halloween stunt in which Epstein walked out of Fenway Park and right past an unknowing media horde, hidden inside a borrowed monkey costume—the Red Sox still looked good on paper.

The starting pitching was bolstered by a risky blockbuster of a trade: minor league shortstop Hanley Ramirez, one of those can't-miss types (and he didn't), was sent to the Florida Marlins in exchange for right-hander Josh Beckett, a throwback pitcher with the kind of game-day bark and snarl once attributed to Jim Bunning, Bob Gibson, and other blasts from the past. In 2003 Beckett, just twenty-three at the time, pitched the Marlins to victory in the deciding sixth game of the World Series over the Yankees—in Yankee Stadium no less.

Included in the deal was Marlins third baseman Mike Lowell, who was coming off an unproductive 2005 season. Lowell had two years and $18 million remaining on his contract, and, really, that's what the Marlins traded: the contract. In order for the Red Sox to land the coveted Beckett, they had to absorb the remaining two years and $18 million still due to Lowell. In time, it would prove to be a bargain.

There were other changes. Popular outfielder Johnny Damon up and signed with the Yankees, instantly transforming himself into a villain in the eyes of Red Sox fans. A year earlier, when Pedro Martinez signed with the New York Mets, he was treated like royalty when Major League Baseball's annual interleague festival landed the Mets in Fenway Park; Damon, though, had committed the unpardonable sin of signing with the Yankees, and Red Sox Nation would never forgive him.

The Sox replaced Damon in center field by obtaining Coco Crisp from the Cleveland Indians. They also had a new double-play combination: shortstop Alex Gonzalez and second baseman Mark Loretta. Epstein liked the pitching staff so much that he traded right-hander Bronson Arroyo, reliable but not a star, to the Cincinnati Reds for outfielder Wily Mo Pena, who, it was said, *would* be a star if he just stopped striking out so much.

When the 2006 season began, the understanding was that Foulke would remain the closer and that Papelbon would work in a setup role. And so it was on Opening Day when the Red Sox played the Texas Rangers at Ameriquest Field: with the Sox leading 7–2, Papelbon worked a 1-2-3 eighth inning. And then Foulke, pitching in a nonsave situation in the ninth inning, gave up a single to Hank Blalock and a double to Kevin Mench, with Blalock scoring on a sacrifice fly.

Foulke got out of the inning without further damage, and the Red Sox had a 7–3 victory. They also had a new closer: two days later, and with no fanfare, manager Terry Francona, a baseball lifer with a reputation for giving his veterans one more chance to redeem themselves, and then one more after that, chose Papelbon to close out the ninth inning against the Rangers, with Boston holding a 2–1 lead. The new closer—though nobody was calling him this at the time—needed just eleven pitches, eight of them strikes, to silence the Rangers.

The Red Sox opened the season 5–1 on the road, with Papelbon saving three games. In the home opener, he fired up the sellout crowd at Fenway Park by closing out a 5–3 victory over the Toronto Blue Jays, after Foulke had given up two eighth-inning runs. It wasn't long before Papelbon mania gripped Boston: by July the hottest-selling Red Sox shirts were those with the rookie closer's number 58 on the back. His shirts were outselling those of Ortiz, Ramirez, Schilling, and other established Red Sox stars.

Scott Saklad of the Red Sox Team Store explained what was happening: "He's new, he's exciting, and he's on fire. Girls like him too, which is a big part of it. And he has a great fastball. People love fastballs and home runs."[4]

But the 2006 season was turning into a disaster for the Red Sox. They had come into the campaign believing that Beckett would be their ace, but he was too often relying on his fastball and too often ignoring the counsel of catcher Jason Varitek, whose reputation for calling a good game was solid gold. Beckett also had an issue with blisters: whereas an NFL tough guy can play with a broken foot (as Los Angeles Rams defensive end Jack Youngblood did in Super Bowl XIV), a blister can land a pitcher on the DL. And so Beckett, 11–4 before the All-Star break, was 5–7 after the break. His ERA for the season was 5.01. He gave up thirty-six home runs, the second-highest total in baseball, and he was fifth in the American League in walks allowed. In short, he won sixteen games and he sucked.

Clement, his shoulder failing him, made just twelve starts. Veteran David Wells, a talented but boorish left-hander who had always talked about how much he hated Fenway Park until the Red Sox offered him a paycheck, spent most of the season on the disabled list; Epstein traded him to the San Diego Padres on the last day of August, an admission that the Sox knew they were out of the playoff fight. Varitek, hobbled by a knee injury, played in only 103 games. Schilling missed three weeks late in the season with a muscle strain, and knuckleballer Tim Wake-field was out nearly two months with a stress fracture in his rib cage.

About all that was left for Sox fans to root for over the last month of the season was a piece of history: no slugger save for Jimmie Foxx had ever hit fifty home runs in a season for the Red Sox—Double X did it in 1938—and now Ortiz, Big Papi himself, had a shot. But in some ways he was on his own: his sometime buddy on the Red Sox, Manny Ramirez, had pretty much called it a season. Hosting the Yankees in a five-game series at Fenway in mid-August, the fast-fading Sox lost the first four games; in the fifth inning of the series finale, Francona removed Ramirez because of "cramping of the right hamstring." The Sox lost 2–1. Ramirez missed most of the last month of the season with what the club called "patellar tendinitis," Manny's pain having moved from his hamstring to his knee; meanwhile, his agent was pressuring the Red Sox to trade the outfielder. It was not the first time Ramirez had been idled by a convenient injury while at odds with management. It would not be the last.

"It was going bad," said Francona, looking back on the 2006 season. "We lost those five games against the Yankees. Shit, we were getting tested. And there are times, looking back, when I'm just as proud of that team as I was of the '04 and '07 teams."

But Francona was unable to convince Ramirez to get back into the lineup.

"I was really aggravated with Manny and had about had it," he said.

Following a game one night late in the season, Francona and Ortiz huddled in the manager's office until about two in the morning.

"Let me have a shot at him," Ortiz told the manager.

The next day Ortiz found Francona and said, "Fuck, do whatever you want."

Ortiz, like Francona, had failed to inspire Ramirez to return to the lineup.

"I think he thought he could probably get him in there," Francona recalled. "It didn't work."

Given the valuable protection Ramirez provided Ortiz when he was in the lineup, Big Papi was at a disadvantage as he chased the record.

But with Manny or without him, Ortiz was taking the chase seriously. A month earlier, admitting he didn't know much about Foxx, he vowed to study up on the slugger once referred to as the right-handed Babe Ruth. Second baseman Mark Loretta, a student of the game who had asked for Foxx's number 3 when he joined the Red Sox (and got it*), offered to provide a tutorial.

"I want to know what he looked like, how big he was," said Ortiz. "I want to know how he swung the bat. I'm telling you, he must have been some fucking good hitter."[5]

It was a difficult last month of the season for Ortiz, and the stress was getting to him. The team was falling apart, he was unable to get Ramirez into the lineup, and now there was this record, this Foxx trot in the last days of a going-nowhere season. In mid-August, Big Papi was admitted to Massachusetts General Hospital for tests after complaining of an irregular heartbeat; a little more than a week later, with the Red Sox on the West Coast playing the Oakland A's, he was scratched from the lineup after having a similar sensation and sent back to Boston for further tests.

Everything came back normal, and Ortiz was cleared to play. "I've been stressing out the way things are going around [here]," he said. "We're trying to make the playoffs, and things are not going well on the field."[6]

Things didn't get much better, except that Ortiz obliterated the Jimmie Foxx home run record. He hit number fifty on September 20 off the Minnesota Twins' Boof Bonser, and the next night he hit two more. When the season was over—the Red Sox slipped behind the Toronto Blue Jays and into third place in the American League East—Ortiz had fifty-four home runs.

But Ortiz wasn't the only Red Sox player whose health was an issue as the lost 2006 season was winding down. For even after Big Papi was

---

* Jimmie Foxx is arguably the greatest player in baseball history not to have had his uniform number retired. He played only seven seasons with the Red Sox and is perhaps best known for his eleven seasons with the Philadelphia Athletics, who eventually moved to Kansas City and then to Oakland. The Oakland A's have yet to retire Foxx's number.

medically cleared to return to the business of swinging for the fences, the Red Sox and their fans were dealing with yet another health crisis.

O n the afternoon of Friday, September 1, with a month remaining in the season, the Red Sox made a startling announcement: Jon Lester, a twenty-two-year-old left-hander in his first season in the big leagues, had been diagnosed with a treatable form of anaplastic large cell lymphoma, an aggressive form of non-Hodgkins lymphoma.

Lester had been selected by the Red Sox in the second round of the 2002 amateur draft. Though his climb through the Boston farm system was slower than Papelbon's, it was steady: he was promoted to a new level each season, making it to Triple-A Pawtucket in 2006. It was little more than finishing school; he was summoned to the big leagues on June 10 and won his first five decisions. At the time of his diagnosis, he was 7–2 with a 4.76 ERA, a star in the making.

The Red Sox already had one concern about Lester: his ability to pitch into the late innings of his starts. Still feeling his way around the big leagues at an age when a lot of pitchers are riding buses through the Eastern League and nursing beers in all those Ale Houses out there, Lester frequently ran up high pitch counts in the early going, the result being that he was gone by the fifth inning.

It was a problem that could easily be solved through experience and coaching, the Red Sox reasoned. Now there was this: cancer. But it's not like the Red Sox didn't know where to turn for help: it was announced that Lester would begin his treatment at Boston's renowned Dana-Farber Cancer Institute, whose fund-raising arm, the Jimmy Fund, has received millions of dollars of support over the years from the Red Sox.

The Jimmy Fund and baseball have always been synonymous. At first, it was the Boston Braves who embraced the Jimmy Fund; when the club moved to Milwaukee in the spring of 1953, owner Lou Perini met with Red Sox owner Thomas A. Yawkey and, as writer Saul Wisnia puts it, "convinced his colleague to take on the cause as his team's official charity."[7] Over the years such Red Sox stars as Ted Williams, Carl Yastrzemski, Mo Vaughn, Roger Clemens, and Tim Wakefield have worked tirelessly on behalf of the Jimmy Fund. The chairman of the Jimmy Fund is Mike Andrews, who played second base for the pennant-winning 1967 "Impossible Dream" Red Sox.

Here now was an active Red Sox player, about to step into the Dana-Farber as a patient.

On the night the statement about Lester was released to the media, the Red Sox were playing the Blue Jays at Fenway Park. Papelbon entered the game in the ninth inning, after seven shutout innings from starter Kyle Snyder and a scoreless eighth from Foulke, but the phenom rookie closer felt an odd pain in his right shoulder while pitching to the Jays' Lyle Overbay. When the odd pain did not go away, Papelbon was taken out of the game.

With the Red Sox unlikely to climb back into the playoff race, it was more or less understood that Papelbon was being shut down for the season. As for Lester, he held an emotional press conference at Fenway Park on September 6 to answer some of the questions that had been swirling nonstop since the announcement about his cancer diagnosis.

"I'm twenty-two years old, and I thought I was in the best shape of my life," Lester told the gathering. "I'm coming out here and pitching every five days, and pitching in Fenway Park. I mean, what could be better? Obviously, there's that denial, that why-did-it-happen-to-me thing, but right now we don't have room for that. Right now we've got to fight."[8]

Meeting with teammates before his press conference, he received words of encouragement from some people in uniform who had battled health problems of their own. Mike Lowell, who had overcome testicular cancer, gave reporters a version of what he told Lester: "Take it for what it's worth, get well, and worry about baseball later."[9]

Manager Francona was particularly moved by Lester's plight, mostly because of his paternal attitude toward younger players, but also because, in addition to having lost his mother to cancer, he was no stranger to receiving sobering news from the doctor. In 2002 he suffered a pulmonary embolism, and, he later acknowledged, probably another one early in the 2006 season. He continues to take blood thinners to control circulation problems.[10]

"You don't get to know every kid's parents, because we're a professional team, this isn't college," the manager would later say. "But we sort of all went through this together. And you're on the phone, talking to his parents, and you're not talking baseball.

"When young kids come up through the organization, you feel a sense of responsibility for them anyway," he said. "But for him to go through what he went through . . . it gets to you."

A week later, at Yankee Stadium, it was now Papelbon's turn to make news. He told reporters he was most likely done as a relief pitcher: in an attempt to remove him from the daily grind of working out of the bullpen, the new plan was for him to return to the starting rotation for 2007.

"I've done it before, so it's not going to be anything new to me," he said. "I'm going to take it just like I did the closer's role this year. I'm going to be going out there knowing I can win."[11]

Perhaps it was fitting that Papelbon spoke these words in the bowels of Yankee Stadium, home of the greatest closer of this era, Mariano Rivera. Papelbon, from the time he moved into the Boston bullpen, wanted to be another Rivera—he liked Mo's style, liked the take-charge confidence Rivera exuded when he came into a game. Rivera was already a Hall of Fame lock. Papelbon had already made the Hall of Fame a goal of his, a brazen goal for one so young.

"I'll miss the adrenaline," he told reporters. "I'll miss the excitement. I'll miss all that. The thought of going out there to get the last, toughest, hardest outs of a ball game, and the challenge of that. Of course I'll miss that."[12]

As they were making their bones in the minor leagues, Papelbon and Lester had often been talked about as though they were a tandem, a modern-day baseball version of Martin & Lewis. This is not uncommon. Daryl Strawberry and Dwight Gooden were viewed as a tandem when they blossomed with the New York Mets in the early eighties, partly because they were young, African American, and enormously talented, but leaving out the fact that one was an outfielder, the other a pitcher, and they were never all that buddy-buddy to begin with. Red Sox fans, too, had their tandems: outfielders Jim Rice and Fred Lynn both made their major league debut in late 1974, and each would win an MVP Award. Broadcaster Ned Martin called them the Gold Dust Twins. In the nineties, a couple of minor league pitching prospects named Brian Rose and Carl Pavano were routinely spoken of in the same breath, to the point that they started to sound like one person: a sweet little old lady named Rose Pavano.

But Papelbon and Lester didn't have much in common. Where Papelbon was funny and loud and unpredictable, enjoying the daily banter with the growing collection of reporters who sought him out, perhaps hoping for some back-page bombast, Lester was no noisemaker. He'd be cordial with the media, dutifully answering questions after each start, but he didn't have much interest in funny stories and brash predictions. The two pitchers were also built differently. Papelbon, with his barrel chest and thick, meaty legs, looked like a pro football player. Lester, when he broke into the big leagues, was lanky by baseball standards, even skinny. He looked more like a high school basketball player.

Yet what they had in common was enormous talent. And this: on September 1, 2006, they were both at a crossroads—Lester about to undergo chemotherapy, Papelbon clutching an aching shoulder and talking about being reborn as a starting pitcher.

In little more than one year's time, they would share the same mound, the same World Series pressure, and, when it was over, the same champagne celebration.

Theo Epstein was named general manager of the Red Sox on November 25, 2002. At the age of twenty-eight years and eleven months, he was the youngest GM in baseball history. A native of Brookline, Massachusetts, who grew up just a few miles from Fenway Park, Epstein was a Yale graduate who'd started out in baseball as an intern with the Baltimore Orioles and made an astonishing climb from gofer to go-to guy.

Discovered by Orioles director of public affairs Charles Steinberg and brought to the attention of club president Larry Lucchino, Epstein followed Steinberg and Lucchino to the San Diego Padres and, eventually, to the team he'd rooted for during his childhood. On the day he was named general manager, Epstein told the media, "We're going to turn the Red Sox into a scouting/player development machine."[13]

Translation: the Red Sox were going to have a better farm system. And it was all boilerplate stuff. Just as candidates for office always promise to lower taxes, just as actors always tell late-night talk-show hosts they took the part because they fell in love with the script, just as superstar athletes insist that "it's not about the money" as they bolt from one team to the next, newly minted general managers always fire up the fan base with bold pronouncements about scouting and development.

The difference here is that Epstein, backing up his bravado, constructed a farm system that would soon be churning out major league ballplayers. In the 2004 draft, Epstein's first selection was a tough little infielder named Dustin Pedroia; within a few years he would elbow his way into the big leagues and become the heart and soul of the Red Sox. Boston's first five picks in the '05 draft—outfielder Jacoby Ellsbury, right-hander Craig Hanson, right-hander Clay Buchholz, infielder Jed Lowrie, and right-hander Michael Bowden—would be in the big leagues within three years. And Ellsbury, like Pedroia, would play an important role on the 2007 Red Sox.

But it was going to take more than fresh-out-of-the-oven graduates of the farm system to make the 2007 Red Sox a contender for another World Series championship. Epstein needed veteran players, and he needed them fast. Fortunately, he was working for a major-market organization that sold out every game and had revenue streams that were the envy of most other teams.

Epstein had money to spend, and now he was going to use it to complete the 2007 Red Sox. Though he shelled out $70 million over five years for right fielder J. D. Drew and $36 million over four years for shortstop Julio Lugo, Epstein's biggest, and riskiest, acquisition was for a pitcher most Red Sox fans had never even heard of, let alone seen in a game.

Twenty-seven-year-old right-hander Daisuke Matsuzaka was already a legend in his native Japan, having starred for eight seasons with the Seibu Lions. By the time he was pitching for Team Japan in the inaugural World Baseball Classic in early 2006, he had already been targeted by the Red Sox, with the team's international scouting director, Craig Shipley, and Pacific Rim coordinator Jon Deeble closely monitoring his career.

That Matsuzaka would pitch Japan to victory over Cuba in the WBC championship game at San Diego's Petco Park and be named MVP of the tournament no doubt had the Red Sox worried that other big league teams would wake up and say, "Hey, this guy can help us." As Shipley told writer Ian Browne, who penned a biography of Matsuzaka, "I think that probably added a few more teams to the mix."[14]

Many teams no doubt had interest in Matsuzaka; only a few had the financial means to go out and get him. Signing a Japanese player of Matsuzaka's acclaim was expensive and complicated, involving an ordeal called the "posting system" in which interested major league teams were required to file a sealed bid by a specified date. And that money wasn't for Matsuzaka, but for the pitcher's Japanese team, the Seibu Lions. If the Lions accepted the offer, it meant only that the big league team could negotiate with Matsuzaka. To make this ever more daunting for the Red Sox, Matsuzaka had chosen as his agent one Scott Boras, a former minor league infielder who had emerged as one of the most powerful negotiators in sports history. He also had become a rather convenient punching bag for sportswriters who viewed him as somehow sullying the great game of baseball, as if the owners were doing God's work. But as Jerry Crasnick wrote in *License to Deal: A Season on the Run with a Maverick Baseball Agent*, "even his detractors, from agents who fear and envy him to club executives who dread his phone calls and interminable 'World According to Scott' soliloquies, respect him for his intellectual motor and attentiveness to detail."[15]

Thus was the obstacle course laid out for the Red Sox. Left out of the equation was the simple fact that the Red Sox wanted the guy much more than did other teams, and in the end it showed. The Sox ponied up a $51.1 million posting bid, easily muscling out the New York Mets, whose runner-up bid was just under $40 million.[16]

Now that the Red Sox were negotiating exclusively with Matsuzaka, it probably didn't hurt any that they had just signed another Japanese pitcher, a wiry left-handed reliever from the Nippon Ham Fighters named Hideki Okajima. But those who thought the Okajima signing was intended as something of a welcome mat for Matsuzaka were missing the point: Okajima could pitch.

And anyway, it was going to take money, not familiar faces from the old sod, to sign Matsuzaka. Negotiations with Boras were laborious and lengthy, with all the predictable down-to-the-wire tension that modern-day sports fans have come to expect, but on December 14, 2006, the Red

Sox and Matsuzaka finally agreed on a six-year, $52 million contract. Factoring in the posting fee, the Red Sox were investing more than $100 million in a man who had yet to throw a pitch in the major leagues.

Overnight the Red Sox were looked upon as an international team. It was estimated that nearly four hundred members of the media attended Matsuzaka's introductory Fenway Park press conference. Recognizing that this was not a one-day event, the Red Sox announced that the Fenway press box would be rebuilt to accommodate the expected surge of Japanese on hand to cover Matsuzaka, whose first name, pronounced "dice-kay," was now being recast as "Dice-K" by headline writers. The Boston chapter of the Baseball Writers' Association of America now included the likes of Dai Yuasa of *Sankei Sports*, Toshimitsu Tanaka of the *Hochi Shimbun*, Hiroki Toda of *Sports Nippon*, and Yoshihisa Miura of the Jiji Press.

Matsuzaka's arrival for spring training made for yet another media sensation. On the morning of February 24, 2007, after Dice-K threw live batting practice for the first time, Red Sox media relations director John Blake made a rather unusual announcement: "Bobby Scales will be available for interviews in the clubhouse in five minutes." It was unusual because at the time Scales was a nine-year minor leaguer now suddenly in great demand because he was the first hitter to test out the new pitcher.

Things grew crazier still when Matsuzaka made his first spring training start, facing Boston College in the annual exhibition game between the Red Sox and Eagles. Leading off for Boston College in the top of the first inning was Johnny Ayers, a two-sport athlete at BC who punted for the football team in the fall and played baseball in the spring. A left-handed hitter, Ayers was expecting a first-pitch fastball and figured it would be his best chance for a hit. He got one and shocked everyone by slicing Matsuzaka's first pitch as a member of the Red Sox down the left-field line for a double.

No matter that Ayers did not score, or that Matsuzaka worked two shutout innings in a 9–1 Red Sox victory. Once the game was over, Ayers got the Bobby Scales treatment: he was ushered into a packed interview room for his fifteen minutes of fame. Years later Japanese baseball fans still visit Ayers's Facebook profile and make friendship requests.

"I never thought I'd experience anything like that in my life," said Ayers, who went on to pursue a master's degree in finance at Boston College. "Every once in a while, someone will come up to me and ask if I'm the guy who got that hit off Daisuke Matsuzaka. And when I watch him pitch on television, I can smile and say to myself, 'I own him.' I'll always have that memory."

Though spring training was going well for the 2007 Red Sox, there were questions. Would Manny Ramirez show up on time? Would he be a spring training distraction?

He arrived on February 26, later than the rest of the position players but one day ahead of his scheduled reporting day, and the grateful Red Sox went along with the story about how the outfielder's absences from the lineup the last month of the 2006 season were due to patellar tendinitis.

More questions: Could rookie Dustin Pedroia handle second base? Having decided not to bring back the veteran Loretta, the Sox were committing to Pedroia, who had struggled offensively during his September call-up to the big leagues and now wasn't hitting much in spring training.

Jon Lester had undergone a successful off-season of chemotherapy and rejoined the team, and though it was understood he would open the season in the minor leagues, everyone was wondering when he'd be allowed to pitch in a Grapefruit League game. And then there was the issue as to who would be the closer. With Papelbon moving to the starting rotation, the Red Sox were sifting through an assemblage of veterans—Joel Pineiro, Brendan Donnelly, Mike Timlin—in search of an answer. There was even some far-fetched speculation that Okajima, who had yet to throw a pitch in the big leagues, might land the job.

The Lester situation was handled magnificently by the Red Sox. Instead of having him make his return in a packed stadium and with a crowd of media blogging each pitch back to Boston, Francona had him pitch in a morning "B" game against a collection of Minnesota Twins rookies at the Twins' spring training complex on the other side of Fort Myers on the morning of March 5.

Pitching in a near-empty Hammond Stadium—the Twins didn't even bother to turn on the scoreboard—Lester began his outing by throwing a fastball to a twenty-two-year-old rookie infielder named Alexi Casilla for a called strike. He pitched one scoreless inning, throwing eight pitches. Everyone was thrilled; he had taken an important step in his comeback.

Before the start of spring training, Lester had telephoned Francona. "You're my second phone call," Lester told the manager, the first call having been to his parents.

His off-season of chemotherapy had been completed. He was cancer-free.

The 2007 season has already been a success, Francona told himself that day. And he sat down and cried. "I didn't want to," he recalled. "It was a phone call, it was quick, and when I hung up I was a basket case."

So Lester was back, and he had delivered the most important one inning of "B" pitching anybody could remember. Now it was Papelbon's turn to deliver some good news. A couple of weeks after Lester's comeback outing, while shagging balls in the outfield, he said to himself, *Fuck this. I'm going to do what I'm going to do.*

He spoke with Varitek, who had spoken with Francona. And then Papelbon walked into Francona's office and said, "I don't know what you guys are thinking, but I can't do this starting thing. Pitching once a week is going to drive me insane. And I don't think I'll be as effective as if you leave me out there three or four times a week."

Papelbon simply couldn't get it out of his head that he was a born closer, that entering a game in the ninth inning, the door to the bullpen swinging open, the crowd roaring, excited him in a way that being a starting pitcher did not. He wanted to be Charlie Sheen in *Major League*. He wanted to be the Wild Thing, only without the wildness.

"I sat there for a week, and went back and forth, back and forth, back and forth," he would later say. "And I was talking to my dad one night, and then my wife, and both of them told me to do what your heart wants you to do. I had to ask myself that one simple question. And then it was easy."

Ten days after Papelbon's announcement about being born to be a closer, the Red Sox traveled to Kansas City to open the 2007 season. It was a bad day all the way around for the Sox. David Ortiz doubled home a run in the first inning, but it would be Boston's only offensive output in a 7–1 loss to the Royals. Curt Schilling lasted only four innings, allowing five runs. Hideki Okajima's first major league pitch was walloped by the Royals' John Buck for a home run.

The Red Sox won their next two games against the Royals, with Matsuzaka winning his major league debut in the series finale. They moved on to Arlington, Texas, and lost two straight to the Rangers. In the final game of the series, Schilling bounced back with a solid outing, Big Papi hit a pair of home runs, and then Papelbon took charge: entering the game with one out in the eighth inning, the tying run on third, he punched out 2005 American League batting champion Michael Young and then got slugger Mark Teixeira on a pop to third baseman Mike Lowell.

In the bottom of the ninth, leading off for the Rangers was Papelbon's old pal Sammy Sosa—the batter against whom Papelbon had made his bones with a spring training brushback pitch two years earlier. This time Papelbon got him on a pop-out. Then the closer closed things out, striking out the last two batters in a 3–2 victory.

Later that night, on the team's plane ride to Boston for the traditional Fenway opener, Papelbon couldn't stop thinking that he was doing what he was born to do.

4

URBAN LEGEND

A ndrew J. Urban II was out of bed with the morning sun and feeling a little fidgety as he arrived in the kitchen for his personal, time-honored breakfast of champions: a plate of leftovers from the dinner his mother had prepared the previous evening, all of it washed down with a nice, cold can of Pepsi. Urban, never having consumed a cup of coffee in his life, had come to find that nothing fired up the burners in the morning like a Pepsi. No Coke. Pepsi, please.

On this day, Opening Day 2007, the house special was Hamburger Helper, a favorite of Urban's. He liberated a generous portion from the refrigerator, gave it a respectable nuking, and then toted his morning meal down the hallway and into what he considers "the world's smallest bedroom."

Could be, could be. His queen-size bed takes up most of his room in the family homestead at 11 Kingston Road in suburban Waltham, Massachusetts, and what little space remains is gobbled up by the basics: an end table, a bureau, and a small writing desk in the corner. And his television: a no-frills thirty-two-inch Sharp that's stationed in front of the window facing the bed. And it was the Sharp that brought Hamburger Helper–toting Andrew J. Urban II back to his bedroom on this morning, for it was time to consult NESN, his favorite TV station, to see if there was anything going on with his beloved Red Sox.

It wasn't just scores, highlights, and postgame interviews Urban was seeking. It was player transactions. He had to know whether the Red

Sox had added any new players since the end of last night's game—a veteran pitcher claimed off the waiver wire perhaps? A slick-fielding kid infielder brought up from Triple-A Pawtucket? If anyone had breaking news on the Red Sox, Urban reasoned, it would be NESN, whose majority owner is the Red Sox, which means it is the cable network that carries any Sox game not scooped up by Fox or ESPN for national viewing.

Urban was partial to *SportsDesk*, NESN's version of ESPN's *SportsCenter*. He had become so proficient at reading the crawl at the bottom of the screen that he'd talk about it as though he had invented the thing: "The crawl," he said, "is where you find out about new Red Sox players. If you look at it long enough you'll find out the information even before the people on the screen start talking about it."

When you consider yourself the best and the brightest of all the autograph collectors who keep daily vigil at the players' entrance at Fenway Park, when you're so good at this game outside the game that even the security guards at the old ballyard have a sort of grudging respect for you, when you can lay claim to the ownership of literally thousands of players' signatures that are securely stored in Tupperware containers in your mother's basement, there is an expectation that you, only you, will know if a new player has been added to the club since the last game.

And if the Urban Legend isn't the best autograph collector at Fenway Park, he is certainly the most recognizable. He is a tall drink of water, six-foot-one and about 145 pounds, a slightly stooped-over collection of elbows and kneecaps that always seem to be moving in several directions at once. With long, straggly, brown hair escaping from every side of his ever-present Red Sox cap and a pair of thick, black glasses sitting at the base of his generous nose, he looks a little like a long-lost fourth Hanson brother from the cult hockey film *Slapshot*.

He dutifully wears a Red Sox jersey when camped out at Fenway Park, but never, never, *never* the same jersey two days in a row. That's a strict policy of his. If the Red Sox have returned to Fenway for a seven-game home-stand, Urban will wear seven different T-shirts, each one freshly laundered for the occasion by his mother. It's a respect thing. You don't approach a major league baseball player for an autograph looking as though you've just finished hot-topping your driveway.

On the day the Red Sox played their 2007 home opener, Andrew J. Urban II was two months shy of his thirty-fifth birthday and had been collecting autographs since the magical summer of 1986. The Red Sox picked up a pennant that year, and Urban, fourteen years old at the time, picked up the autograph of a rookie outfielder named Mike Greenwell. He also presented himself to pitcher Calvin Schiraldi and came away with an autograph.

And it's funny—a Curt Schilling can tell you who he whiffed for his first big league strikeout (Todd Benzinger, September 7, 1988), and a Mike Lowell can name the pitcher against whom he registered his first major league hit (Kelvim Escobar, September 13, 1998), but here's Urban, veteran big league autograph collector, and he's uncertain about his first connection: Greenwell and then Schiraldi? Or was it Schiraldi and then Greenwell?

But the way he sees it, that was so many autographs ago. Since then he has collected more than five thousand of them.

And each autograph has a story.

One day he met Shonda Schilling, Curt's wife, as she was taking part in a Red Sox wives food drive outside the park. Urban asked to have his picture taken with her, whereupon Mrs. Schilling said, "Wouldn't you want to get a picture of my husband?"

"I'd love to," he said. "Except he never comes over here."

The next day Schilling, accompanied by his wife, navigated his SUV down Yawkey Way and took the right through the gate onto Van Ness Street.

A few minutes later, security guard Paul Anderson, who was working the gate, stepped out and gestured for Urban to step inside.

Urban figured he had done something wrong and was about to be dressed down. Had he lingered too close to the gate? What about the meeting with Shonda Schilling from the day before? Had that been viewed by Fenway Park's gendarmes as some breach of etiquette? Had he crossed a line? Literally? Figuratively?

Urban looked at Anderson, bracing for the news.

"Go in," he said.

"What?"

"Go in."

Urban stepped through the gate, and immediately saw Schilling approaching him.

"I understand you talked with Shonda and you want a ball," Schilling said.

That's not exactly what Urban had said. A baseball? *I had not asked for a baseball*, Urban said to himself. It's just that he and Shonda Schilling had been talking, see, and . . .

"What's your name?" Schilling said.

"Andrew J. Urban II."

"Here," Schilling said, producing a baseball. He took Urban's pen and wrote, "To Andy, God bless. Curt Schilling."

Urban thanked Schilling, and they shook hands, and then the ball-player turned and walked toward the players' entrance.

And there is the Manny Ramirez story.

One day the Red Sox slugger pulled up at the players' lot at Fenway Park in his fine ride, and Urban was as Urban is: he approached the car in search of an autograph. But just as he reached his target, Ramirez gave the pedal a little nudge, and the car moved up a few feet. Unfazed, Urban made a second attempt, and again Ramirez moved forward. Urban tried yet again, only this time Ramirez pulled past the barrier and was now off-limits to the huddled, autograph-seeking masses.

Urban didn't mind. *Just Manny being Manny*, he thought.

Now it was Opening Day, or what Urban lovingly refers to as "the beginning of summer." Never mind that it was only April, or that Opening Day at Fenway Park can sometimes be cold, even wintry. Urban, like thousands of Red Sox fans, had come to regard the traditional Fenway Park opener as not just a holiday but as baseball's version of a holy day of obligation. On Opening Day in Boston, grown-ups suddenly discover sore throats and disordered stomachs that necessitate a sick call to the office. Students engage in good old-fashioned hooky, though that's probably an overstatement given that many parents, caught up in their own Opening Day nostalgia, know perfectly well what's going on.

By Opening Day 2007, the Boston sports community had entered an era when three teams, the Red Sox, Celtics, and Patriots, were selling out all their games. And the Bruins, after years of producing boring, lackluster teams, were starting to play winning hockey again and, hence, winning back their fans.

But it all began with the Red Sox. While Andrew J. Urban II represents die-hard Red Sox fans of the present day, it is important to understand just how this love affair between Bostonians and their sports fans came to be.

For those who believe in karma, for those who believe in cosmic clickers falling into place, for those who believe in friendly ghosts guiding us through life, perhaps it is no coincidence that the first batter ever to step to the plate at Fenway Park was a Boston kid. The new yard was christened on April 9, 1912, with the Red Sox reaching across the Charles River to Cambridge and inviting the Harvard University varsity squad over for a preseason exhibition game, after which the Sox were to travel to New York to open the regular season against the Highlanders. (They would be renamed the Yankees a year later.) On a cold, snowy day at the new yard, Harvard's leadoff hitter in the top of the first inning was a sophomore third baseman with the appropriately Ivy League–sounding name Dana Joseph Paine Wingate. Born and raised in Winchester, Massachusetts, a leafy suburb a few miles north of Boston, Wingate was the son of Charles E. L. Wingate, editor of the *Boston Journal* and, later, Sunday editor of the *Boston Post*. He, too, was a Harvard man.[1]

As for the Harvard boy, Dana Joseph Paine Wingate didn't have much success as Fenway's first batsman, striking out against Casey Hageman, a twenty-four-year-old right-hander with a reputation for wildness. Three seasons earlier, while pitching for the Grand Rapids Stags of the Ohio State League, Hageman had sailed a pitch in on the head of second baseman Charles "Cupid" Pinkney of the Dayton Veterans. Pinkney died the next morning.[2]

Wingate came out of the Fenway Park unveiling with his head on straight and went on to have a standout career at Harvard, settling in at shortstop and emerging as captain for both his junior and senior years. He graduated in 1914 and, according to stories in the local papers, turned down a chance to sign with the Chicago Cubs in order to accept a position with the New England Coal and Coke Company.

But Wingate didn't live long enough to see Fenway Park become a baseball shrine or come to appreciate that by merely stepping up to the plate on that freezing April morning in 1912 he'd made history. On June 13, 1918, just four years after graduating from Harvard, Dana Joseph Paine Wingate, suffering from tuberculosis, died at a sanitarium at Saranac Lake, New York. He is buried in the family plot at Wildwood Cemetery in his hometown, his name and his deed largely lost to the passage of time.

It would have been fun for Red Sox fans in the ensuing generations to see Old Man Wingate kicking back and chillin', snapping at his suspenders and speaking breathlessly and endlessly about how, back in the day, he was the first man to step up to the plate at Fenway Park. Given what the writers said about him when he died—he was "that rare, clean athletic type" and was "immensely popular," wept the *Herald*—one gets the impression he'd have made for great copy as an old codger. Had Wingate made it into his seventies—likely as a retired Boston businessman, a pillar of the community, a doer of good deeds, and an enthusiastic regular at Fenway Park—he might have been on hand to see the 1967 "Impossible Dream" Red Sox defy the oddsmakers and capture the American League pennant. It was that year, 1967, that Fenway Park began its transformation from just another old ballpark to its present status as a baseball shrine for fans throughout New England—and beyond.

It was not always so. Though many a misguided baseball poet has advanced the ever-spreading myth that today's Red Sox fans are simply walking in the steps of their parents, grandparents, and great-grandparents, the prose so fantastical that you'd think the first Thanksgiving is connected to the first World Series (both, after all, having taken place in what is now Massachusetts), it is all just that—a myth.

It is true that, in 1903, the Boston franchise in the newly formed American League won the first World Series, with Big Bill Dinneen and Cy Young combining for five victories in the best-of-eight showdown against Honus Wagner and the Pittsburgh Pirates.

It is true that, in the early days, the Americans (they would not be called the Red Sox until 1907) had as loyal a following as existed anywhere in America. Their every accomplishment was applauded, and their every failure dissected and analyzed, by a spirited bunch who called themselves the Royal Rooters and whose ringleader, Michael "'Nuf Ced" McGreevey, remains, more than a century later, the most famous Red Sox fan in history.

Cheering for the Americans was good community spirit on McGreevey's part, but it was also good business. Decades before Boston fans could criticize or applaud, condemn or salute, cry or laugh, simply by dialing in to one of the fire-breathing talk-show hosts at all-sports WEEI radio, they would do their venting at any of hundreds of watering holes around town.

And McGreevey's establishment, Third Base, located at various locations before settling in at 940 Columbus Avenue in Roxbury, was the place to be for the serious fan. Even its name had the ring of final judgment to it, third base being the last stop on the way home. And McGreevey's nickname came about for no other reason than because the respected, well-known barkeep felt empowered to end any and all baseball arguments by slamming a hand down and announcing, "'Nuff said!" McGreevey, writer Dan Shaughnessy suggests, "may well be the man who invented the sports bar."[3]

It is also true that the early Red Sox were one of baseball's first powerhouses, winning the World Series five times between 1903 and, fatefully, 1918. But then Red Sox owner Harry Frazee made what is inarguably the worst transaction in the history of professional sports, selling the man-child Babe Ruth to the New York Yankees following the 1919 season.

And the debate lingers: did Frazee sell Ruth to the Yankees in order to raise the cash needed to produce the Broadway play *No, No, Nanette?* Glenn Stout and Richard L. Johnson, whose *Red Sox Century: One Hundred Years of Red Sox Baseball* is the bible for anyone wishing to know the history of Boston's American League ball club, argue that "this version of history, like a third-rate melodrama that supplies an obvious villain, is spurious on its face and virtually unsupported by any factual evidence apart from a series of misconceptions and distortions."

Stout and Johnson maintain that "the truth is a more complicated story," noting that Frazee was not cash-poor at the time of the Ruth sale, and anyway, *No, No, Nanette* didn't even open until 1925—five years after the Babe was sent to New York.[4]

But Shaughnessy, whose best-selling *The Curse of the Bambino* set in motion the myth that Boston's decades-long hunger for a World Series championship was the product of an angry, vengeance-fueled Babe cursing the Red Sox from the great beyond, posits that Frazee was "strapped for cash" when he made the deal.[5] And the late, great David Halberstam concurred in *Summer of '49*, writing that Frazee was "desperate for funds."[6]

As for *No, No, Nanette* being the reason Frazee needed to raise cash, Leigh Montville, author of *The Big Bam: The Life and Times of Babe Ruth*, argues that there is a connection. "*No, No, Nanette* was indeed part of the deal," Montville writes. "Frazee did use the money to keep his theatrical interests afloat. The picture that had been handed down to New England schoolchildren was essentially correct: Harry Frazee was the bad guy."[7]

Montville unearthed an interview given to the Baseball Hall of Fame by pitcher Waite Hoyt, who was himself sold from the Red Sox to the Yankees a season after Ruth was. Hoyt recalled seeing a notice on the bulletin board prior to a Red Sox–New York Giants exhibition game at the Polo Grounds in the spring of 1920 stating that players "were invited to a theatrical performance, a light comedy, called *My Lady Friends*, that Harry Frazee was producing. There would be tickets at the box office." Hoyt, who apparently attended the play, said, "That show was put to music in 1924 and became *No, No, Nanette*. . . . If you trace it back, it was the sale of Babe Ruth that provided Harry Frazee with the $125,000 to produce that show."[8]

Whatever his reasons for selling Ruth, and however deep (or shallow) his pockets, Frazee had set in motion a series of events that would transform the Red Sox into a laughingstock.

By 1922 the Red Sox had hit rock bottom, losing 93 games and finishing in last place in the American League. And attendance fell off accordingly. Having led the majors in attendance in 1915, drawing 539,885 fans to Fenway Park, the Red Sox drew only 259,184 that year. And with the last-place Boston Braves of the National League attracting just 167,965 fans to Braves Field, the total combined attendance for the city's two big league teams—427,149—was less than every other team in baseball save the Philadelphia A's.

Red Sox Nation indeed.

From 1922 through 1933, the Red Sox finished last in the eight-team American League nine times, with two seventh-place finishes. It must have been a cause of celebration in 1931 when the Red Sox actually chugged to a *sixth*-place finish. But whatever optimism there may have been was short-lived, as the 1932 Red Sox lost a franchise-record 111 games. Attendance for the 1932 season was 182,150, the lowest in the history of the franchise—even including the inaugural 1901 season at the Huntington Avenue Grounds.

The ravages of the Great Depression surely played a role in holding down attendance. But lousy management, which acquired lousy players, did more than anything to discourage would-be fans from investing their hard-won entertainment dollars in a team that rarely won.

Had Andrew J. Urban II been around in the early 1930s, he'd have been out shooting pool, not collecting the autographs of crummy Red Sox players.

SAVIOR?

Which brings us to . . .

Thomas Austin Yawkey,
Owner, sportsman, fan.
Baseball lives in Boston
Through the efforts of this man.

This homage to the longtime owner of the Red Sox was written in 1967 by John Connelly, an obscure news writer at the original WHDH-TV in Boston, Channel 5. The 100–1 long-shot Red Sox had just completed their "Impossible Dream" campaign, winning the American League pennant on the final day of the season, and Connelly was asked to provide the script for a television special honoring the team. What he came up with was a punchy, breezy poem with lyrics so memorable in the local baseball community that many aging Sox fans are able to repeat them to this day:

Sure the Tigers lead,
Chicago has speed,
And the Twins still have Oliva.
But with Yaz and Scott,
and what we've got,
just feel that pennant fever.

The script—paired with player interviews, game highlights, and a serenade to Red Sox left fielder (and 1967 Triple Crown winner) Carl Yastrzemski that Connelly and his wife wrote one night in the living room of their home in suburban Norwood—was eventually turned into a record album, titled, naturally, *The Impossible Dream: The Story of the 1967 Boston Red Sox.* Jess Cain, a hugely popular radio presence on morning drive, was brought in to record what came to be known as "The Yaz Song," knocking it out in one take at the studios of Fleetwood Records. The album's narration was provided by Red Sox play-by-play barker Ken Coleman.

"The two big albums for people from New England in 1967 were *Sgt. Pepper's Lonely Hearts Club Band* and *The Impossible Dream,*" said writer Richard Johnson, also curator of the Sports Museum. "It came out for Christmas, and everyone had a copy. I still have mine."[1]

The album is important on many levels, but chiefly as a reminder of how the 1967 Red Sox captured the collective imagination of New England sports fans and blazed a trail for such future devotees as autograph collector extraordinaire Andrew J. Urban II. It also serves as an example of how, back in the day, fans and media alike gently pulled on their kid gloves in any discussion of Tom Yawkey, owner of the Red Sox from 1932 until his death in 1976.

Baseball lives in Boston
Through the efforts of this man.

A more accurate verse would have been: baseball somehow survived in Boston despite this man. For while it is true that Yawkey invested time, money, and passion when he purchased Boston's laughingstock American League franchise in 1932, it is also true that he, more than any other man, contributed to the so-called curse that denied the Red Sox a World Series championship for eighty-six years.

Born in 1903 as Thomas Yawkey Austin, the future owner of the Red Sox was not yet seven months old when his father died. He was adopted by his mother's brother, Detroit Tigers owner William Yawkey, and eventually took his uncle's last name as his own. And like his uncle, Tom Yawkey invested in baseball: when he turned thirty and collected his inheritance, this lifelong child of privilege became one of the boys of summer, albeit at the corporate level, with his purchase of the Red Sox.

In the early days, Yawkey was a maverick owner and a godsend to Red Sox fans. He invested in a major renovation of Fenway Park, which until then had been unchanged since Dana Joseph Paine Wingate dug in against Casey Hagerman in 1912, and then he invested in players. During his first decade as owner, he waved his checkbook under the noses of the owners of cash-poor teams and purchased such stars as first baseman Jimmie Foxx, left-hander Lefty Grove, and shortstop Joe Cronin, the last serving double duty as manager. All three would later be enshrined in the Hall of Fame.

Yawkey also hired scouts to hit America's heartland in search of future stars, and in 1938 the Red Sox hit the mother lode when a scrawny, left-handed-hitting outfielder from San Diego's Hoover High School arrived for his first spring training. Ted Williams would go on to become one of the greatest hitters in the game's history, an iconic player who feuded with sportswriters, refused to doff his cap to the fans, and, in between all that, managed to become the last player in history to hit .400, going 6-for-8 in a doubleheader against the Philadelphia Athletics on the final day of the 1941 season to close out at .406.

Since then, no player has come close to hitting .400. Since then, few players have come close to matching the Williams swagger.

But it wasn't just Williams who turned the Red Sox into a team to be reckoned with. In 1936 a sturdy and stoic second baseman named Bobby Doerr debuted with the Red Sox. He, too, would one day be enshrined in Cooperstown. Johnny Pesky, a onetime clubhouse boy with the Portland Beavers of the Pacific Coast League, became a fixture at shortstop, logging three 200-hit seasons. Had he not lost three seasons serving in the Naval Air Corps during World War II, he might have joined Williams and Doerr in Cooperstown. And the Red Sox signed the youngest of the three baseball-playing brothers from an immigrant Italian family from San Francisco: Dominic DiMaggio would roam center field for ten seasons.

It took until after the war was over—by which time Foxx and Grove were gone and an over-the-hill Cronin had at last stopped playing and was now managing the team full-time—but in 1946 the Red Sox won their first pennant since 1918.

They lost the World Series to the St. Louis Cardinals in seven games, but Boston baseball fans knew they had a team worth following. True, it was an era of heartbreak for this new breed of Royal Rooters: two years after their World Series loss to the Cardinals in '46, the '48 Red Sox lost a one-game playoff to the Cleveland Indians for the American League pennant when aging manager Joe McCarthy made the preposterous decision to start journeyman Denny Galehouse.

The playoff loss to the Indians denied Boston sports fans what would have been the city's only subway series, as the Braves captured the National League pennant. The Indians went on to defeat the Braves in the World Series, a last hurrah of sorts for Boston's National League ball club, which in 1953 gave up trying to compete with the Red Sox and moved to Milwaukee.

With two games remaining in the 1949 season, the Red Sox went into Yankee Stadium needing just one victory to secure the American League pennant. They lost both of them. The Sox had another strong season in 1950, putting together an offense so powerful that three players drove in 100 or more runs, with Williams, playing in just 89 games, driving in 97. The *team* batting average was .302. The *team* on-base percentage was an off-the-charts .385. Yet the Red Sox still finished four games behind the pennant-winning Yankees and a game behind second-place Detroit. Do the math: in 1948, '49, and '50, the Red Sox finished a *combined* six games out of first place. It was a dynasty of frustration for Sox fans.

And then, just like that, the Red Sox returned to being irrelevant. They were mostly a middle-of-the-pack outfit through the 1950s, usually finishing above .500 but getting no closer to first place in the final standings than eleven games out. The customers took notice. The team had set a franchise record by drawing 1,596,650 fans to Fenway Park in '49, but attendance dipped in each of the next five seasons. Even in 1953, with the exodus of the Braves making Boston a one-team town, the Red Sox drew nearly 100,000 fewer fans than in the previous season.

By the 1960s, Tom Yawkey had more or less given up on the team and retreated to his South Carolina estate, and the Red Sox had become the laughingstockings all over again. In 1960, Williams's final season, the Red Sox won just 65 games, finishing 32 games out of first place.

In 1961, Williams's perch in left field was assumed by rookie Carl Yastrzemski, who would play twenty-three seasons for the Red Sox and one day join Teddy Ballgame in Cooperstown. But it made little difference in '61 as the Red Sox went 76–86, a whopping 33 games behind the Yankees.

In 1965, the Red Sox lost 100 games for the first time since 1932, the year before Yawkey bought the team. Not only had the Red Sox become bad, they had become boring. Even taking into account that attendance at major league ball games was not what it is today, the Red Sox simply were not connecting with their fan base. They *averaged* only 8,052 fans per game in 1965. In 1966 that figure jumped to 10,014 fans per game. Their total attendance for 1966—811,172—was nearly 200,000 off the major league average.

For years Yawkey had trusted an assortment of cronies and drinking buddies to run his team. But while mismanagement can be looked upon as comical when played out by the Three Stooges or the Marx Brothers, there was—and is—nothing funny about the sad reality that Red Sox management, under Yawkey's watchful eye, did its best work when it came to making sure that no black man wore a Red Sox uniform. In what remains the sorriest episode in the history of the franchise, the Red Sox were shamed by a local politician into granting an April 1945 tryout to three Negro League players—Sam Jethroe, Marvin Williams, and an infielder with the Kansas City Monarchs named Jackie Robinson.

The Red Sox said they'd be in touch. Naturally, they never were. And Robinson, who two years later made history when he debuted with the Brooklyn Dodgers, hated the Red Sox for the rest of his life. "For all the talk about Boston's Curse of the Bambino," wrote Jonathan Eig in *Opening Day: The Story of Jackie Robinson's First Season*, "the curse of Jackie Robinson hurt them far more."[2]

It was not until 1959 that the Red Sox promoted an African American to the big leagues, infielder Elijah "Pumpsie" Green. This was more than twelve years after Jackie Robinson had played his first game with the Dodgers. Every other team in baseball had already promoted black players, with the likes of Willie Mays (Giants), Ernie Banks (Cubs), Frank Robinson (Reds), Henry Aaron (who had originally signed with the Boston Braves in 1952 and now was starring in Milwaukee), and Bob Gibson (Cardinals) establishing their credentials for future enshrinement in Cooperstown. With Willie O'Ree making his National Hockey League debut in 1958, the Boston Bruins had a black player on their roster before the Red Sox did.

To be sure, race issues would continue to haunt the Red Sox right into the 1980s, but the Red Sox of the 1960s began to look like other teams. Thanks to a new breed of baseball operations executives, notably general manager Dick O'Connell and scouting director Neil Mahoney, the Red Sox began to sign and develop black players. They even had a black minor league coach of sorts when Billy Harrell, who played in thirty-seven games for the Red Sox in 1961, emerged as a player-coach with the team's Double-A Pittsfield club in 1965.

While the biggest stars of the pennant-winning 1967 Red Sox were Most Valuable Player Carl Yastrzemski, Cy Young Award winner Jim Lonborg, and fiery Hall of Fame–bound rookie manager Dick Williams, the team owed much of its success to African American players who wouldn't have been given a chance a decade earlier: Joe Foy at third base; rookie Reggie Smith in center field; first baseman George "Boomer" Scott, who hit .303 and drove in eighty-two runs; veteran John Wyatt, acquired from the Kansas City Athletics, who pitched sixty games in relief, winning ten of them.

"What they now call Red Sox Nation, we think we started that in 1967," said Dick Williams. "I think there were only eight thousand fans there on Opening Day that year. There were a lot of empty seats. But you could see the change midway through the season."

At the All-Star break, the Red Sox were just six games out of first place. In August, matinee idol right fielder Tony Conigliaro was hit in the left eye by a pitch thrown by California Angels right-hander Jack Hamilton, forcing the twenty-two-year-old Massachusetts native out for the remainder of the season and derailing what up until then was a career on the fast track to Cooperstown. Still, the Red Sox went into

September clinging to first place in what was turning out to be a scramble in the ten-team American League. The race was so tight that the *fourth-place* White Sox were just one and a half games out of first.

The Red Sox needed victories over the Minnesota Twins in their final two games of the regular season to earn at least a tie for first place. Unlike the '49 Red Sox, who closed out the season with those two losses to the Yankees, these Red Sox took care of business and swept the Twins; later that afternoon, when the Tigers lost the second game of a doubleheader to the California Angels, the pennant was Boston's.

Never mind that the Red Sox lost the World Series to the Cardinals in seven games. While the seeds of Red Sox Nation were planted by the Royal Rooters, the Nation was reborn in 1967. After six straight seasons of drawing fewer than one million fans, the Red Sox drew a franchise-record 1,727,832 fans to Fenway in '67, tops in the American League.

And the crowds have been coming ever since. Though the history books are filled with the many near-misses and tragic endings that became a sort of Red Sox tradition in the '70s and '80s and '90s—Luis Aparicio tripping as he rounded third in '72, a September collapse in '74, losing Game 7 to the Reds in the '75 World Series after Carlton Fisk's home run for the ages in Game 6, Bucky Dent in '78, Bill Buckner in '86, being swept by the Oakland A's in '88 and '90, losing to the Cleveland Indians in '95 and '98, and to the hated Yankees in '99, culminating with Grady Little leaving Pedro Martinez on the Yankee Stadium mound to fry in Game 7 of the 2003 American League Championship Series—the fans kept showing up and asking for more.

Their faith was rewarded in 2004, when the Red Sox, having staged their history-making comeback against the Yankees in the ALCS after losing the first three games of the series, went on to sweep the Cardinals for their first World Series championship in eighty-six years.

B ut in the opinion of some observers, Fenway Park was not the same after the modern-day Red Sox finally won a World Series. Some preferred the time when Fenway had been a temple of hardball wisdom, a meeting place for serious, well-read baseball fans who were convinced they had a better handle on things than the manager. Rare indeed was the Red Sox skipper who could serve out his term without suffering the wrath of the fans. In 1976 a tavern owner from South Portland, Maine, named Eddie Griffin took out an ad in the *Portland Press Herald* claiming he would not attend another Red Sox game until manager Darrell Johnson was fired.

The man who replaced Johnson, Don Zimmer, fared even worse. Johnson at least got the Red Sox into the '75 World Series. Zimmer was at the controls when the '78 Red Sox blew a fourteen-and-a-half-game lead over the Yankees in the American League East, leading to the one-game playoff game and Bucky Dent's home run.

"I would have to say there's no tougher town to manage in than Boston," states Zimmer in his book *The Zen of Zim: Baseballs, Beanballs, and Bosses.* "The fans there are as knowledgeable as you'll find anywhere in America, but they're also the most frustrated. As in eighty years of frustration. There's an unofficial Baseball Hall of Infamy in Boston filled with fans' villains from over the years who played a part in Red Sox heartbreak—and I'm probably one of 'em."[3]

Zim's book was published in the summer of 2004—just a few months before those years of frustration would be wiped off the books. But even before the Sox won the 2004 World Series, a kinder, gentler Red Sox Nation was awakening. When the estate of Tom Yawkey's widow, Jean Yawkey, sold the team following the 2001 season, new owners John Henry, Tom Werner, and president/CEO Larry Lucchino brought sweeping changes to Fenway Park.

For one thing, they cleaned the joint up. Lucchino had run the Baltimore Orioles from 1988 to 1993 and was instrumental in the creation of Oriole Park at Camden Yards, a glitzy but old-timey-looking ballpark that was shoehorned into the city's urbanscape. With ripping down Fenway apparently not an option, Lucchino sought to modernize and expand it. He brought in Janet Marie Smith, with whom he had worked in Baltimore, as vice president of planning and development, and soon they were ripping down walls aplenty at Fenway and adding new amenities. While the park remained cramped, with seats in some sections being impossibly uncomfortable, it now offered bigger, cleaner restrooms, an array of concession venues, and an exciting new tier of seating atop the original grandstand.

The new owners also wanted to change the *mood* of Fenway Park. The previous ownership had trumpeted the old ballpark as "Friendly Fenway" when in reality it was anything but. Longtime employees were often indifferent to the wants and needs of modern-day fans, and in-game entertainment did not extend much beyond old show tunes being pumped out on the organ between innings.

The new owners changed that, beginning with the hiring of Charles Steinberg, another old Lucchino lieutenant from the Baltimore days. A Baltimore native and baseball zealot whose introduction to the Orioles was as a teenage intern, Steinberg remained with the club through college and beyond. Even after he had become a practicing dentist, Steinberg continued to work for the Orioles, both in public relations and, naturally, as team dentist.

A baseball impresario who created lavish pregame ceremonies with the precise choreography of a Broadway musical, the jaunty Steinberg brought his panache to the Red Sox and to Fenway Park. He hired an array of musical notables to perform before, during, and after Sox games, from Ray Charles to the Cowsills. Following the death of Ted Williams on July 5, 2002, he staged a lavish, night-long celebration of the Splendid Splinter's life, right down to famed broadcaster Curt Gowdy re-creating his call of the home run that Teddy Ballgame hit in his final big league at-bat. The man who threw the pitch, sixty-three-year-old Jack Fisher, was brought in to stand on the mound, decked out in his old Baltimore Orioles shirt.

Steinberg kept tweaking the Fenway presentation. He enlisted young children to scream, "Play ball!" into a field mike before each game. He resurrected an old Orioles gimmick of costuming an attractive young woman in a uniform from the All-American Girls Baseball League and having her sweep off the bases between innings.

Suddenly, it wasn't all about the baseball. The Red Sox had become chic, sexy. And Fenway, no longer just a haven for hard-core, educated *baseball fans*, now was a social center, a place to see and be seen. Beginning on May 15, 2003, when 33,801 fans turned out to see Pedro Martinez submit six shutout innings in a 12–3 rout of the Texas Rangers, the Red Sox began a streak of consecutive sellouts at Fenway Park that by the end of the 2008 season would reach 469, a major league record.

Not everyone liked the team's newfound popularity. As tickets became increasingly harder to get, the old-time fans Zimmer wrote about were being squeezed out by the smart set. And thus was created a local catchphrase: the Pink Hats. The term took its name from the trendy pink Red Sox caps now being hawked at the souvenir stores; to be called a Pink Hat, whether you owned one or not, was to be branded a tourist.

"They show up like every day is Christmas, and you know what that means: you just lost your seat at church," wrote Tony Massarotti in the June 2, 2006, issue of the *Herald*. "You have shown up week after week, year after year, and now you have to stand behind the last pew because of some lady with an obnoxious pink hat.

"The Red Sox are trendier than a Louis Vuitton handbag these days, more than three years removed from their last baseball-free October," continued Massarotti. "The championship season of 2004 extinguished years of agony and decades of self-doubt, and it rewarded long-suffering loyalists who knew what it meant to hurt. Unfortunately, it also gave birth to an entirely new generation of wannabes, a nouveau riche that shows up at Fenway Park and acts like Paris Hilton.

"The rest of us? We are starting to get a little tired of it all."[4]

Andrew J. Urban II, no student of class warfare, didn't give a damn. "Bring 'em on" was his mantra. If these newbie fans were having a good time and bringing a new kind of electricity to Fenway Park, then what was wrong with that?

In Urban's worldview, there was only one subspecies of fan out there who merited scorn and ridicule: the professional autograph collector.

Like Joe McCarthy (the alcoholic onetime U.S. senator, not the alcoholic onetime manager of the Red Sox) talking about the spread of communism, Urban gets mighty worked up when he talks about the spread of professional autograph collectors.

And just as Joe McCarthy famously said he had in his pocket a list of Communists working in the State Department . . .

"I know who the professional collectors are," Urban will tell you. "On any given day, I can weed out who's selling. I can weed out who's lying. They disgust me. You can always tell the guys who are there to buy and sell, because all they carry are baseballs, and maybe seven or eight bats that they just want to get single-signed.

"And they're only after a select group. If it was between David Ortiz signing and Kevin Cash signing, they would all rush up to Ortiz because he's a starter and Cash is just the backup catcher. And that's being very disrespectful to Cash. I see it happen all the time, and it makes me mad. It's not enough to ask them to sign. They'll tell them *where* to sign, and then they'll tell them to sign a second bat. That's another way you know they're just there to make a buck."

Not once in his life has Urban sold an autograph. Hasn't even considered it. Even were he down to his last nickel, with no shelter, no food, no hope, he would not sell an autograph. To do so, he reasons, would be to violate something special, something sacred.

Urban was thinking about the professional autograph seekers as he prepared for the 2007 home opener. They'd be out in force, like locusts, he reminded himself. But he was not going to let them ruin this, his favorite day of year.

Just as big league ballplayers have their Opening Day rituals, so, too, does Andrew J. Urban II. There is, for instance, the equipment check. Look, he may not be one of those slimy professionals, but he is no rookie. Just as a sport fisherman would be viewed as an amateur if he were to head off for Golden Pond without his lures and hooks, an autograph collector would be viewed similarly if he didn't leave the house with the following:

1. A pen that works. ("It bothers me," he says, "when someone asks a player for an autograph and hands him a pen that doesn't work. That's a sign of a person who is unprepared, and it's disrespectful. It makes us all look bad.")
2. A disposable camera. ("Sometimes if I can get next to a player I'll hand the camera to someone and ask them to take a picture. That means more to me than an autograph.")
3. Baseball cards.
4. Five or six regulation major league baseballs. ("I've had some bad experiences with cheap baseballs, so I only get the best. I

try to buy them at Target, because they're cheaper. No offense
to the souvenir store at Fenway, but I never buy baseballs there.
They charge double.")
5. A Sharpie. ("I use the Sharpie when players are signing a card,
but never on a baseball. A Sharpie will bleed on the baseball,
and over time it will expand.")

Urban was ready for Opening Day, ready and excited. And a little nervous. Opening Day jitters. He stepped outside into the morning springtime chill, turned left, and walked one block to the bus stop on Trapelo
Road. No way was he going to drive to Fenway Park today, not with all
the zanies who don't even have tickets but will mill about outside the old
ballpark just for the Mardi Gras feel of the scene.

Urban would not be on the outside looking in, not today. He had
scored a ticket from a friend, and he planned on being inside to watch
the game after he had checked out the autograph scene outside. He
hopped aboard the 70-A bus to Watertown Square. From there, he
caught the 57 bus to Kenmore Square. After a short walk over a bridge
under which run some old railroad tracks and the Massachusetts Turn-
pike, he had arrived.

As he expected, it was a bad day for autographs. Too many hooky-
playing kids hanging around. Too many pain-in-the-ass grown-ups who'd
called in sick. The gates finally opened, the early arrivals cheering, and
Urban stepped inside with the masses. He walked around the old park,
taking in all the sights, sounds, and aromas. He did an inventory to see
what was new in the park since last season. He looked up to the roof
in right field, where a set of temporary bleachers had been erected, the
club calling it Tony C's Corner, in memory of Tony Conigliaro. Urban
approved.

Scouting around for celebrities, he caught a glimpse of actor-comedian
Tom Arnold. He ran into Fred Smerlas and Steve DeOssie, a pair of onetime professional football stars and now popular yakkers on local radio
and television. His next stop was Autograph Alley, a Fenway Park contriv-
ance of recent vintage located at the end of a ramp where, before each
game, a former Red Sox player would be enlisted to meet fans and sign

autographs. Sometimes you'd get a famous ex-player, such as Rico Petro-celli or Oil Can Boyd; other times it might be, say, Billy MacLeod, a native of Gloucester, Massachusetts, whose big league career consisted of two mound appearances with the Red Sox in 1962.

Though Autograph Alley was a gathering place for fans who would not otherwise be collecting autographs—amateurs, if you will—Urban rather liked seeing these old-timers return to Fenway. He once met Ted Lepcio, an all-purpose infielder who played for the Red Sox in the 1950s. Another time he met Billy Conigliaro, Tony's kid brother, who played a few years with the Red Sox.

On a normal game day, Urban would have gone home more than an hour earlier; when your main purpose for being at Fenway Park is to stand outside and collect autographs, your mission is complete once all the players have gone inside to change. But Urban settled back and watched the Red Sox roll to a festive 14–3 victory over the Seattle Mariners. Josh Beckett allowed just one run in seven innings, striking out eight Mariners and walking nobody. The Boston offense banged out fourteen hits, including a two-run homer by J. D. Drew in his Fenway unveiling. Varitek was 3-for-4 with three ribbies, and first baseman Kevin Youkilis had three hits.

What troubled Urban, though, was the little rookie at second base, Dustin Pedroia. He had gone a combined 5-for-10 in the season-opening series at Kansas City to begin his tenure as Boston's everyday second baseman, but now he was struggling some; having gone a combined 0-for-6 in the series at Arlington, Texas, and then 0-for-4 in the home opener, he was now hitless in his last ten at-bats.

A small, almost irrelevant sampling to be sure. Still, Urban had a right to his opinion, and he had his doubts about this Pedroia kid.

6

SWINGING OUT OF HIS ASS

I n the seventh round of the 2003 amateur draft, Theo Epstein's first as general manager of the Red Sox, the club selected a sturdy, power-hitting first baseman out of Arizona State University named Jeremy West. In the early going, it looked like a solid pick: debuting that summer for the Lowell Spinners, Boston's farm club in the rookie New York–Penn League, West drove in forty-three runs in seventy-one games. Though he hit just .280, his on-base percentage was .368.

For his efforts, West was named the Spinners' Player of the Year. While the honor included a nice plaque for West to hang in the family room back home in Las Vegas, Nevada, the real prize was a September trip to Fenway Park for a pregame ceremony in which the big club's top prospects for 2003 would be introduced.

When West arrived at Boston's Logan International Airport, he was met by Amiel Sawdaye, at the time an intern in the Red Sox scouting department. Sawdaye helped West stow his luggage in the back of a car he had borrowed from one of the scouts, and then the baseball executive in training and the baseball player in training pulled out of Logan Airport, sped through the Sumner Tunnel into the city, and picked up Storrow Drive. Destination: Fenway.

As they were passing Massachusetts General Hospital near the Longfellow Bridge, Sawdaye, with scouting on his mind, began quizzing West about Jeff Larish, a power-hitting infielder entering his junior year at Arizona State.

"Larish is very good," said West, "but he's not their best player."

Sawdaye played along.

"Oh? And who *is* their best player?"

"Dustin Pedroia."

Sawdaye was familiar with Pedroia, ASU's diminutive, tough-as-nails shortstop. The Red Sox had scouted Pedroia the previous season, and liked him. At the time, though, Larish was the higher-profile prospect, the player to keep an eye on.

"If you ever need a big hit at any point in the game," West said, "Dustin Pedroia is your man."

"Really?" asked Sawdaye. "What kind of hitter is he?"

Replied West, "He swings out of his ass."

It was not the first time such a comment would be made about Dustin Pedroia. Nor would it be the last. Sometimes the remark was made as a compliment, the idea being that Pedroia, generously listed at five-foot-nine, 180 pounds, in the *2005 Red Sox Media Guide*, managed to generate more power with his swing than players twice his size. Others used the remark as a criticism, shaking their heads and wondering why such a small player was taking such big cuts instead of doing what pint-size players are *supposed* to do: hitting 'em where they ain't, the way Wee Willie Keeler did in the 1890s.

It boiled down to this: Pedroia's feisty swing, coupled with his feisty nature, worked at the college level. Would it work at the major league level? After checking Pedroia out, the Red Sox determined that, yes, absolutely, the kid's act could work in the big leagues.

"I remember Amiel coming back and saying, 'This kid's numbers are ridiculous,'" said Red Sox assistant general manager Jed Hoyer. "That was the first time we really started looking at him. We obviously knew him, but hearing that, we thought, okay, maybe this guy's a little different.

"Numbers-wise, he jumped off the page. And when we started scouting him, we had remarkably consistent reports on him. You'd think it wouldn't be like that, but everyone was very confident he was going to be a big leaguer, period. The debate was over the impact he'd have . . . but we knew if we took him, we'd have a guy who was definitely going to play in the big leagues."

Nobody had to tap Theo Epstein on the shoulder and tell him about Pedroia's potential. He, too, was impressed.

"His performance really stood out," Epstein recalled. "While he lacked standout tools, his defense stood out, and his makeup stood out. But we figured he was probably going to be gone before we got a chance to draft him."

By the spring of 2004, plenty of other teams were interested in Pedroia. Having already been named Pac 10 Co-Player of the Year in 2003, he returned for his senior year and lit up opposing pitchers, hitting .445 with five home runs and eighteen doubles.

Having forfeited their first-round pick, the twenty-fourth pick overall, to the Oakland A's as compensation for signing free-agent reliever Keith Foulke, the Red Sox wouldn't even be stepping up to the table until pick number sixty-five at the 2004 amateur draft; by that time, went their reasoning, Pedroia would already have been gobbled up by another team. Thus, the Red Sox went into the draft not thinking too much about such players as Pedroia and Old Dominion right-hander Justin Verlander.

As expected, Verlander went high, taken by the Detroit Tigers with the second pick. And the Tigers made a splendid pick: within two years, Verlander was a big league ace, fashioning a 17–9 record in thirty starts as Detroit made its first World Series appearance since 1984. As the draft moved along, Pedroia remained on the board. The first round came and went, and Pedroia went unclaimed. It was looking more and more as though talent evaluators throughout the game were being turned off by Pedroia's diminutive size and big-ass swing.

After some fifty-five players had been taken, and with Pedroia and Cal State Fullerton catcher Kurt Suzuki still available, the Sox baseball brain trust, sitting in a conference room at Fenway Park, had some reevaluating to do.

"Shit, one of these two guys is going to be left," Epstein said to his staffers.

And Epstein liked both players. A lot.

The draft reached the sixty-second pick, whereupon the Philadelphia Phillies returned to an old passion, taking catcher Jason Jaramillo of

Oklahoma State. Three years earlier, when he was a Wisconsin high school senior, Jaramillo was selected in the thirty-ninth round by the Phillies. Not high enough for Jaramillo's taste. He chose to attend Okie State. Now he was back. So, too, were the Phils.

Following the Kansas City Royals and Houston Astros, the Red Sox were up. The Sox had already boiled their debate down to two players: Suzuki, a Hawaii native who had already won the Johnny Bench Award, presented annually to the nation's top collegiate backstop, or Pedroia.

"It was a no-brainer that we were going to take whichever of those two players was still available," Epstein recalled. "There was a high school infielder we were going to take if all those guys were gone. A couple of scouts really liked him. But a few didn't. I didn't feel real good about it. So we hoped that someone else would still be there."

After much discussion—"We had better reports on Pedroia," Epstein said—the Red Sox decided they would pick the feisty little infielder from ASU. Two picks after the Sox grabbed Pedroia, the Oakland A's drafted Suzuki. He was in the big leagues within three years.

Pedroia began his professional career with a twelve-game hitting streak for the Red Sox Single-A club in Augusta, Georgia, registering a .400 average in 50 at-bats. The Red Sox quickly moved him up to their "high" Single-A club in Sarasota, Florida, where he was reunited with his former Arizona State teammate Jeremy West, whose conversation with Amiel Sawdaye had helped place Pedroia on Boston's wish list. And the hits kept coming at Sarasota, with Pedroia logging a .336 average in 107 at-bats, including a twelve-game hitting streak.

Just as the Red Sox had invited Jeremy West to visit Fenway Park at the end of the 2003 minor league season, now it was Pedroia's turn. On September 20, 2004, with the Red Sox less than two weeks from beginning a postseason that would prove to be history-making, Pedroia stepped into the batting cage at Fenway to take some cuts with the big boys.

As Pedroia confidently pounded line drives all over the old ballyard, Red Sox legend Johnny Pesky, a few days shy of his eighty-fifth birthday, shouted out words of encouragement.

"There it goes—another one!" yelled Pesky, a leathery old ballplayer who takes pride in his role as a walking, talking link to the 1940s, which is to say Ted Williams.

"Another one!" he yelled again. "And another one!"

Pedroia's presence did not go unnoticed by the local media.

"It's awesome being here," the *Globe* quoted him as saying. "I wanted to see the Monster after having seen it so much on TV. It's pretty cool."[1]

Steven Krasner of the *Providence Journal* noted that Pedroia "managed to clout one over the Green Monster."[2]

The *Herald*'s Michael Silverman played on Pedroia's size, writing: "Pedroia cuts a less-than-imposing figure on the field, but his credentials are weighty enough."[3]

Pedroia apparently chose not to act like he was visiting Fenway Park solely for the $5 tour. With barely a summer of low-level minor league baseball under his belt, he was issuing a challenge to the cynics.

"Every day, people are still doubting me," he said. "A guy my size, 'He can't do it, he can't do anything.' I've got to prove people wrong."[4]

Later that night, sitting in a private box with Red Sox officials, Pedroia was even more direct. When someone noted that he'd been the sixty-fifth player selected in the draft, Pedroia said, "Yeah, fuck those other sixty-four guys. I'll get to the big leagues before all those guys anyway."

However one chooses to define this—cockiness, bravado, a Napoleonic Complex, Little Man's Disease—it was pure Pedroia. And the anecdotal evidence abounds. He kept a list of those members of the media who he believes doubted he could play in the big leagues; later, when a reporter asked if he really remembered the names of the doubters, Pedroia's response was "You mean, like you?"

As for those scouts who doubted him, "I don't listen to any of that crap," he told the *Globe*. "Scouts, they're going to doubt me. They're just upset because they don't have the ability to be in the major leagues. That's why they're scouting."[5]

Amiel Sawdaye, whose own playing career didn't last beyond high school ball in Baltimore, found the Pedroia quote to be hilarious. He keeps a copy of the newspaper article in his office, as do several other scouts. In a weird way, they're rather proud of it.

The Red Sox promoted Pedroia to the big leagues on August 21, 2006, and he made his debut the next night against the Angels. The Sox were fading fast in the American League East, and recognizing there would be no return to the playoffs that season, the club saw a perfect opportunity to audition Pedroia for a possible starting job in 2007.

The incumbent second baseman, Mark Loretta, had played his entire eleven-year major league career in the National League before signing with Boston for the 2006 season. He was voted by fans to represent the American League in the 2006 All-Star Game. He was also going to be a free agent following the season and would be looking to make somewhere in the neighborhood of the $3.25 million he was being paid by the Red Sox. And he was thirty-five years old. Pedroia, who had just turned twenty-three when he was promoted to the big leagues, would be making the major league minimum—about $380,000—if he made the team in 2007.

Pedroia appeared in thirty-one games in the last weeks of 2006, hitting just .191. But Red Sox fans suspected a change was about to take place at second base: on the last day of the season, in what would be a 9–0 rain-shortened victory over the Baltimore Orioles in which rookie Davern Hansack submitted a five-inning no-hitter, the crowd bestowed a standing ovation on Loretta when he was called in from second base in the top of the fifth. He was replaced by Pedroia. The masses were certain Loretta would not be back. They were right: he eventually signed a one-year, $2.5 million deal with the Houston Astros.

The Red Sox were committed to Pedroia as their second baseman for 2007. Now they waited for him to start hitting.

Had Pedroia been willing to do some homework and extend his list of media doubters to include skeptical Red Sox fans, it would have included Andrew J. Urban II.

But for all his baseball knowledge, after all those years of watching the games, keeping the stats, collecting the signatures of stars and scrubeenies alike, Urban had it wrong, all wrong, about Dustin Pedroia.

Like all learned fans, Urban had been hearing and reading glowing reports about Pedroia ever since the 2004 amateur draft. Some two years later, he remained skeptical. But not content with merely standing outside Fenway Park to meet and greet established big leaguers

Urban would climb into his 2001 Ford Focus and go off on personal scouting missions. Three of the Red Sox minor league teams are within easy driving distance of Fenway Park, with the Lowell Spinners of the rookie New York–Penn League in nearby Lowell, the Double-A Portland (Maine) Sea Dogs just a two-hour trip up Interstate 95, and the Triple-A Pawtucket Red Sox an hour away in the other direction.

Urban went to McCoy Stadium a couple of times to watch the Pawtucket Red Sox. Even then, with Pedroia en route to tearing up the International League with a .305 batting average and a .384 on-base percentage (third highest in the league), Urban didn't like what he saw—just a skinny little kid with a big man's swing.

If Pedroia even got to the big leagues, Urban felt, he'd get eaten up.

"The kid isn't going anywhere," Urban proclaimed.

After all his years following the game, Urban was confident in his ability to determine who had it and who did not. He knew his stuff. And it made him wonder: Why? How was it that he had become so passionate about baseball? He enjoyed the other sports and, naturally, had a rooting interest in the Patriots, Celtics, and Bruins. But it was not the same. Baseball was his rocket fuel, right up there with those cans of Pepsi he'd gulp down with his leftovers for breakfast.

Yes, his father, Andy Urban, was a big baseball fan. The old man also had an impressive card collection. Still, something else tugged at Urban, drumming a steady baseball beat. Baseball. Always. It was in the walls.

And then one day, when Urban was around twelve years old, his mother made a casual comment about how the family home at 11 Kingston Road was once lived in by a major league ballplayer.

What?

Could it be possible that Andrew J. Urban II, a man who has made collecting baseball players' autographs his life's work, his mission, his giving-back to society, was living in the very house in which a *player* once lived?

Urban began researching the matter, and it turned out to be true: Don Nottebart, who pitched nine years in the major leagues in the 1960s, almost all of them in the National League, lived for a time at 11 Kingston Road. Nottebart grew up on a small farm his family owned in nearby Lexington and was a three-sport star at Lexington High School; later, after he had gone off to play professional baseball, his family sold the farm and moved to the house at 11 Kingston Road in Waltham. In the early years of his career, it was to 11 Kingston Road that Nottebart traveled as soon as the season was over.

Nottebart is known for having pitched a no-hitter in 1963 and, in 1965, for giving up Willie Mays's five-hundredth career home run. At the tail end of his career, he pitched for the Yankees, and on April 22, 1969, he stood on the mound at Fenway Park for the first time as a major leaguer. Entering the game in the seventh inning in relief of starting pitcher Stan Bahnsen, the first batter he faced was Carl Yastrzemski, who homered. Though Nottebart returned in the eighth inning and struck out Yastrzemski in the rematch, there must have been a lot of joking later on at 11 Kingston Road. He finally gets to pitch at Fenway Park, and—*bang! zoom!*—he gets taken out of the yard by Yaz.

Having made this startling discovery about Don Nottebart, twelve-year-old Andrew J. Urban II took appropriate action: he wrote a letter to the man, asking for an autograph. A fellow autograph hound from outside Fenway Park had loaned him a book that contained the home addresses of hundreds of retired baseball players, and Nottebart was listed as residing in East Wakefield, New Hampshire.

In his letter, Urban explained to Nottebart their common thread as residents of 11 Kingston Road, and, oh, by the way, please send an autograph. Nottebart responded by sending back a nice letter and a couple of signed baseball cards.

I n the first days of the 2008 season, Urban's take on Dustin Pedroia's ability to play in the big leagues was spot-on. The kid just wasn't hitting.

The Red Sox had a fine backup infielder in Alex Cora, a onetime everyday player with the Los Angeles Dodgers who was now making a nice living as an all-purpose reserve. The younger brother of former major league infielder Joey Cora, who by now was a coach with the Chicago White Sox, Alex Cora wasn't much of a hitter, but he earned his keep with solid defense anywhere in the infield and a measure of game awareness that can't be taught. He was being looked upon as a future big league manager.

Only now there was rumbling that Cora should step in as the everyday second baseman and that Pedroia, deemed not ready for the big time, should be returned to the minor leagues.

"I wanted to impress everyone all at once—the whole Red Sox Nation, the media, my teammates," Pedroia would later say. "It took too much out of me. There were many, many sleepless nights. I'm the type of guy, if things aren't going well, I take it personally, deep inside. This isn't just a game for me. It's my life, and I take every part of it to my heart. That's what drives me to be successful. I don't want to be just a normal player. I want to be a great player. And that comes from taking things personally.

"I'd sit out on the couch, late at night, and I thought about *everything*. If I tried to get into bed, I'd get back out in five minutes. Those nights were definitely tough."

Francona confidently told members of the media that there would be no change, that Pedroia was his second baseman. And that was that. Privately, Francona, too, was anxious to see some of the offensive thunder the scouts claimed Pedroia was capable of delivering.

"They all said this kid was a keeper, but that there's the potential for him to struggle some because of his unique swing," Francona recalled. "I'd seen the struggling in September, I'd seen it in spring training. And you try not to make evaluations based on September and spring training. But it would have been nice to see him hit.

"We were worried, yeah," he said. "We're human."

Worries or no worries, the Red Sox weren't going to scrap the Pedroia plan after one month. And even had Francona wanted to, what was the alternative? Alex Cora?

"First of all, and it's not a knock on Cora, but he's not an everyday player," Francona said. "Okay, we could have gone with Cora in April. But where does that get us? We were supposed to take a guy who plays once a week and play him every day? Well, then what do we do? It just wasn't going to happen."

Francona had another reason to be patient with Pedroia: the Red Sox were winning. The Yankees arrived at Fenway in mid-April for the first series of the season between the two historic rivals, and the Sox won all three games. Beckett won the middle game to improve his record to 4–0; Matsuzaka, in his first career start against the Yankees, allowed six runs in seven innings but came away with the win in the series finale, thanks to a Boston offense that abused rookie lefty Chase Wright. Making only his second major league appearance . . . against the Red Sox . . . at Fenway Park . . . after being jumped from Double-A Trenton to the big leagues . . . in a game televised nationally on ESPN . . . Wright became the second pitcher in history to allow home runs to four consecutive hitters. In the third inning, Manny Ramirez, J. D. Drew, Mike Lowell, and Jason Varitek all socked home runs off the twenty-four-year-old in a span of ten pitches.

Until Chase Wright stumbled into the history books, the only pitcher to submit this kind of an inning was a fellow named Paul Foytack, who was on the mound for the Los Angeles Angels on the night of July 31, 1963, when four consecutive Cleveland Indians took him out of the yard. One of them was Tito Francona, whose son Terry, future manager of the Red Sox, was four years old.

As soon as Varitek's home run went into the books, Foytack, seventy-six years old and long, long retired from baseball, began receiving phone calls at his Tennessee home.

"I'm going to send that kid a note," he said, referring to Wright. "I'm going to tell him to hang in there. It must be tough for him. I was at the end of my career when I did it. He's just starting out."[6]

Hopefully Foytack sent his "Dear Chase" note to Trenton, New Jersey, which is where the Yankees sent Wright after the game.

A week later the Red Sox and Yankees hooked up at Yankee Stadium. The Red Sox again won the series, taking two out of three games. Leading off the top of the first inning in the second game, shortstop Julio Lugo lined a single off the right leg of Yankees starter Jeff Karstens. The right-hander pitched to one more batter before being removed from the game; good thing too, as it was later determined he had suffered a broken leg. And it's funny how things worked: with Karstens out, Yankees manager Joe Torre summoned *his* team's Japanese import, twenty-seven-year-old Kei Igawa, who pitched six shutout innings, helping the Yankees to a 3–1 victory.

As for Pedroia, he ended April hitting .182, and the kid who swung out of his ass was still looking for his first home run of the season. But Francona had been right: the Red Sox *were* winning, so there was no urgency to make a switch at second base. With a 7–4 victory over the Yankees in the series finale, the Red Sox went into May with a 16–8 record and in first place in the American League East.

Beckett was already 5–0 and establishing his credentials as a candidate for the Cy Young Award. Ortiz had seven home runs. Lowell was hitting .314. Papelbon, the returning closer, had yet to allow a run in nine relief appearances. After giving up that home run to John Buck on his inaugural major league pitch, Okajima made eleven more appearances in April without allowing a run.

And now, as the season moved into its second month, Boston's scouts—those guys who couldn't play this game, which, you know, is why they became scouts in the first place—were shown to be accurate in their assessment of Dustin Pedroia. As though some switch had been pulled upstairs in Baseball Operations, the kid began to hit.

Francona had sat Pedroia for two games over a three-day period, and the rookie used the time to work with Dave Magadan, the team's newly installed batting coach. During his own playing days, Magadan had been an entirely different kind of hitter from Pedroia: swinging from the left side of the plate, he used his bat like a surgeon's blade, slicing pitches the other way, working the count, eschewing the long ball. And it worked: Magadan was a .288 career hitter, including a .328 average with the Mets in 1990. He never did hit for power, accumulating just forty-two career home runs.

Many years from now, when Pedroia is inducted into the Hall of Fame, historians will regard May 5, 2007, as the date when he delivered on all that college and minor league promise. Facing Minnesota Twins ace Johan Santana at the Hubert H. Humphrey Metrodome, Pedroia singled to right in his first at-bat. In his next at-bat, he banged out a double. In the next game, a Sunday matinee at the Metrodome, Pedroia went 3-for-4, including a sixth-inning double off Sidney Ponson.

The Red Sox moved on to Toronto, and Pedroia kept hitting. He went 2-for-4 in Boston's 9–2 pasting of the Blue Jays at Rogers Centre, including a three-run homer off Jays starter Victor Zambrano. The next night, he had two more hits.

"I got away from Fenway Park and all that stuff that goes along with Boston, and kind of relaxed and played baseball," Pedroia recalled. "By the time I got back, I was on fire. I think that's when everyone started to say, 'Hey, this guy can play.' When we got back to Boston, I felt I didn't just have my teammates behind me. I had a whole city behind me."

The Red Sox won twenty games in May, including a 6–5 decision over the Baltimore Orioles at Fenway that was instantly and appropriately dubbed the Mother's Day Miracle. Trailing 5–0 through eight innings, Orioles starter Jeremy Guthrie having allowed just three hits, the Red Sox caught a break in the bottom of the ninth when Coco Crisp reached first on a dropped pop by catcher Ramon Hernandez. Here, Orioles manager Sam Perlozzo made the preposterous decision to remove Guthrie from the game. The Red Sox proceeded to have their way with relievers Danys Baez and Chris Ray, coming away with a 6–5 victory.

Pedroia hit .415 in May. Ramirez, who had also slumped in April, hit .327 with five home runs in May. Lowell sizzled in May, hitting .343 with six home runs. Matsuzaka wasn't pitching great, but he was winning. Beckett improved to 8–0.

Following an 11–6 victory over the Yankees at Fenway on June 2, Lowell driving in four runs against the team that nine seasons earlier gave him his first taste of the big leagues, the Red Sox were 37–17 and had an eleven-game lead in the American League East. Lowell also proved to be a one-man wrecking crew that day, introducing Yankees second baseman Robinson Cano to his shoulder and elbow while breaking up a double play. In the seventh inning, he collided with the Yankees' Doug Mientkiewicz, landing the Yankee first baseman at Massachusetts General Hospital.

The Mientkiewicz incident was a freak play; even the Yankees understood it was simply a case of two players landing in the same place at the same time. With Cano, it was impossible not to believe Lowell was retaliating for the previous night's game, when Yankees pitcher Scott Proctor rode a pitch up and in on Kevin Youkilis.

Lowell, who was high-fived by teammates after taking out Cano, was coy about the play when talking with reporters, explaining that, as an ex-Yankee, "that's what they taught us in the minor leagues. . . . It's a clean play. They taught me how to do it."[7]

7

THERE ONCE WERE THREE FANS FROM NANTUCKET

To judge from the television commercials that air during the games, fans of the National Football League are a bunch of Budweiser-drinkin', Hummer-drivin', Bridgestone-tires-buyin', Wrangler-jeans-wearin', Doritos-eatin' guys who possess Old Spice swagger, who send lots of packages that absolutely, positively have to get there overnight, and who, by the way, should really start thinking about life insurance. Because, after all, life comes at you fast.

The ad execs who buy airtime during NFL telecasts apparently look upon football fans as little more than overstuffed ex-frat boys. The Madison Avenue suits do not know, or do not care, that there are fans out there, hard-core fans, fans with heart, with passion, with pure fire escaping from their nostrils when the game isn't going their way, who in the end have absolutely no idea what the big deal is with the Bridgestone-Brand Potenza RE050A Tire.

Joan Fisher, born in 1930 on the island of Nantucket, thirty miles off the coast of Cape Cod, is a card-carrying Patriots fan who has had season tickets since 1995. She loves her Beringer merlot, which she buys at the Islander on Polpis Road on Nantucket, yet she's never seen the stuff advertised during an NFL game.

She has two younger sisters, also Nantucket natives. Jeanne Dooley, born in 1932, wouldn't know what to do without a steady supply of Kenra Perfect Spray, which she buys at Suzanne's Hair

Salon on Surfside Road. Not once has she seen a commercial in which Donovan McNabb, Mike Ditka, or any of the various members of the Manning Football Family have stood before the cameras, a gleam in the eye as they proudly hold a container of Kenra. And the baby of the family, Jane Hardy, born in 1939, makes regular pilgrimages to the Stop & Shop on Pleasant Street to do her grocery shopping, including two necessities: Smucker's Natural Peanut Butter, which she "puts on everything," and Sunkist lemons, which she uses for her beloved gin and tonics—or as she calls them, her enthusiasm mixed with reverence, "my toddies." She's never seen a Smucker's ad while watching a game, and the only ads she's seen for lemons are for those produced in Detroit.

But as football fans go, Joan and Jeanne and Jane are real, and they are spectacular. They are wives, they are mothers, and they are grand-mothers. Joan is even a great-grandmother. And they are Pats fans right down to their Tom Brady game jerseys. When getting to a game begins with crawling out of bed at 4:30 AM to catch a 6:30 AM car ferry from Nantucket to Hyannis, followed by an hour-and-a-half drive to Gillette Stadium, your opinions, from standard X's and O's to the newfangled logo that in 1993 replaced the old-timey "Pat Patriot" on the side of the team's helmets, are just as valid as those delivered by good old boys who play touch football in the same kind of Wrangler jeans Brett Favre plugs on television.

And the Nantucket Gals' trips to Gillette Stadium are not sporadic. Save for the 2006 season, which Jane missed while being treated for a life-threatening staph infection, the three sisters/pals have been regulars at Pats games since 1995, first at Foxboro Stadium and later at Gillette Stadium. In 2005 they were the proud tri-recipients of the Patriots' annual "Fan of the Year" competition. But their unique brand of fanhood predates their actual attendance at Pats games by more than three decades: they signed on with the fledgling American Football League in 1960, a three-pronged act of rebellion that did not go over well with their father, old Matt Jaeckle, whose football passion was limited to just two teams: the Nantucket High School Whalers and the New York Giants. And not in that order. Old Matt, whose roots were in New York City, loved his Jints.

But the Nantucket Gals held their ground on this one. They were going to be Pats fans, and that was that. To them it made sense: the Patriots were based in Massachusetts, and the Nantucket Gals, unlike old Matt, were natives of the Bay State.

Boston had had flirtations with professional football before the birth of the Patriots—including the Redskins in the 1930s and the Yanks a decade later—but by the 1950s most fans with a jones for the pro game used geography as their guidepost and latched on to the nearest team: the New York Giants. To this day there remain some scattered, old-timey New Englanders who have a soft spot for the Giants and remember watching their games on television when the NFL took off in the late fifties.

The Patriots were founded by William H. "Billy" Sullivan Jr., a one-time sportswriter and public relations man who was as much carnival barker as businessman. A Boston College graduate, the jovial, balding Sullivan had a variety of jobs in his early years that did not suggest he'd one day be the owner of a professional sports franchise. He was the ghostwriter for Frank Leahy, the legendary Boston College and Notre Dame football coach whose column was syndicated nationally. He worked as the public relations man for the old Boston Braves base-ball team and liked to tell the story about how a sprucing-up of Braves Field in the spring of 1947 included a fresh paint job on the old park's seats—which, regrettably, did not dry in time for Opening Day. When fans complained that their clothes were damaged by the offending seats, Sullivan seized the opportunity for a publicity grab and announced that the Braves would pay any cleaning bills that came their way.

When the Braves departed for Milwaukee in 1953, Sullivan remained in Boston. He tried his hand in television, producing a football highlight show that never really took off, after which he took jobs with United Airlines and the Metropolitan Coal Company. On November 16, 1959, he scraped together $25,000, only about $8,300 of which was his own money, and lined up additional investors, including retired Red Sox out-fielder Dominic DiMaggio, and landed the last available franchise in the original American Football League.

Though it would be years before they actually attended a game, the

Nantucket Gals, believing they owed their loyalty to this new team from Massachusetts, were Pats fans beginning with the AFL's inaugural 1960 season. A sort of gridiron détente eventually was established, with Matt—everyone called the old man Matt, even his daughters, even the grandkids, "even the grandkids' friends," says Jane—extending a grudging diplomatic recognition to the Patriots.

Still, the old man must have gotten quite a chuckle as the Patriots stumbled through their early years. The Patriots had some quality seasons in the '60s—they played the San Diego Chargers for the 1963 American Football League championship, losing 51–10—but by the end of the decade they were AFL cellar dwellers. From 1967 through 1975, playing in four different stadiums and under five different head coaches, the Pats were a combined 37–88–1.

In 1976, with the multitalented Steve Grogan settling in for his second year at quarterback, the Patriots exploded into prominence with an 11–3 record. However, New England's Super Bowl dreams were dashed in a controversial 24–21 playoff loss to the Raiders at the Oakland Coliseum in a game that to this day has aging Pats fans gnashing their teeth as they spit out the name of one Ben Dreith. The veteran official flagged Patriots tackle Ray "Sugar Bear" Hamilton for roughing the passer after Oakland's Ken Stabler had thrown an incomplete pass late in the fourth quarter, giving the Raiders a first down on the New England 13-yard line. Five plays later, and with ten seconds remaining in the game, Stabler bounded into the end zone for a touchdown, propelling the Raiders to victory.

The Giants, meanwhile, stumbled to a 3–11 record in 1976, their fifth losing season in six years. But old Matt Jaeckle never changed sides; when he died in 1977, he went to the grave a Giants fan.

Thirty years later, when the Patriots announced the acquisition of a controversial but supremely talented wide receiver named Randy Moss, Joan was seventy-six. Jeanne had just turned seventy-five on April 1, and Jane had turned sixty-nine a little more than a week later.

Naturally, they all had their opinions about this new player who seemed to have a gift for making news on two fronts: on the field . . . and off.

Naturally, they rang one another up on the telephone to share and compare those opinions.

To them, it all came down to Bill Belichick. They agreed that the man was a coaching genius, that he and he alone could take a talented player with a troubled past and show him the way to the winner's circle. He had done it a few seasons earlier with running back Corey Dillon, who left the Cincinnati Bengals on bad terms and then played on a Super Bowl winner with the 2004 Patriots, and, yes, absolutely, Belichick would do it now with Randy Moss.

"He's a troublemaker," Jane remembers saying to her sisters when she first heard the news that Randy Moss was coming to New England. "It always has to be about Randy. But I think it's a great idea. It will be the Belichick way or the highway. There won't be any trouble because Belichick won't let it happen. And Tedy Bruschi and Richard Seymour and the rest of the old-timers. You'll see. They'll make Randy Moss feel at home."

Joan had her doubts. And said so.

"I always thought he was kind of a show-off and not a team player," she told her sisters. "But then, of course, we all have trust in Bill, don't we? It's 'In Bill We Trust,' I always say. Just wait. What's the worst that can happen? If he doesn't work out, they'll just get rid of him. If it does work out, Tom Brady will have a pretty good receiver to throw to."

Jeanne agreed.

"Bill has a way," she said. "I feel that anyone that Belichick takes on seems to have a way with him, and he can kind of mold them—make them feel like that's the place they should be. I think this will work."

They were three little old ladies from Nantucket who grew up in an era when Jack Benny was jousting with Fred Allen on the radio. When Joan was born, Herbert Hoover was in the White House. Jeanne remembers when the telephone number at the Jaeckle house consisted of just three digits—5-7-M—and how it was a party line shared with the folks over at the neighboring Bartlett farm. Jane's first car was a 1947 Willys Jeep, in which she tooled around the island while being courted by her future husband, Ralph Hardy, when they were students at Nantucket High School in the fifties.

The Nantucket Gals had gray hair and they had glasses and they had their old-time, hard-line Nantucket values. Yet when it came to football, they were not unlike a couple of burly electricians from East Boston who drive to Gillette Stadium in a Ford F-150: they loved their Patriots. And if Randy Moss was going to become a Patriot, then, well, past transgressions, real or imagined, would be wiped off the books.

The catchy, modern-day phrase for this phenomenon—in which fans embrace a newly acquired player whom they once booed—is "rooting for laundry," the evolution of a routine made famous by the comedian Jerry Seinfeld. The legendary Johnny Most, radio voice of the Boston Celtics for more than thirty years, routinely fired verbal roundhouses at ruffians from opposing teams—until said ruffian was acquired by the Celtics, at which time Most allayed any fears his listeners might have about the transaction by pointing out that the fellow "has changed his ways." Red Sox fans enjoyed unleashing a series of long, whiny "Sterrrrrrrrrrrrrrr-roids!" chants at Jose Canseco when the Oakland A's slugger popped his head out of the third-base dugout at Fenway Park, but the venom went away when Canseco joined the Red Sox. Chris Nilan, a native of Boston's West Roxbury neighborhood, was viewed as a thug and a cheap-shot artist when he played for the Montreal Canadiens; when the man affectionately known as Knuckles became a Bruin in 1990, he was recast by his fellow Bostonians as a hustling, chippy player who got more out of his abilities than most players.

Now it was time for a Moss makeover. He was coming to New England, and the Nantucket Gals approved.

As they continued to pile up the victories, the Red Sox became the only show in town. It had been a familiar springtime routine in recent years: the Patriots would be in between seasons, and the two Garden teams, the Bruins and Celtics, rarely made much noise. They'd be lucky just to make the playoffs, and if they did, they never went very far.

And so it was in the spring of 2007. The Bruins had undergone a dramatic organizational makeover before the season—including the installation of Peter Chiarelli as general manager and former NHL defenseman Dave Lewis as head coach, along with the dramatic jettisoning of aging hockey sage Harry Sinden as president—and they had added a marquee attraction with the signing of free-agent Zdeno Chara, a six-foot-nine, 255-pound defenseman from Slovakia. But it was the same old stuff in a shiny new box: the Bruins did not qualify for the Stanley Cup playoffs. They hadn't been to the postseason since 2004, hadn't *won* a playoff series since 1999, hadn't won *two* playoff series since 1992. And of course, they hadn't won the Stanley Cup since 1972, when Bobby Orr and the Big Bad Bruins toppled the New York Rangers in six games in the Cup finals.

The Bruins had closed out the 2006–2007 season with a 4–3 loss to the Atlanta Thrashers, and that was that for professional hockey for the year.

The Celtics were even worse. Intentionally or not, they had been a smashing success in being truly bad, thus positioning themselves for a generous collection of Ping-Pong balls at the NBA's draft lottery, scheduled for May 22 in Secaucus, New Jersey. The hope was that the Celtics would come away with either the first or second pick in the draft and thus be able to land either of the nation's two hugely touted college phenoms, Greg Oden of Ohio State or Kevin Durant of the University of Texas. But the lottery was still a ways off; in the meantime, there was the matter of concluding the going-nowhere 2006–2007 season. Losing a franchise-record eighteen consecutive games along the way, the Celtics closed at 24–58, the second-worst record in the NBA.

But just when it should have been all Red Sox all the time on the local professional sports scene, their daily adventures commanding the back page of the *Herald*, their games getting the "A" block treatment on NESN's *SportsDesk*, Comcast's *New England Sports Tonight*, NECN's *Sports Late Night*, and other nocturnal television fixes for the serious fan, along came the Patriots with an announcement that over the next several weeks would be among the dominant topics throughout the region.

On April 29—the same day the Red Sox closed out their first Yankee Stadium series of the season with a 7–4 victory, thus completing their April schedule with a 16–8 record—the Patriots held a press conference to introduce Randy Moss.

That Moss was a supremely talented football player was not in doubt. Here was a man who could outrace his defenders with embarrassing ease. Here was a man with the smarts to make instant reads of opposing defenses, to deploy a zig here, a zag there, and thus become precisely what his quarterback was looking for: the open man. Here was a man capable of making acrobatic, one-handed catches so eye-popping that to see them on television was to wonder if they were perhaps created on a computer by some idling tech guys from the last *Star Wars* film. If anyone wanted to draw artistic comparisons between being an athlete and being, say, a ballet dancer, then the place to begin on the athletic side would be with the graceful, talented, *artistic* Randy Moss.

Eliot Feld, a trim, energetic sixty-seven-year-old who serves as artistic director of the New York–based Ballet Tech, is able to judge the artistry of Randy Moss from two perspectives: as the choreographer of more than 133 ballets . . . and as a hard-core football fan.

"I always root against him because I'm a Giants fan," said Feld. "And when you're not rooting for somebody, their virtues irritate you because they're working against your team. But the year he had in 2007 was unbelievable, one of the most prolific years ever. And that really pissed me off.

"But he's fabulous, the bastard," said Feld, who as a sixteen-year-old in the late fifties performed in the original Broadway production of *West Side Story*, and later in the film version. "Many of the same attributes of physical grace, coordination, and a kind of somatic sophistication are all the same ingredients, but put to different purposes. The most important thing, if you want to be a dancer, is the desire to be a dancer. And if Randy wanted to be a dancer, I have little doubt he would have been a wonderful dancer."

Yes, he was that good. But the issue was this: Randy Moss also had a reputation for being a pain in the ass, a troublemaker, a bad seed . . . the descriptions just go on and on. After spending the first seven years of his NFL career with the Minnesota Vikings, the six-foot-four, 210-pound wideout was traded to the Oakland Raiders, for whom he played in 2005 and 2006. A once-proud franchise that dates back to the original American Football League, the Raiders won Super Bowls in 1977, 1981, and

1984 under the aggressive, sometimes visionary stewardship of general partner Al Davis.* But as Davis aged and his management skills eroded, the Raiders dissolved into a pro football laughingstock; following the 2002 season, which culminated in a 48–21 loss to the Tampa Bay Buccaneers in Super Bowl XXXVII, the Raiders failed to win as many as six games in each of the next six seasons. In the 1970s, the Raiders had a four-year stretch in which they went 12–2, 11–3, 13–1, and 11–3; now they were in the midst of a four-year stretch in which they were 4–12, 5–11, 4–12, and 2–14. This included Moss's two seasons in Oakland, during which the Raiders went a combined 6–26.

Moss was viewed as a malcontent playing for a bad team. It didn't help his case when, halfway through his second season in Oakland, he said that being a Raider was no fun. Appearing at a press conference in conjunction with the unveiling of "the Randy Moss Award," to be given to the top return specialist in college football, Moss, asked to comment on the number of dropped passes he'd been accumulating, said, "Maybe because I'm unhappy, and I'm not too much excited about what's going on, so my concentration and focus level tends to go down when I'm in a bad mood. So all I can say is, if you put me in a good situation and make me happy, man, you get good results."[1]

True, there were fans and sportswriters who took the position that Moss was simply being brutally candid about the state of affairs with the Oakland Raiders. Dave Del Grande of the *Oakland Tribune* was among them:

> *Randy Moss bites his tongue and gets criticized for keeping his feelings inside.*
>
> *Then he spills his guts and gets ripped for going public with his thoughts.*
>
> *Which is it, people?*
>
> *I, for one, give Moss a big thumbs-up for coming clean on his*

---

* The Oakland Raiders won Super Bowls XI and XV. The Raiders played in Los Angeles from 1992 to 1994; thus, it was the Los Angeles Raiders who won Super Bowl XVIII.

lack of interest in the current Raiders product. At least he has the guts to admit he's not trying.[2]

Elsewhere, the media was killing Moss. A year-end piece penned in tongue-in-cheek style by Bud Geracie of the *San Jose Mercury News* announced that the "newly established Randy Moss Award will be given to the college player who drops the most passes and generally doesn't seem to give a damn."[3] Columnist Mark Purdy, also of the *Mercury News*, wrote, "It was clear early on that Moss' mind was more on his new fruit smoothie venture[†] than on buckling down to make the Raiders better. [Raiders coach] Art Shell needed to find someone on his staff who could motivate Moss. Instead, Moss kept losing interest and kept dropping passes."[4]

Phil Barber of the *Press Democrat* of Santa Rosa weighed in with: "He clearly wants out of Oakland—he has done everything but solicit one-way Southwest Airlines tickets on his FOX Sports radio show," adding that Moss's standing as a Raiders offensive captain "is a nationwide joke."[5]

This certainly wasn't Moss's first visit to controversy. Perhaps most famously, there was a September 2002 mishap that began when a Minneapolis traffic officer stepped in front of Moss's car after the then-Vikings star made an illegal turn. Moss pushed his car onward, knocking the traffic officer to the ground. In addition to being charged with careless driving and failure to obey a traffic officer, both misdemeanors, he was also charged with drug possession when police found a joint in his car.

Five nights later, the Vikings were in Seattle to play a nationally televised game against the Seahawks. The Vikings were roundly criticized for allowing Moss to play in the game, and Seahawks fans had as much fun jeering Moss as in cheering for the hometown team. Moss had been in the news all week—in addition to the incident with the traffic officer in Minneapolis, ESPN, citing unnamed sources, reported that he had

---

† In June 2006, amid much fanfare, including an article in *USA Today*, Moss opened a pair of Inta Juice franchises in his native Charleston, West Virginia.

tested positive for marijuana during the 2001 season[6]—and Seahawks fans let him hear about it. Moss responded by dropping four passes in the end zone and catching just six passes for fifty yards in a 48–23 loss to Seattle.

"It was just one of those nights where whatever could go wrong did," Moss said after the game.[7]

The comment could have nicely summed up his week. Moss hadn't had merely a scrape with the law, but one that was easily retooled as professional sports vaudeville, what with the irresistible image of a meter maid sliding off the hood of a car being driven by a marquee football player. As Rick Morrissey put it in the *Chicago Tribune*, Randy Moss "was arrested for being an idiot."[8]

The case with the traffic officer was settled out of court. But it was not the first time Moss's name had been attached to some unpleasant, eyebrow-raising piece of news. Some of the stuff was merely silly, such as the time at Green Bay's Lambeau Field when he did a sort of virtual mooning of Packers fans, turning his backside to them and pantomiming the pulling-down of his pants. For this, he was fined $10,000. Some of it was appallingly bad sportsmanship, as in the time he walked off the field with two seconds remaining in the final game of the 2004 regular season as his Vikings comrades were lining up for an onside kick in what would be a 21–20 loss to the Washington Redskins. And some of it was no more complicated than a remark being taken out of context, as when he was famously quoted as saying, "I play when I want to play."[9]

The quote paints Moss as a lazy, me-first player who would deign to play only when the mood suited him. But the *Herald*'s John Tomase, in a lengthy piece after the receiver was acquired by the Patriots, made the case that Moss was merely responding to a question about whether playing with Vikings receiver Cris Carter, a future Hall of Famer, inspired him to play better. As in: *He doesn't play because of Cris Carter. He plays when he wants to play.*

Tomase also did some digging and revisited a sorry chapter from the new Patriot's days at DuPont High School in Rand, West Virginia, when Moss was sentenced to thirty days in jail after pleading guilty to misdemeanor battery following a fight that had racial overtones. The incident also cost Moss a scholarship to take his considerable talents to Notre Dame. While most reporters have chosen to go with the basics—Randy Moss, fight, racial overtones, jail—Tomase looked a little deeper into the incident. Moss was certainly not blameless, but Tomase points out that "the belief is that a student . . . scrawled the words 'all [n-word] must die,' on the desk of Moss' girlfriend, along with the name of one of Moss's friends, Rayeshawn Smith. The two confronted [the student]. Smith knocked him out. Moss stomped on him.

"[The student] spent a week in the hospital with injuries to his head, kidney and spleen."[10]

Tomase quotes an unidentified teacher as saying, "That kid had it coming," referring to the student Moss assaulted.[11]

The list of Moss's transgressions—some of them quite real and horrifying, some of them imagined, some of them blown out of proportion—went on and on. Plus, there was speculation that the on-field version of Randy Moss was no longer all that: Tom Walsh, offensive coordinator of the Raiders for most of 2006, would later say that Moss "is a player whose skills are diminishing, and he's in denial of those eroding skills."[12]

And now the Patriots were willing to bring him into their locker room. Though they were coming off a painful 38–34 loss to the Indianapolis Colts in the American Football Conference championship game three months earlier, the Pats, with their three Super Bowl victories and combined 70–26 regular-season record since 2001, remained the NFL's premier franchise. They had a quarterback for the ages in Tom Brady. Bill Belichick, though unloved by many members of the media for failing to turn his press conferences into fireside chats with the requisite one-liners and witty observations, was nonetheless regarded as the best coach of his generation. The September 2005 edition of *Forbes* magazine named the Patriots "the Best Team in Sports." Robert Kraft, the onetime Patriots season-ticket-holder who bought the franchise in 1994 for $172 million and later replaced austere Foxboro Stadium with glitzy Gillette Stadium, appeared on the cover of the magazine with the two Super Bowl trophies the team had won by then.

Kraft grew up in a second-floor apartment at 131 Fuller Street in Brookline, less than a mile from Braves Field, Boston's National League ballpark. He was a devoted Braves fan as a kid, a passion he maintains played a role in his decision later in life to purchase the Patriots. After graduating from Columbia University and Harvard Business School, he went to work for Rand-Whitney Group, a paper business owned by the father of his wife, Myra. Kraft later acquired the company and joined it with other ventures, forming what is now known as the Kraft Group.

He then introduced his money to his heart, purchasing the Patriots in 1994 and vowing to keep the team in New England. And did. In a funny way, then, the demise of the Boston Braves played a role in the salvation of the New England Patriots; the franchise became Kraft's signature investment, his baby. Now "the Best Team in Sports" was going to embrace . . . Randy Moss?

And then there was the Patriots' locker room, a place said to be filled with "character guys" who put team ahead of self. Tedy Bruschi. Rosevelt Colvin. Dan Koppen. Mike Vrabel. And, of course, Brady.

But it was painfully obvious to anyone watching the 2006 Patriots that they had a Hall of Fame–bound quarterback throwing passes to a collection of receivers who, while good enough for the National Football League, were not in Brady's league.

New England's 2006 receiving corps included the popular Troy Brown, who had been with the team since 1993; Reche Caldwell, who had played four seasons with the San Diego Chargers; Jabar Gaffney, coming off four seasons with the Houston Texans; and tight end Benjamin Watson, drafted by the Patriots out of Georgia in the first round of the 2004 draft. It was a cast that inspires a visit to a comment made nearly a quarter-century earlier by longtime NBA coach Del Harris. Following the Houston Rockets' tenth consecutive loss to open the 1982–83 season, Coach Harris took a jab at his team's personnel with the observation: "All of our players belong in the NBA. I'm just not sure they all belong on the same team."[13]

And so it was with Brown, Caldwell, Gaffney, and the rest. They all belonged in the NFL; they just didn't belong on the same team.

For the Kraft family, the Patriots' loss to the Colts in the AFC championship game on January 21, 2007, was painful on a variety of levels. The Patriots had a 21–3 lead in the second quarter and were seemingly on cruise control for another trip to the Super Bowl, but the Colts roared back in the second half, taking the lead on a three-yard touchdown run by Joseph Addai. The Pats got the ball back with one minute remaining, but this time there was no heroic, game-saving drive from Brady; this time he got his team down to the Indianapolis 45-yard line and then threw a pass intended for Benjamin Watson that was instead intercepted by the Colts' Marlin Jackson. Only twenty seconds remained on the clock; the game was over. The roar of jubilant Colts fans shook the RCA Dome; a few of the rowdies discovered members of the Kraft family and began pelting them with debris. It was a decidedly inglorious end to a season that had seemed destined to end at Miami's Dolphin Stadium, site of Super Bowl XLI.

The Krafts, and by extension the Patriots, quickly regrouped. Less than forty-eight hours into the free-agent signing season, they signed Adalius Thomas, a hardnosed linebacker who had been a two-time Pro Bowl selection during his seven seasons with the Baltimore Ravens. Two days later, on March 5, the Pats announced that they had acquired Wes Welker, a five-foot-nine, 185-pound wide receiver, from the Miami Dolphins. On the thirteenth, they announced the signings of free-agent receivers Donte Stallworth and Kelley Washington.

Brady, recalling a conversation he had with Belichick at the end of the 2006 season, said, "He asked me what my thoughts were when we had a year-end evaluation. He said there were some receivers we might try to approach.

"And then we went out and got Wes, and we got Kelley Washington, and at that point I was, like, great. Awesome. And then it was Stallworth, and I couldn't believe that. Coach had brought up all those names at one time or another before we got them. The one name he never brought up was Randy Moss."

It was all a warm-up for what took place during the early morning hours of April 29. The first three rounds of the 2007 NFL draft took place the previous day, with the Pats taking University of Miami defensive back Brandon Meriweather with the twenty-fourth overall pick, but now they were trying to liberate Moss from the Raiders.

Brady remembered getting a phone call from Belichick.

"The way it works is, he'll call me and say, 'Hey, this is what we're thinking,'" Brady said. "When he tells me that, I know what decision he's making."

Belichick had done his homework on Randy Moss, but in this case the assignment did not include talking with Art Shell or Tom Walsh, two disgruntled members of the Oakland coaching staff who'd had their fill of the wide receiver.

"I know there was some public stuff out there from Art Shell and Tom Walsh," said Belichick. "I didn't talk to either one of them. I obviously don't have a lot of respect for what either one of them thought. And I had a lot more respect for what other people told me about Randy. . . . I don't know Walsh or Shell other than to say hello to them. But I know other people that have been with them, and they didn't say anything close to what those two guys said."

So much had to happen. The Raiders would have to be compensated. Moss would have to agree to ripping up the remaining two years on his contract and working out a new deal with the Patriots. And there was this: Papa Bear Robert Kraft needed to be convinced that Moss would arrive in Foxboro with his luggage, but with no baggage.

Belichick was on the phone with Al Davis at two-thirty in the morning, East Coast time, working out the deal. After receiving permission to speak with Moss, Belichick was soon on the phone with his prospective new wideout. The timing was tight. If the trade were to be made, Moss would have to fly to Boston, undergo a physical at Massachusetts General Hospital, and then . . . well, there was no other way to put it: he had to meet with Kraft.

The Raiders agreed to surrender Moss for a fourth-round pick in the draft, which was to resume on Sunday. Moss agreed to shed a contract that would have paid him $9.75 million in 2007 and $11.25 million in

2008 and instead signed a one-year deal for $3 million, plus an additional $2 million in incentives.[14]

Belichick told Moss there was a commercial flight leaving Houston at six o'clock in the morning that would get him to Boston in time for a physical and the all-important meeting with Kraft.

Moss told Belichick he didn't need a commercial flight; he would leave immediately on a chartered plane he had at his disposal. He arrived in Boston early Sunday morning, underwent his physical at Mass General, affixed his signature to a batch of preliminary paperwork, and then was driven to Gillette Stadium.

Vice president of player personnel Scott Pioli, who worked as well with Belichick as it was hoped Moss would with Brady, busily worked out the salary cap details to create space for the new wide receiver. Assuming, of course, the new wide receiver's meeting with Robert Kraft went well.

Moss was accompanied to Kraft's office by Berj Najarian, a onetime media relations director for the New York Jets who had come to New England with Belichick.

Jonathan Kraft, Robert's son, sat in on the meeting and remembered his father saying, "The Patriots' name and logo and brand is completely associated, in my mind, with my family. This is an extension of my family name. And anybody that doesn't understand the responsibility isn't somebody that I want on this team."

Jonathan Kraft said he was looking at Moss and that he "didn't blink . . . he was completely into the conversation and looking straight ahead like an investment banker trying to close a deal."

Robert Kraft, the onetime Boston Braves fan, the onetime Patriots season-ticket-holder, had this memory of the meeting: "I looked him in the eye and said, 'If you come here, you have my family name. Your name is Randy Moss Kraft.'"

The meeting lasted around twenty-five minutes; when it ended, Moss was a Patriot.

Kraft recalls Moss saying, "I want to be a part of the family. You won't be disappointed."

Though he did not sit in on the meeting, Belichick believes it was more of a meet-and-greet, that the trade had already been made and Moss and Kraft were simply saying hello to each other.

"There was never any 'you better do this' and 'you better do that,' 'you better not do something else,'" Belichick said. "I don't think there was ever any need for that.

"In my career I've coached plenty of bad guys, and he's not one of them," Belichick said of Moss. "And you see some of the other people in this town, guys like Manny [Ramirez] and fucking guys like that. There's no comparison. There's no *comparison*."

8

COURTSIDE

Donnie Wahlberg was already an international star before he reached his twentieth birthday. Born in Boston's gritty Dorchester section, the eighth of Donald Sr. and Alma Wahlberg's nine children, he was also a born performer, with a natural attraction to the stage. When he was sixteen, he showed up at an audition in Boston for some kind of new boy band and came out of the experience as one of the original members of a hot-off-the-presses group that would eventually become New Kids on the Block.

The group's second album, *Hangin' Tough*, released in 1988, sold more than eight million copies, and that's when Joey McIntyre, Jordan Knight, Jonathan Knight, and the so-called bad boy of the bunch, Donnie Wahlberg, became instantly recognized celebrities, their weekly fan mail reaching into the tens of thousands.

Wahlberg eventually made it to Hollywood, but he never truly *went* Hollywood. His acting career flourished, with critically acclaimed performances in such movies as *Southie*, *Ransom*, and the HBO miniseries *Band of Brothers*. His screen time in M. Night Shyamalan's *The Sixth Sense* is only about four minutes, but his portrayal of the tragic Vincent Grey explodes off the screen. The grown-up Wahlberg evolved into an intense, driven, highly intelligent but slightly rough-around-the-edges *Dorchester guy* who, despite his film credits and all that goes with it, remained true to his roots, devoted to old pals and old haunts.

His credentials as a true Boston sports fan never fell into disarray.

Or to put it in ESPN-esque, his fanhood is beyond reproach. Ask him about onetime Red Sox slugger Jim Rice and he'll tell you, "He was my Mickey Mantle." Ask him about the Bruins and he'll take you on a trip back to that December 26, 1979, night at Madison Square Garden when Terry O'Reilly, Stan Jonathan, and some of the other boyos climbed into the stands and wailed on some Rangers fans. "That one's on YouTube," Wahlberg was quick to point out. "I show it to people from time to time."

Of the 1984 Thanksgiving Day showdown that the New England Patriots lost to the Dallas Cowboys, Wahlberg said, "I cried. And I'm not just saying that. I really did cry."

His earliest sports memory is of the Celtics winning the 1976 NBA championship. He was seven years old. Two years later, when the Red Sox met the Yankees in a one-game playoff for the American League East title, crumbling under the weight of Bucky Dent's three-run homer off Mike Torrez, he "felt the emotional tug of that team and was hooked." But his coming-of-age moment as a Boston sports fan took place when the Celtics won the 1981 NBA championship. He was eleven years old now and could better understand and appreciate the intricacies of the game.

"I remember everything about it—how they were down 3–1 against the 76ers in the conference finals and came back to win it, how Cedric Maxwell had a fight in the stands, I think it was in Game 3 in Philly," he said. "This guy threw a pencil or something at Max, and he went after him."

(Indeed, the video suggests that the fan threw something at Maxwell, who said that, actually, nothing was thrown.)

"There was this song that year about the Celtics called 'No More Games.' At the end of the song, they announce the starting lineup for the Celtics. It went, 'Ladies and gentlemen, for the Boston Celtics, number 7, Tiny Archibald,' and all that. It was a local hit. They played it on KISS 108 all the time. We used to sit by the radio and wait for that song to come on. And we'd be all fired up. That season, that year, that playoff series, is when I really became passionate about the Celtics.

"I'm passionate about all the Boston teams. But the Celtics have always been the team I want to devote the most time to."

Pre—New Kids, when he was just another kid from Dorchester, his older brother Jim told him there was a way to watch the Celtics and Bruins for free by sneaking into Boston Garden, the ancient and aching arena located on Causeway Street, near Boston's old West End. Call it the dark side of Norman Rockwell: instead of an oil color of a young Donnie Wahlberg and his friends shooting marbles or skinny-dipping at the local pond or ordering up a milk shake at the corner drugstore, we see a gang of Dorchester guttersnipes climbing a fire escape out behind the Garden, opening up an old, creaky door, and emerging high above courtside, up by the rafters.

But Wahlberg never did find the door, and try as he might, he never did sneak into a Bruins or Celtics game. And it's funny how things happen: a few years later, famous by now, he didn't have to check for unlocked doors at the Garden because doors would be opened for him. He was a celebrity; tickets would just appear, tickets to good seats.

The way things played out, though, he'd have been better off climbing those stairs and sneaking in through the old, creaky door.

"I was in a teenage boy band, and because of that sporting events became a good place for me to get into trouble," he said. "It wasn't teenage girls up in the rafters yelling down at me. It was drunken guys looking to cause trouble. So I really avoided going to big sporting events. I just didn't feel comfortable being out in the crowd. I felt like a target. I'd gotten into a few fights during the New Kids' heyday, and I didn't want to subject myself to problems with belligerent fans. I was really insecure, to be honest.

"I'm not bothered by fans. I'll pose for fifty pictures a night. No, my problem was that I can't walk away from trouble. I'm a Dorchester boy. Somebody yells an obscenity at me, and I'm going to yell one back, and then it's going to get complicated. Sporting events were on my list of places to avoid if I didn't want to be sued every three months because I'm getting in fights."

Years later he invested in courtside season tickets for Celtics games during the disastrous mid-1990s reign of Rick Pitino as head coach. But even then, his boy band days behind him, pushing thirty years old, he rarely showed up for the games. He still followed the Celtics and had a special appreciation for forward Antoine Walker, but Wahlberg, mindful of the fights and near-fights with beery fans, remained a fan in exile. He'd read about the team in the papers and watch the games on television, but he was not a courtside presence.

All that changed in 2002 when Mike Rotondi arrived in Donnie Wahlberg's life. A successful Boston businessman who had been sitting courtside at Celtics games for years, Rotondi met Wahlberg's brother Jim at a local charity event, and the two men instantly hit it off. Few things give Rotondi greater pleasure than extending an invite to sit with him in his cherished courtside seats for a Celtics game, and so he reached out to Jim Wahlberg, asking if he'd like to join him one night.

Sure, Jim Wahlberg said. But then, remembering his brother's status as a lapsed Celtics fan, he had an idea: "Why don't you invite my brother Donnie?"

There were two famous Wahlbergs by now. Donnie was a successful actor, and their brother Mark had climbed the ladder from rapper Marky Mark to iconic underwear model to his own successful career as an actor and film producer. But Mark Wahlberg was in Los Angeles at the time Jim Wahlberg met Rotondi. And anyway, there was talk that Marky Mark had become something of a . . . Lakers fan.

Donnie was visiting friends and family in Boston, stashing himself at his mother's house for a few days, and the idea of stepping out and going to a Celtics game appealed to him. He made contact with Rotondi, who, as it turned out, would be passing near where Wahlberg's mother lives.

"I'll pick you up," said Rotondi.

They were a courtside Odd Couple: Rotondi, a married businessman from the Boston suburbs who'd seen a lot of Credence Clearwater Revival and Grand Funk Railroad back in the day but now, as he approached his sixtieth birthday, wasn't one to truck with the fast crowd, and Donnie Wahlberg, in his early thirties at the time, married to the singer Kim Fey, the father of two small children, and spending most of his time in Hollywood.

They attended a game against the Sacramento Kings, and Wahlberg came out of the experience as a reinvigorated Celtics fan. He called a buddy in L.A. who produced custom-made leather jackets and ordered one up for his new friend Mike Rotondi. The jacket was eye-poppingly slick, a jet-black job with a dazzling Celtics logo on the back. Naturally, Rotondi hardly ever wore it. Too beautiful to wear, he'd say when asked about it by Donnie.

But they kept attending Celtics games together, the entrepreneur and the entertainer. Soon the evenings evolved into elaborate pregame dinners and occasionally some stepping-out afterward. Wahlberg was older now, more mature, and he blended in nicely with the Garden masses.

"We just hit it off," Wahlberg said of Rotondi. "He was one of those nice guys. It's hard to explain. It's like he was a celebrity without being a celebrity. The ushers all knew him by name. The guy in the elevator. The waitresses. He was the mayor of Celtics games. Watching him walk through the arena, it gave me a chance to see what my life is like when I walk into an arena to do a concert. I know this guy, and that guy, and the security guys, and everyone goes out of their way to say hello . . . that's what it was like with Mike."

The twosome very quickly became a threesome. During one of his early games with Mike Rotondi, Wahlberg recognized the fan seated to his right as someone he'd seen on television so many times he felt he knew him. And when the man introduced himself as Marty Joyce, Wahlberg thought: *Maybe I do know this guy.*

"I'm thinking, his last name is Joyce, and I know a ton of Joyces in Boston," Wahlberg recalled. "Turns out I didn't know him personally, but I did know him as this big Fred Flintstone guy sitting on the court, always up on his feet, screaming at the refs. Everyone knew him. I said, 'Shit, you're that guy!'"

A few years earlier, there were some tense moments when Joyce first met Mike Rotondi. Whereas Rotondi fashioned himself a regular guy from humble roots who brought a measure of decorum to his courtside seats, Joyce, a Boston stockbroker, was a one-man demolition derby who screamed at referees, mocked opposing players, and, during pregame warm-ups, slapped the backs of his favorite Celtics players. In that respect, Rotondi and Joyce could not have been more different. But they worked things out and became friends; now Wahlberg was in the mix, and soon phone calls were being made, schedules changed, in order that they might all watch the Celtics . . . side by side by side.

All this was happening at a time when the Celtics were long on tradi-tion, sure, but woefully short on modern-day delivery. By the 2006–2007 season, they were at rock bottom, losing a franchise-record eighteen games in a row. But while Wahlberg, Rotondi, and Joyce longed to see the Celtics return to the top of the world—as they were in the days of Bird, McHale, and Parish and, before that, Havlicek and Cowens and, before *that*, Russell and the Cooz—the Celtics' drought didn't stop them from meeting in the North End for a fine dinner at Nebo or Ristorante Limoncello and then heading down to Causeway Street to bleed some Green for a couple of hours.

"The Celtics were so bad the first couple of years that it allowed us to develop a friendship," Wahlberg said. "The games were kind of dull. We knew what was going to happen. They were going to get killed nine out of ten games. So we got to know each other.

"I felt comfortable. I felt like I was with friends."

The Celtics finished the 2006–2007 season at 24–58, second only to the Memphis Grizzlies, who were 22–60, for the worst record in the NBA. But the team's losing season did offer one major perk: with the league's draft lottery scheduled for May 22 in Secaucus, New Jersey, Boston fans believed that the Celtics could turn things around if the proper distribution of Ping-Pong balls yielded the first or second pick in the draft, which would be held on June 28 at Madison Square Garden.

Everyone agreed that the upcoming draft offered two prospects who would be NBA superstars the day they walked onto the floor. If your team landed presumptive number-one-pick Greg Oden of Ohio State or Kevin Durant of the University of Texas, the number-two lock, your team was going to get good fast.

Here was a chance, after more than two decades of failing to deliver banner number seventeen, for the Celtics to land that one player with the talent to return them to their rightful perch as an NBA power.

All they needed was some help from those Ping-Pong balls.

Each of Boston's four big league sports franchises is blessed with an iconic ex-player who has seemingly been around forever in one role or another, his very presence providing a feel-good connection between the present and the past.

On the Red Sox, that man is Johnny Pesky, a .307 lifetime hitter who played for the Red Sox from 1942 to 1952 (not counting three years he missed while serving in World War II) and who was later manager, coach, broadcaster, minor league instructor, and front-office assistant. As he approached his ninetieth birthday, Pesky was still serving the Red Sox in a role best described as goodwill ambassador. Johnny "the Chief" Bucyk, the forever captain of the Bruins, was a key player on the team's Stanley Cup–winning teams in 1970 and '72. He played twenty-one of his twenty-three NHL seasons for the Bruins, scoring 556 career goals, and then stayed on as a broadcaster and front-office executive. Gino Cappelletti was a quarterback/kicker who broke in with the original Boston Patriots of the American Football League in 1960 and who closed out his career in 1970 when the team debuted in the National Football League. Like Pesky and Bucyk, he then went to the broadcast booth.

And then there is Tommy Heinsohn, a tough kid from New Jersey who starred at Holy Cross and then earned NBA Rookie of the Year honors for the 1956–57 season, with the Celtics taking out the St. Louis Hawks in a grueling seven-game series for their first championship. During his nine seasons as a Celtic, the team won eight NBA titles. He coached the Celtics to championships in '74 and '76 and went on to a phenomenally successful career as a broadcaster, nationally as well as locally. He enjoys a cultlike popularity among younger fans who never saw him play but who watch Celtics games on Comcast's *SportsNet* to listen to him berate officials and bestow "Tommy Points" on players who put in that extra special effort.

When the Celtics traveled to Secaucus, New Jersey, for the 2007 NBA draft lottery, Tommy Heinsohn was the perfect choice to be the face of the franchise for the glitzy, high-tech televised production. The actual lottery would take place in a backroom, with the Celtics represented by managing partner and CEO Wyc Grousbeck.

Symbolic or not, Heinsohn was deeply touched by the honor. For all the high-energy, hometown boosterism he displayed on television, Heinsohn was dealing with problems at home: his wife, Helen, an outgoing, outspoken woman known as "the Redhead from Needham," was dying of cancer. The two were famously inseparable at Celtics games, with Helen a good bet to offer a pregame opinion or two on a variety of topics as she held court in the media dining room, and now here was an opportunity for them to fly on a jet chartered by Grousbeck to New Jersey—Tommy's turf—and hopefully put some of the old Celtic magic into play. And Helen surely did her part: "She came up with all kinds of good-luck charms and various religious ornaments," Heinsohn recalled. "She was going to take this very seriously. You couldn't even joke about it with her."

The decision to choose Heinsohn for this honor was arrived at about a month earlier when Grousbeck and managing partner Stephen Pagliuca were seated with the Celtics legend at a charity event for the Perkins School for the Blind, a fabled institution located in Watertown, Massachusetts, whose graduates include Annie Sullivan and, later, a young girl named Helen Keller, whom Sullivan famously mentored. Grousbeck, whose father, H. Irving Grousbeck, was a cofounder of Continental Cablevision, grew up in the Boston area and was an enthusiastic follower of the Sox and Pats, Celts and Bruins; in pickup street hockey games at the Noble and Greenough School, he pretended to be Gerry Cheevers, the fabled Bruins goaltender. His favorite Sox player was left fielder Carl Yastrzemski. Grousbeck moved on to Princeton, where he starred on the crew team, followed by law school at the University of Michigan and an MBA at Stanford Business School, after which he settled in California. His family had made several inquiries into buying professional sports teams over the years, including the Red Sox, but it was not the Sox that brought Grousbeck back to Boston. And it was not the Celtics, Bruins, or Patriots.

It was the Perkins School.

Wyc and Corinne's second child, Campbell, was born blind in 1992. They met with doctors, talked with consultants, and did countless hours of research, with the singular goal of doing what was best for their son, which led them to Perkins. There was no debate: Wyc and Corinne pulled up stakes and moved their young family back to Boston to make things as seamless and stress-free as possible for their infant son. They became proactive in raising money for the school and for the National Braille Press (as well as the Boston Children's Hospital, Horizons for

Homeless Children, and many other charitable concerns), and they have been involved in a program, along with scientists at Harvard, Yale, Penn, the University of Iowa, and other colleges and universities, that they hope will make possible retinal transplants. "The goal," said Grousbeck, "is to have gene therapy designed and safely in humans" by 2013.

Pagliuca, a managing partner at Bain Capital, was a onetime freshman basketball player at Duke University who remains fixated on the game: "I grew up a gym rat, and I spent more time playing basketball than anything else," he said. "I had four kids that played, and I was coaching AAU. So the game was still with me as an adult."

As it happened, Steve and Judy Pagliuca's daughter, Stephanie, and the Grousbecks' daughter, Kelsey, attended the same school. In 2002, when Wyc Grousbeck was looking into purchasing the Celtics and seeking partners, it was his wife who told him about Pagliuca, noting that the man's interest in basketball extended to building a half-court in his basement.

Pagliuca, who was also involved in a variety of philanthropic pursuits, including the chairmanship of the Massachusetts Society for the Prevention of Cruelty to Children, was interested as soon as Grousbeck spoke the word "Celtics." More than being a mere investor, Pagliuca later helped soften the financial load for both himself and the Grousbecks by lining up an additional $100 million in minority investors.

On December 31, 2002, Boston Basketball Partners, whose principals included Wyc Grousbeck, H. Irving Grousbeck, Steve Pagliuca, and a Boston-based real estate management and development company called the Abbey Group, completed its purchase of the Celtics for $350 million from the Gaston family based in Greenwich, Connecticut. Donald F. Gaston, a former executive with Gulf & Western Industries, was the leader of a 1983 group that had purchased the Celtics. In 1993 the elder Gaston moved his son, Paul, into the ownership as chairman of the board. But both Gastons were largely absentee owners; it was said that team employees often used Paul Gaston's office as an informal lunchroom. What Grousbeck and Pagliuca brought to the Celtics, went the logic, was that they had settled in the Boston area and were hell-bent on restoring the dignity of the franchise.

Partly out of respect, partly because of tradition, but also because they believed it to be good business, Grousbeck and Pagliuca made it a point to travel to Washington, D.C., to seek the blessings of the patriarch of the Celtics, eighty-five-year-old Arnold "Red" Auerbach.

A one-step-ahead-of-the-competition, cigar-smoking, referee-baiting genius of the hardwood, Auerbach was one of the most successful general managers in sports history. From 1957, when they captured their first championship in that bloody seven-game series with the old St. Louis Hawks, to 1986, when the Hall of Fame–bound trio of Larry Bird, Robert Parish, and Kevin McHale led the Celtics to a six-game dismissal of the Houston Rockets in the NBA Finals, a record sixteen championship banners were raised to the rafters at the old Boston Garden. What every one of those teams had in common was that they were assembled by Auerbach, an old-time wheeler-dealer who for sixteen seasons also coached the Celtics. Nine of the team's championships were secured while Auerbach paced the floor, tightly gripping a rolled-up game program; with victory at hand, Red would light up his trademark cigar, a tradition that riled opponents but endeared him to Boston sports fans. His chief talent, though, was that he knew how to *acquire* talent: on April 29, 1956, for example, he traded Easy Ed Macauley and Cliff Hagan to the St. Louis Hawks for the Hawks' first-round draft pick, which Auerbach used to land a University of San Francisco center named Bill Russell. During Russell's thirteen seasons with the Celtics, the team won eleven championships.

By the mid-1980s, Auerbach was ceding more and more of the day-to-day operations of the franchise to young suits, though he remained on the masthead as club president. But the title was ripped away from him in 1997 when Paul Gaston reached into the college ranks and hired Kentucky coach Rick Pitino as coach, de facto general manager . . . and president. When Pitino's tour of duty with the Celtics ended in 2001, Auerbach, though by then spending most of his time at his Washington, D.C., home, was reinstated as president.

To Pagliuca, Auerbach's home office "resembled the bomb shelter in the TV show *Lost*, with lots of old letters, magazines from the fifties, an old radio. He was still using a rotary telephone. Going into Red's office was like going back in time. It was a tremendous experience."

These meet-and-greets with freshly minted owners were nothing new to Auerbach, who, since joining the Celtics in 1950, had worked under seventeen different ownership groups.

"Why don't you sit down and we'll talk some basketball," he said, but it was more of a pop quiz. After asking some break-the-ice questions about which team Grousbeck and Pagliuca believed would win the NBA championship, he got down to business: Did the new owners have a plan? A philosophy? Auerbach knew changes would be made, among them the exodus of general manager Chris Wallace, a holdover from the Pitino regime. Did the new owners have a new general manager in mind?

Auerbach listened intently to the new owners, just as he had done with Harry Mangurian and Robert Schmertz and Marvin Kratter and all the others who had come and gone over the years. But the new owners added this: because of their respect for Auerbach, they planned to consult him on all major decisions. Auerbach would not have final say, his presidency being of the emeritus variety, but he would be kept in the loop. Auerbach was flattered. Like an aging Mafia don—indeed, *Boston Globe* columnist Dan Shaughnessy once compared him to a retired Don Corleone "playing with his grandson in the vegetable garden"[1]—Auerbach gave the new owners his blessing.

A few months after meeting with Auerbach, Pagliuca met with Danny Ainge, a onetime basketball-baseball star at Brigham Young University who in 1981 gave up a major league career with the Toronto Blue Jays when Auerbach selected him in the NBA draft. Following some protracted legal wrangling with the Blue Jays, Auerbach bought out the remainder of Ainge's baseball contract, and a new Celtic star was added to the mix. Ainge, who played on two championship teams during his eight seasons with the Celtics, was by now working as an analyst for basketball games televised by the TNT network, and Pagliuca, who knew him from various charitable projects, wanted to sound out the former Celtic on a list of candidates he was considering for general manager. In what turned out to be a critical juncture in the Celtics' future, Ainge picked up Pagliuca at the Phoenix Sky Harbor International Airport;

from there, they were supposed to head to a series of golf dates with some of the men being considered to replace Chris Wallace, a pleasant native of West Virginia with a solid reputation as a talent evaluator who had nonetheless failed to restore the Celtics to their past glory.

But Ainge, mulling over his previous conversations with Pagliuca, had come to the conclusion that *he* was interested in being the next general manager of the Celtics. Pagliuca and Ainge kept driving around the airport, talking about the job opening, and then they dropped the matter and played golf. After a meeting on the links with one would-be general manager, Pagliuca had another talk with Ainge about moving to Boston.

A scheduled golf date with another of the GM candidates was no longer necessary, but Pagliuca kept the appointment.

"I wound up playing eighteen holes of golf with this other person who was not going to be the next general manager of the Celtics," Pagliuca recalled.

That job would go to Danny Ainge.

W yc Grousbeck is a man of tradition: talk to him about his college crew days and his eyes widen as he waxes nostalgic about Princeton capturing the 1983 lightweight rowing national championship.

"It's a hypercompetitive sport," said Grousbeck. "The only way to beat somebody is to be in better shape than they are and to have a higher pain tolerance. A boat is a machine that sucks all the life out of you, and if I beat you in rowing it's because I'm in better shape than you are. You just kick someone's ass. That's the whole sport. And you take someone's shirt and you wear it. So you wear a Yale or a Princeton shirt around if you're the Harvard guy who won."

It was this taste for competition, and a belief in tradition, that helped throw Grousbeck into the frenzy of being an owner of the Celtics. One of his first tasks was to set up a series of lunch meetings with the various club executives he and Pagliuca had inherited and to ask them what needed to be done to create a Celtics buzz in the Boston sports market.

During one such meeting, a longtime club exec said to him, "This is a Red Sox town."

Replied Grousbeck: "Well, be that as it may, and I'm a Red Sox fan too, but they don't play in the winter. The World Series ends the day before our season begins. How do you sell Celtics tickets? Who are your buddies in the league that you call about ticket-pricing specials?"

"I just do it by the seat of the pants," came the reply, remembered Grousbeck.

The new owner proceeded to ask his lunch guest what arenas he liked in the NBA, which teams had the best halftime shows, the best concessions stands. . . .

The executive told Grousbeck he hadn't been to a road game in six years.

The guy didn't know it yet, but he had just lost his job.

Though Grousbeck understood that the best way to get the natives' buttons popping over the Celtics was to put a good team on the court, he took additional steps. He required all of his employees to place Celtics bumper stickers on their cars. He had specially designed CELTICS STAFF shirts made, and then he said, "Wear them. And you're not eating lunch in the office. You're going out to lunch every day, and people will ask you about your shirt, and you will tell them about the Celtics."

Four years later, sitting with Tommy Heinsohn at the Perkins School charity function, Grousbeck and Pagliuca agreed that, yes, absolutely, here was the perfect representative for the Celtics at the NBA's upcoming draft lottery: Heinsohn was loyal, he had a reputation as a grinder, and he was a winner. One didn't need to see what kind of shirt Tommy Heinsohn was wearing to know he was a Celtic, though he *did* wear his love for the team on his sleeve.

But while most folks with any interest in the Celtics were hoping that Tommy Heinsohn's grit and Helen Heinsohn's charm—and her charms—would somehow vault the Green into one of the top two picks in the draft, Danny Ainge had different ideas.

In the weeks leading up to the 2007 draft lottery, Ainge was in constant touch with his onetime Celtics teammate Kevin McHale, now general manager of the Minnesota Timberwolves. He wasn't calling to talk about the good old days: Ainge wanted to talk about McHale's best player, Kevin Garnett. The Timberwolves had drafted the demonstrative, superbly talented forward directly out of high school with the fifth pick in the 1995 draft, and for twelve seasons Garnett was the face of the franchise. Yet the Timberwolves never won an NBA championship during that period, and now McHale was looking to rebuild. And so the two onetime Celtics players from the glory years discussed the possibility of a deal: if the Celtics landed the first or second pick in the lottery, perhaps they could send it to Minnesota for Garnett.

But the Ping-Pong balls did not bounce the right way for the Celtics. In the no-cell-phones-or-pagers-allowed backroom where the actual lottery took place, the Celtics, with a 19.9 percent chance of getting the first pick, ended up with the *fifth* selection. The Seattle Sonics, with an 8.8 percent chance of getting number one, landed the top pick. The Portland Trail Blazers collected the number-two pick. For the televised portion of the lottery, each team's representative sat behind a little podium on a set resembling a game show, with Heinsohn sporting a grim, whoop-de-doo expression as the Celtics' number-five pick was announced.

Until that point, the only representative of the Celtics who already knew the team's poor fortune was their man in the backroom, Wyc Grousbeck. Danny Ainge was in his office at the Celtics' training facility at HealthPoint in Waltham, Massachusetts, joined by Steve Pagliuca and several staffers.

But even before the game show began, Ainge had a good idea of how things were going to turn out.

"They flashed a picture in there of the vault room, and we saw a glimpse of Wyc, and we knew it was not good," he recalled. "Wyc is just a high-energy person, an animated person. We saw a quiet and subdued Wyc in that setting. He would have been holding up a sign or giving the world a thumbs-up if we had won the lottery.

"All it did was clarify things," Ainge said. "It took options away from us. And we had to get to work on what our next step would be."

Ainge still wanted Garnett, but he knew he would have to offer a different package to Kevin McHale. And there was another problem: Garnett would have to sign a contract extension with his would-be new team, since the Celtics planned on keeping him for more than the one year remaining on his current deal. That was key. And the way things looked now, Garnett didn't believe even he could make the Celtics a championship contender.

Ainge had covered all his bases in advance of the lottery.

"I was always thinking, 'Here's what we'd do if we had number one,' 'Here's what we'd do if we got number two,' and, 'Here's what we'd do if we didn't get one of those,'" Ainge recalled. "We had had conversations with teams about making trades with the idea that we would *not* get number one or two."

One of those conversations was with the Seattle Sonics. As with Garnett, Ainge had had an interest in acquiring the Sonics' veteran shooting guard Ray Allen since long before the draft. Allen had something else in common with Garnett: he was hard not to notice. But whereas Garnett was an emotional, high-strung, on-the-court presence who seemed to pour every ounce of his soul into every game, Allen had a smooth, regal way about him, gliding effortlessly up and down the court.

Appearances, however, can be deceiving: Allen, a onetime University of Connecticut star, was a veteran of eleven NBA seasons and had plenty of wear and tear on his body. Following the end of the 2006–2007 season, he underwent surgery on both ankles to have bone spurs removed.

On the night of the NBA draft at Madison Square Garden, Ainge packaged veteran small forward Wally Szczerbiak (a Celtic for parts of two seasons), point guard Delonte West (the team's fiftieth overall pick from the 2004 draft), and the rights to number-five pick Jeff Green of Georgetown University and made a deal with Seattle that brought Ray Allen to Boston. Along with Allen, the Celtics also received Louisiana State University forward Glen "Big Baby" Davis, who had been drafted by Seattle with the thirty-fifth overall pick and then flipped to Boston.

The trade almost did not happen, because the Sonics preferred center Theo Ratliff, who had just one year remaining on his contract, over Szczerbiak.

"It was critical that we not give up the Theo contract," Ainge recalled. "But Seattle was adamant about not taking Wally's contract and wanting Theo's contract. Up until the very end there was not going to be a trade for Ray Allen, but there was no way we could make the further deal."

The "further deal" was with Minnesota for Kevin Garnett. Ainge tried again on the day of the draft to swing the deal. In holding back

Theo Ratliff, he recognized that he would likely have to make the painful decision to part with forward Al Jefferson, whom he had drafted out of Prentiss (Mississippi) High School with the fifteenth overall pick in the 2004 draft.

"I always had a Kevin Garnett trade on my mind," Ainge said. "When the deal on draft day fell through, Kevin [McHale] gave me no indication that there was no longer a deal. I just felt that Minnesota loved Al Jefferson. We had the Ratliff contract. I felt we could make this happen."

About three weeks after the draft, Donnie Wahlberg traveled to Bristol, Connecticut, to make a live appearance on ESPN's *First Take*. The main purpose of the trip was for Wahlberg to plug his latest acting project, *Kill Point*, a television series for Spike TV about a gang of military veterans who return from Iraq and then reunite to stage a bank robbery. But the ESPN appearance was also an opportunity for the die-hard Boston sports fan to talk about his favorite teams.

What he said turned out to be so stunning a forecast of the Celtics' 2007–2008 season that nearly two years later, when Ainge watched a recording of the show, he said, "My initial thought is: *Is Donnie tapping my phone lines?* He got some inside information that the rest of the world didn't have."

The interview opened with host Jay Crawford lobbing a softball, asking Wahlberg to name his greatest Boston sports moment.

"The generic answer would be the Red Sox winning in 2004," he replied. "But I'm going to reserve that. I have a top-three list."

"I'd love to hear your top-three list," Crawford said.

Wahlberg went in descending order, placing the Patriots' 20–17 victory over the St. Louis Rams in Super Bowl XXXVI at number three, and the Red Sox' four-game sweep of the St. Louis Cardinals in the 2004 World Series at number two.

"Number one, I'm going to reserve it, because I think something very special is going to happen very soon," he said.

Crawford: "As in this year?"

Wahlberg: "I think this year we may have three world champions."

Crawford: *"Three?"*

Wahlberg: "Three."

Crawford: "I can give you the Patriots and the Red Sox. . . ."

Wahlberg: "Yes, and see how easily you did that?"

Crawford: "Yeah, now where is that third one coming from, 'cause, Donnie, I'm not seeing it."

Wahlberg: "I gotta tell ya, I think the Celtics are going to do something really special."

(*Jay Crawford chuckles*)

Wahlberg: "Danny Ainge has something up his sleeve, and I think something special's gonna happen."

Crawford: "As in an NBA championship?"

Wahlberg: "Yes."

When Crawford tsk-tsked his guest, reminding him that the Celtics did not get Greg Oden in the draft, Wahlberg said, "We don't need Greg Oden. Greg Oden is six years away. And I'm so insulted every time [people] put Greg Oden on a magazine cover next to Bill Russell. How could they do that?"

Crawford drifted on to some other sports topics, and then they discussed Wahlberg's television series. But in closing, the host couldn't resist returning to this nonsense about three Boston teams winning championships . . . with the Celtics on the list.

"You don't acquire Theo Ratliff's contract unless you want to do something with it," Wahlberg said of Ainge's earlier acquisition of the well-traveled center. "We still have it. We still have some young chips to trade. We've already got Ray Allen. We've got Paul Pierce, we've got Al Jefferson. There's a major thing that could happen. Still.

"Danny Ainge's tenure will be judged on this year, and I think something great's gonna happen."

⑨
KID STUFF

The Red Sox came into the 2007 season with a player payroll estimated at $143 million, the second highest in baseball. They weren't spending as much money as the Yankees ($195.2 million), yet their payroll was significantly higher than those of the game's other big spenders, including the Mets ($117.9 million), Angels ($109 million), White Sox ($109.7 million), and Dodgers ($108.7 million).[1]

There was no getting around it: part of the reason the Red Sox were so good was that they were willing to spend money in the pursuit of excellence. Manny Ramirez, J. D. Drew, Curt Schilling, Jason Varitek, and David Ortiz were all earning in excess of $10 million per season, and Mike Lowell and Julio Lugo were pulling in about $9 million apiece. Daisuke Matsuzaka was a $6-million-a-year "rookie." Far from being scrappy underdogs, the Red Sox had money to spend, and did.

Yet as the 2007 season moved toward the warmth of summer, it was becoming more apparent that the Red Sox were also getting younger, ever younger. Whereas the World Series–winning 2004 Red Sox were a team of loud, swaggering veterans, with not a single rookie emerging with an everyday job,* the 2007 Red Sox were turning into baseball's version of the New Frontier. They had three rookies in key roles—second baseman Dustin Pedroia, starting pitcher Daisuke Matsuzaka, and

---

* Rookie infielder Kevin Youkilis, shuttling back and forth from Triple-A Pawtucket, appeared in seventy-two games for the 2004 Red Sox, and rookie southpaw Lenny DiNardo made twenty-two relief appearances.

left-handed reliever Hideki Okajima—and outfielder Jacoby Ellsbury, a twenty-three-year-old speedster in just his third professional season, was on the way.

Papelbon, now in his second full season in the big leagues, was no longer content to just *be* a closer; he was now looking like one. Before delivering a pitch, he would look down to the ground and then slowly lift his head, his eyes sneaking a look at the plate from below the brim of his cap. He looked . . . scary.

"It all started with trying to figure out how to focus," Papelbon recalled. "It was something in my pre-pitch routine that I developed. Basically I would look down on the ground where my land foot would go, and I'd draw my imaginary line where I wanted that ball to go. I don't remember exactly when it started. It just fucking started one day."

On June 30, Red Sox fans got their first look at Ellsbury, the gifted outfielder from Oregon who was the club's first pick in the 2005 draft. Promoted to the big leagues when pitcher Joel Pineiro went on the disabled list, Ellsbury reached on an infield single in his second major league at-bat. He had a six-game cup of coffee with the Red Sox before being returned to Triple-A Pawtucket, but he hit .375 (6-for-16) in those six games. It was apparent to anybody following the Red Sox: Ellsbury could play . . . and soon would play.

And then there was Jon Lester. He began the season on the disabled list and remained there until June 11, at which time the Red Sox finally activated him and sent him to Triple-A Pawtucket. Given that he was making a return from his off-season treatment for lymphoma, the team was in no hurry to rush the young lefty back to Boston. Lester finally returned to the big leagues for a July 23 start against the Cleveland Indians at Jacobs Field, allowing two runs in six innings in a 6–2 victory.

"I figured the day would come, I just didn't know when," Lester told reporters after the game. "I'm just fortunate it was this early on. There's just a lot of fun, a lot of excitement right now."[2]

Papelbon. Pedroia. Ellsbury. Lester. Prospects from the farm system continued to arrive—not just spare parts or question marks, but players whom the club was counting on to be major league mainstays.

"It felt like the whole game of baseball was changing," said Pedroia.

"The style of baseball we were playing was, from the first pitch to the last pitch, we were going to come out and play like maniacs. Papelbon doing his whole gig, Lester out there throwing great stuff. Ellsbury, with the fire on the bases. Me, doing the little things to help our team win. You could tell that the style of the game was a little bit different than on other teams."

Even after all his success, Pedroia still ran into critics. One of them was a Hall of Famer, George Brett of the Kansas City Royals. Like Red Sox hitting coach Dave Magadan, Brett had been a precision hitter from the left side of the plate, the difference being that, while Magadan carved out a respectable major league career, Brett's career landed him in Cooperstown. He was a .305 lifetime hitter with some power, hitting 317 career home runs. In 1980 he made a run at becoming the game's first .400 hitter since Ted Williams in 1941, settling at .390.

And Brett, by 2007 working for the Royals as vice president of baseball operations, hated Pedroia's swing.

"You swing too hard, but you don't swing and miss. It's kind of weird," Brett told Pedroia when they were introduced by Terry Francona before a game at Kansas City's Kauffman Stadium. "You got too big of a swing for how small you are."

Pedroia, feeling sufficiently comfortable in his shoes to be able to argue with a Hall of Famer, said, "You did it your way, and I'm going to do it my way."

Pedroia recalled the conversation as "kind of kidding but serious."

These new Red Sox were exciting young players, with unique personalities and interesting backstories. Lester had overcome lymphoma. Pedroia was proving that size does *not* matter. Papelbon was emerging as one of the game's true characters, delivering as much flash and fire with his postgame commentary as he delivered on the mound. Ellsbury, whose mother is a full-blooded Navajo, was believed to be the first major league baseball player of Navajo descent.

But while these kids represented the future of the Red Sox and were of course contributing to the present, it was also true that the veterans, the big-money guys, still had to put up the big numbers if the Red Sox hoped to return to the late-October stage.

One of those players was David Ortiz, whose late-inning heroics over the years inspired favorable comparisons with the 1967 Carl Yastrzemski. Though Big Papi was not going to match the fifty homers he hit in 2006, he was still having a fine season. But in the fifth inning of a 10–3 victory over the White Sox on July 20, Ortiz had to leave the game after straining his left shoulder during a head-first slide into second base.

He missed the next four games. "The first day, when I went down to second, I thought I wasn't going to play again this year," Ortiz told reporters on the afternoon of Lester's comeback. "That's how bad it felt."[3]

Ortiz and Manny Ramirez represented the best 3-4 hitting tandem in baseball, and one of the finest in the history of the Red Sox. Numbers aside, they were electrifying players, pure entertainment. Ortiz had his flair for the dramatic, including his game-winning home run in the bottom of the twelfth inning of Game 4 of the 2004 American League Championship Series against the Yankees and his game-winning single in the bottom of the fourteenth inning of Game 5. And Ramirez, once you got past the baggy pants and the puzzling behavior, such as the July 18, 2005, game against the Tampa Bay Devil Rays when he ducked inside Fenway's Green Monster and made it back out the door to his position just as Sox pitcher Wade Miller was about to deliver a pitch, had a lightning-quick swing and was known to go on prolonged offensive tears. Tall or short, lefty or righty, grizzled veteran or apple-cheeked rookie, Ramirez wrecked them all when he was up to it.

So far this season he had been up to it. His absences from the lineup in the last weeks of the 2006 season made for a caution flag going into 2007, but Ramirez played in all twenty-four games on the April schedule and in all but one game in May. He got off to a slow start, hitting just .202 in April, and then got hot. Real hot. He hit .327 in May, .322 in June. In July, he hit .340 with seven home runs and twenty-five RBI. Ortiz and Ramirez were back in business: during a three-month stretch from the beginning of May and right on through July, they hit a combined .330.

The biggest disappointment of the season was that the team's two big off-season free-agent signings, J. D. Drew and Julio Lugo, were not playing in a fashion commensurate with their lofty salaries. Lugo hit just .209 in May and only .089 in June, and his defensive play tended toward the erratic. Drew was all over the map—.171 in May and then .325 in June, followed by .213 in July. And he wasn't hitting for much power, with just six home runs by the All-Star break.

Where the Red Sox continued to get stellar—and, really, inspiring—play was at third. It had been well documented that the Red Sox had to absorb the remaining two years and $18 million on Mike Lowell's contract in order to swing the Josh Beckett deal, but now Lowell was looking like a steal. En route to fashioning what would turn out to be a career year, Lowell was hitting .300 with fourteen home runs and sixty-three RBI at the All-Star break. He also was displaying remarkable leadership abilities. Born and raised in Puerto Rico to parents who were from Cuba, Lowell was as fluent in Spanish as he was in English; thus, he moved seamlessly within the various factions in the clubhouse—which exist in every major league club—and was respected by all. He was particularly good with young players; more to the point, *all* the veterans on the 2007 Red Sox coexisted peacefully with the ever-growing cast of rookies in the clubhouse, offering advice to the very players who were looking to take away their jobs.

Relief pitcher Manny Delcarmen, who was raised in Boston's Hyde Park neighborhood and drafted by the Red Sox in 2000, was a nervous rookie who was comforted by the support he received from the veteran pitchers when he made his major league debut in 2005. Returning to the big leagues in 2007, he continued to be treated well by such old-timers as Mike Timlin, Tim Wakefield, and Curt Schilling.

Timlin, who turned forty-one during spring training and had been pitching professionally since 1987, was beginning to wear down some. He began the season on the disabled list with a strained left oblique, and he went back on the DL in early May with shoulder tendinitis. He made only fifty relief appearances in 2007—a lot for some pitchers, but for Timlin the fewest in a season in twelve years.

"After I came up to the big leagues and Mike got to know me a little," recalled Delcarmen, "he told me he hoped I'd be the guy who replaced him as the setup guy someday. For him to say something like that to me, with everything he had going on, it's something I'll remember for the rest of my life."

* * *

Given his own medical history, Andrew J. Urban II has empathy for injured ballplayers. Though never much of a ballplayer himself —"I had a tendency to strike out," he said—he understands what it means to cope with injury, rehabilitation, and the many unexpected setbacks that can keep a star on the sidelines.

Urban was born three months ahead of schedule. "There must have been a Red Sox game down at Fenway, and I couldn't wait to get there," he explained.

Not exactly. The Red Sox actually had a day off on June 5, 1972, having moved on to Chicago after splitting a Sunday afternoon double-header with the Kansas City Royals at old Municipal Stadium. But it's just as well the Red Sox were not playing that day, because the team's newest fan was not in game shape.

At the time he was born, his parents were living on the third floor of a three-decker on E Street in South Boston. His mother, Jane Urban, hadn't been expecting to give birth for another three months, and his father, Andy Urban, a driver for B. Stimpson & Son Movers, was in New York City helping the newly installed president of the Massachusetts Institute of Technology transport his belongings to Cambridge. Jane was home alone when she went into labor; she called for an ambulance, but none were available, she recalled, so she was "rushed to the hospital in a paddy wagon. They got me there, and they had to knock me out. I didn't know I had had a baby until two days after he was born."

Andrew J. Urban II came into the world with lungs that were not fully functioning, a condition that would plague him throughout his childhood. He had frequent bouts of pneumonia, and because of this he was kept inside a lot. Baseball—and by extension, baseball cards—became an early passion. His dad was also a card collector, so father and son had something in common. That, and darts: they'd play for hours in the basement of the family home at 11 Kingston Road, and the boy was getting good.

When he was seven, his parents took him to meet Red Sox stars Jim Rice and Butch Hobson, who were making an appearance at the local Star Market. A photo in the family album shows a starstruck young Andrew posing with Rice, a future Hall of Famer.

It didn't take long for Urban to become a Red Sox fan and to select a favorite player. And while the trip to the Star Market was an unforget-table experience, neither Hobson nor Rice made the cut.

The boy had always been relegated to playing right field whenever the neighborhood kids got up a game, because, as he'll tell you, "nobody ever hits the ball out there. I stood out in right field for a whole game once, and nobody hit a ball to me. I wanted to be the guy who dives and makes the great catch, but you can't do that when nothing gets hit to you." And so the first time Andrew J. Urban II ever stepped inside Fenway Park—on a Cub Scout field trip—he looked out toward right field and pronounced himself a Dwight Evans fan for life. Evans won eight Gold Gloves during his nineteen seasons with the Red Sox, and his running, leaping catch to rob the Cincinnati Reds' Joe Morgan of a home run in the eleventh inning of the epic Game 6 of the 1975 World Series remains one of the memorable defensive plays in baseball history. He's the best right fielder Urban ever saw. Nobody else comes close.

In the early morning of April 9, 1985, Urban, twelve years old at the time, was in front of his house at 11 Kingston Road when he spotted a friend, Kevin O'Neil, across the street. He went to the corner and started to cross Trapelo Road. He didn't make it. He was struck by a car, so hard that his sneakers remained on the street at the point of impact. Waltham Police were at the scene at 7:18 AM, and Urban was rushed to Waltham Hospital.

"On contact, I was dead," Urban recalled. "I don't remember being hit. I always tell people I was apparently hit, because apparently I was."

Andy Urban remembered being told by a police officer that his son had missed flying into a tree by about a foot. Nonetheless, the boy lay in a coma; when Andy Urban arrived at the hospital, doctors told him it would help if he talked to his son, talked to him about normal, everyday things. So Andy said, "We're going to play darts," and he kept saying it, over and over. Occasionally he'd change up, asking the boy if he wanted to help tend the garden they kept out back of the house.

Two days later, Urban came out of his coma. Miraculously, he'd suf-fered no broken bones. Not yet, anyway. After eventually being allowed to return home, he was in bed, playing cribbage, when, inexplicably, his wrist broke. He was rushed back to the hospital.

Later that summer, while still recovering from the accident, he attended a local day camp. When the campers were asked by their counselor to write an essay, Urban chose as his theme, "The Worst Day of My Life."

"The worst day of my life was on April 9, 1985 at 7:15 in the morning," he wrote.

I was crossing the street to get my friend for school and I got hit by a Lincoln Continental. I don't remember anything because I was dead. (I didn't see a Devil or Angel.) They said they had to cut off my clothes. (Don't worry, they put a towel over me.) On the way to Waltham hospital I died four times. They said they would do their best to bring me to life.

And the kicker:

I went a total of 20 feet, clearing a chain-link fence. There is one thing I'll remember: I WILL LOOK BEFORE CROSSING THE STREET!

Urban made a full recovery and returned to school. He hadn't planned on any additional academic pursuits after graduating from Waltham High School in 1990, but decided to enroll in Middlesex Community College in Lowell to please his maternal grandmother, Grace Sinclair. He earned his associate's degree in 1992 and then moved on to Bentley College, earning a degree in business management.

Yet Urban never took a job in business—leastways, not on the management end. He was content to pursue a string of blue-collar jobs, explaining, "I just wasn't built to sit behind a desk all day. That's just not me. I believe in being active. When you sit around, you just put on weight."

His father, Andy Urban, saw it this way: "He's doing what he wants to do. He never wanted to go to college, but he only did that to accommodate his grandmother. He was her only grandchild, and she wanted him to be a college graduate."

When the 2007 baseball season began, Urban was working at one of the big-box discount department stores, stocking shelves on the midnight-to-8:00 AM shift. It was, he believed, a good arrangement: he'd knock off work just as the rest of the world was heading to the rock pile, and then sleep until the early afternoon, grab something to eat, and, during baseball season, head over to Fenway Park to greet the arriving ballplayers. For day games, the routine would change accordingly.

His parents divorced in 1998. As is his nature, Urban gets along with both his parents, as well as his mother's second husband, Paul Lamontagne. He pays his mother $125 a week for room and board at 11 Kingston Road, a good deal, he said.

There was a time, back in the day, when folks called him Drew. He didn't much like it, and said so. And to this day he gets in a genuine snit when someone sidles up and dares address him as "Autograph Andy." Or "Andy," for that matter. Andy, he'll tell you, is his father.

Funny: He's devoted to a baseball team whose players have such nicknames as Pedie, Big Papi, Schill, 'Tek, Dice-K, Youk, and Okie. A perusal of the *Baseball Encyclopedia* turns up the likes of Joltin' Joe, Rapid Robert, the Duke of Flatbush, and Boston's very own Splendid Splinter, Ted Williams. Or Teddy Ballgame.

"But I am one of the few people you'll find at Fenway Park without a nickname," he said. "I don't want one, don't care for one. My name is Andrew J. Urban II."

The Red Sox were 13–14 in June, and only a little better in July, going 15–12. Yet they had jumped off to such a fast start to the season (16–8 in April, 20–8 in May) that even a two-month stretch of slightly above .500 baseball had failed to dislodge them from first place in the standings. In fact, after April 17 the Red Sox were never again out of first place in the American League East.

Their largest lead was twelve games, which they reached on July 5 at Fenway Park via a 15–4 victory over the Tampa Bay Devil Rays. It was the eleventh straight loss for the lowly Devil Rays, but nothing but good times for the hometown nine. Mike Lowell had five hits, raising his average to .307. Center fielder Coco Crisp hit a grand slam. David Ortiz went 3-for-5 and scored four runs.

And Josh Beckett, continuing his Cy Young–caliber season, worked six innings against the Rays in improving his record to 12–2. Though it would have been presumptuous for the Red Sox to begin talking about playoff pitching assignments this early in the season, it was obvious that Beckett had emerged as the ace of the staff. Curt Schilling remained one of the great postseason pitchers of his generation—and he could still bring it, as shown on a June afternoon at Oakland when he lost a bid for his first career no-hitter with two out in the ninth inning—but he landed on the disabled list on June 22 and did not return until August 6.

Daisuke Matsuzaka was pitching as well as could be expected, but he was still running up high pitch counts in the early innings. He remained a work in progress, a good pitcher but not an ace. Veteran Tim Wakefield was fashioning another fine season—he would finish with seventeen victories, matching his career high—but you just don't march into October with a forty-one-year-old knuckleballer as the ace of your staff. Julian Tavarez, who earned a spot in the starting rotation by default when Papelbon returned to his closer's role at the end of spring training, was back in the bullpen by mid-August. Jon Lester was going to be in the mix, that much the Red Sox knew. But they had no way of knowing what kind of shape he'd be in by October.

All the Red Sox knew was that Josh Beckett was number one.

"It's awesome to be on a team that wins a lot of ballgames," Beckett said after beating the Devil Rays. "To be able to come every day, whether it's my turn to pitch or someone else's, and see what we're capable to do with the bats. The same thing goes with our starting pitching. You have a chance to win with whoever is on the hill. We're riding that wave right now. It's a fun time."[4]

10

TERRY'S CLOTH

B y late August, as the 2007 baseball season was heading into the home stretch, so, too, was a special commission that had been established by Major League Baseball to root out the rampant use of performance-enhancing drugs.

But while everyone from fans and players to sportswriters and umpires was anxious to learn what would be unearthed by former U.S. senator George Mitchell, who was heading up the investigation, Major League Baseball officials were also working hard to find and suppress other forms of illegal activity that might destroy the national pastime.

An episode that Red Sox manager Terry Francona would later describe as "Shirtgate" took place on Wednesday, August 29, prior to the second game of a three-game set between the Red Sox and Yankees at Yankee Stadium. Francona was standing behind the cage during batting practice when he was approached by former big leaguer Bob Watson, a bear of a man whose official title with Major League Baseball is Vice President of Rules and On-Field Operations, though he is known casually as the game's Dean of Discipline.

Beyond casual pregame chitchat, Watson wanted to make sure Francona was wearing his regulation uniform shirt underneath his fleece pullover, which over the years had become standard on-field attire for the Boston manager. Francona started wearing a pullover during his days managing the Philadelphia Phillies, "and the fans hated it," he recalled. "And it was probably stubbornness, my 'Fuck you.' The hotter it was, the more I wore it. Just because it pissed people off."

Francona was hardly a trailblazer; by the first decade of the twenty-first century it had become common practice for managers to wear some kind of jacket or sweatshirt in place of those clingy uniform tops, all the better to camouflage their middle-aged, ex-athlete's girth. As then–Toronto Blue Jays manager John Gibbons told the *Herald*'s Rob Bradford, "I'm one guy who also never wants to wear [a uniform top]. My reason is when I wear a uniform top my belly is a little too big and it looks bad. That's the sole reason."[1]

The reality, in Francona's case, is that neither vanity nor a chance to stick it to Phillies fans had anything to do with the Boston skipper's decision to wear a pullover. Unlike some managers, he didn't have any girth to hide; he was in tremendous athletic shape for a man his age, adhering to a daily workout regimen that helped keep the pounds off. As for his general health, that was another matter. Francona had been taking blood thinners to help with his circulation, along with occasionally wearing special nylon leggings under his uniform. The fleece pullover afforded him the luxury of either not wearing a belt or even keeping the top of his uniform pants buttoned.

The lords of Major League Baseball, while not keen on the idea of their managers concealing themselves under fleece pullovers, had decided that, so long as their dugout strategists were wearing their official uniform tops underneath, all would be right in the world of hardball. It seemed a goofy compromise considering that Francona and his managerial comrades could have been wearing Homestead Grays throwback jerseys or Def Leppard T-shirts under their fleeces and nobody would have been the wiser.

Francona had been going the pullover route for so long that few fans even knew his uniform number—number 47, known best to Red Sox followers as having been worn by left-hander Bruce Hurst from 1980 to 1988. Aside from photo ops, nobody could remember ever seeing Francona in a uniform top. But now MLB was choosing to enforce its invisible uniform top policy, which apparently was what brought Bob Watson to Yankee Stadium on August 29.

During that casual pregame discussion with Francona, Watson asked the Boston manager whether he was wearing his uniform top.

"I pulled my [shirt] down, and he kind of did a double-take," Francona said. "I said, 'I told you I would.'"[2]

On to the game. Beckett was on the mound for Boston. Pitching for the Yankees was Roger Clemens, the onetime Boston hero who, having made his latest un-retirement, would be pitching against the Sox in this, his sixteenth start since returning to baseball.

Red Sox versus Yankees.

Josh Beckett versus Roger Clemens.

Yankee Stadium, packed house.

It was baseball at its riveting, plot-twisting finest. What more could it need?

Enter Major League Baseball's Fashion Police.

In the bottom of the second inning of what would be a 4–3 loss to the Yankees, Francona was suddenly approached in the dugout by a Major League Baseball security official named Eddie Maldonado.

Maldonado, a New York City police lieutenant, was working for Major League Baseball as a resident security agent, or RSA. The Yankees were up at the time of Maldonado's dugout visit, with Bobby Abreu at bat and Derek Jeter leading off second base. The Yankees already had scored three runs in the inning.

Francona was pacing the dugout, the predictable chaw of tobacco stuffed into his cheek. He was looking suspiciously at second base, wondering if Jeter was going to break for third.

And then: "Excuse me, Mr. Francona, we need to see your shirt."

"This is no exaggeration—I was trying to get Pedroia to hold Jeter on," Francona recalled. "And I can't really get his attention. I'm waving. All of a sudden this guy walks out and he says, 'I need you.' And I said, *Now?*' He looked a little embarrassed. He said, 'Can you step over here?' And I remember going around the corner thinking, 'If this fucking guy steals third I'm going to kill you.'"

As requested for the second time that day, Francona pulled up the fleece, revealing the uniform top. Once Maldonado had determined that Francona wasn't breaking any baseball laws, he left the dugout . . . Francona cursing him all the way up the runway.

Francona made no mention of the dugout incident during his

postgame remarks to the media. For all he knew, it had gone unnoticed, and he wasn't about to bring it up in front of a roomful of sportswriters. But in the next day's *New York Post* a short story appeared under the headline: "Watson's Visit Irks Francona." The article reported that "Bob Watson entered the Red Sox dugout during last night's game to talk to Terry Francona about not wearing a uniform jersey while managing. . . . Upon seeing baseball's top cop, who was ushered into the dugout by an MLB resident security agent, Francona snapped at Watson."[3]

The *Post* had Francona saying to Watson, "Get out of the dugout during the game."[4]

When the Red Sox arrived at Yankee Stadium that morning for what would be an afternoon getaway game against the Yankees in the series finale, all the reporters wanted to ask Francona about was the dugout incident from the previous night. A story about a shirt had become a story with legs. But though Francona was clearly upset about what had happened—he made no secret of that—he was even more perturbed that the *Post* had reported that he'd thrown Watson out of the Boston dugout. Explaining that it had been a security guard who entered the dugout, Francona said he was angry that "some moron" reported it had been Watson.

Francona is as much a baseball lifer as anyone who has ever played the game. His father, Tito Francona, logged fifteen seasons in the major leagues, playing for nine different teams. His best season was '59, when he hit .363 in 122 games with the Cleveland Indians. As he was closing out his career in 1969 and '70 with jumps from the Atlanta Braves to the Oakland A's to the Milwaukee Brewers, his son, Terry, had become old enough to hang around big league clubhouses. And don't think the experience wasn't lasting: in a short piece in the December 27, 2007 edition of *Sports Illustrated*, Francona answered a question about the best Christmas gift he ever received: "Easy. I was 10, and I got an Oakland A's warm-up jacket. My dad was playing with Oakland. They wore white spikes and green jackets. This was in the day [1969] before they sold those things, but I got a jacket that fit me. It was green, in that shiny, satiny material. I wore it to school every day."[5]

Having been around the game so long, Francona has an acquired understanding as to what constitutes proper decorum in a big league dugout. And just as he would never suffer security guards gladly if they dared to give him a clothing inspection during a game, he also knows it would be a serious breech of etiquette for a former big leaguer (who presumably would know better) to be traipsing into the dugout after the first pitch.

So Francona boiled.

"For somebody to say that I yelled at Bob Watson, somebody owes Bob an apology and probably me," Francona said during his pregame media gathering. "Because that's bad. That's not being professional."[6]

Just like that, the dugout inspection by the MLB Fashion Police, along with the *New York Post* mistakenly placing Bob Watson at the scene of the crime, had added yet another dimension to the biggest rivalry in sports history. Everyone had something to say about it. Nick Canepa, writing in the *San Diego Union-Tribune*, predicted that Watson would soon be fining Francona $10,000 "when a surprise underwear inspection reveals the Boston manager isn't wearing any."[7] Wrote Jeff Gold in *Newsday*, "It seemed like the perfect MTV 'Punk'd' setup: a public figure put in an absurd situation at the most inconvenient time. Terry Francona soon realized this was no practical joke. Ashton Kutcher didn't suddenly appear and there were no hidden cameras."[8]

Noting that Watson was upset about what had happened, saying the matter should have been kept "in-house," John Ryan of the *San Jose Mercury News* chimed in with, "No, that's in-sane."[9]

This support for Francona marked a brief departure by the national sports punditry from what rapidly was becoming an anything-but-Boston attitude. Sportswriters everywhere seemed to understand the obvious: for anyone to inspect a manager's clothing during a big league baseball game was indeed embarrassing. And though Major League Baseball would quickly apologize for what had happened—"Terry got upset, and he was within his rights to be upset," MLB executive Jimmie Lee Solomon said[10]—Francona's latest visit to the Bronx was a miserable experience. In the series opener, a 5–3 Boston loss, Manny Ramirez had to leave in the seventh inning with what was later determined to be a strained left oblique, and nobody knew how long the slugging outfielder would be idled. And Bobby Kielty, a versatile journeyman outfielder who had joined the team earlier in the month, left the same game because of lower back pain.

The Red Sox were swept in the three-game series, losing 5–0 in the finale. And Francona wasn't even around when it was over, having been ejected in the seventh inning for arguing with umpire crew chief Derryl Cousins after Youkilis was called out for running too far wide of the base path between second and third.

Francona was not alone in being ejected from the game. In the eighth inning, Yankees rookie phenom Joba Chamberlain, a beefy twenty-one-year-old Nebraskan who looks eerily like Babe Ruth, threw two pitches over the head of Youkilis and was tossed by plate umpire Angel Hernandez.

"If that young man's intention was to get our attention," said Francona, "he did a very good job."[11]

The Red Sox could have all but wrapped up the American League East with a three-game sweep of the Yankees. But it was the Yankees who swept the series, moving to within five games of the Red Sox as September loomed.

Boston sports fans tuning in to the six o'clock news in the early evening of Saturday, September 1, would have been thrilled to learn that Boston College's football team had opened its season with a 38–28 victory over Wake Forest at Alumni Stadium. Eagles quarterback Matt Ryan, who within seven months would be selected third overall in the NFL draft by the Atlanta Falcons, completed 32 of 52 passes for 408 yards, including five touchdowns—the first BC quarterback to do so since 1984, when Heisman Trophy winner Doug Flutie threw *six* touchdown passes in a 52–20 dismantling of North Carolina.

By the time the eleven o'clock news aired on the Boston TV stations, Matt Ryan's crisp passing against the Demon Deacons of Wake Forest had been relegated to second-tier status on the sports budget. Some seven miles from Alumni Stadium, twenty-three-year-old right-hander Clay Buchholz, recalled that very day from Triple-A Pawtucket and making only his second major league start, pitched a no-hitter in the Red Sox' 10–0 victory over the Baltimore Orioles at Fenway Park.

In becoming the first Red Sox rookie to pitch a no-hitter—in 1967, lefty Billy Rohr came within one out of no-hitting the Yankees in his major league debut—Buchholz struck out nine Orioles, including a punch-out of Nick Markakis on his 115th and final pitch, a big round-house curve. When plate umpire Joe West rung Markakis up, pulling back his arm as though starting a lawn mower, Fenway Park erupted.

Buchholz was pitching as a fill-in. A day earlier, knuckleballer Tim Wakefield had to be scratched from his Friday night start against the Orioles because of a sore back, with journeyman/funnyman Julian Tavarez, Saturday's scheduled starter, moved up a day to take Wakefield's place. So the Sox summoned Buchholz, idling at Pawtucket, to Boston to pitch against the Orioles.

Buchholz, generously listed as six-foot-three and 190 pounds in the media guide—though he had the look of a high school kid in need of a good steak—was known to Red Sox fans only by reputation. And the reputation wasn't entirely good. Four years earlier, back home in Lumberston, Texas, Buchholz was arrested for his part in a caper that involved the swiping of twenty-nine laptop computers from a local school. The Red Sox investigated and came away with the belief that the episode was very high on the punk meter but not enough to brand Buchholz a hardened criminal. They selected him forty-second overall in the 2005 amateur draft, and in just over two years he was no-hitting the Orioles.

"We brought him in to Boston before we drafted him," said Red Sox scouting director Jason McLeod. "We wanted to see him throw, but there were also some very pointed questions directed at him. We needed to be satisfied that it was a onetime thing, that it was something that would not happen again. And we did come away satisfied. We've never had a problem with him with regard to anything like that."

Even as Buchholz was making history that night, it was clear to the Red Sox that the young right-hander wouldn't be included in their post-season plans. Francona and pitching coach John Farrell were in the early stages of mapping out their postseason pitching plans, but Buchholz, whose combined 148 innings pitched with Portland, Pawtucket, and Boston were more than he'd ever pitched in a single season, was being shut down.

Another young player emerged that night, however, and he *would* play a role in the team's postseason plans. Jacoby Ellsbury, also recalled from Pawtucket that day and entering the game as a defensive replacement in left field, doubled home two runs in his only at-bat, the beginning of a thirteen-game hitting streak. Over the next three weeks, it would become apparent to Red Sox Nation that Ellsbury belonged on the postseason roster.

It so happened that Andrew J. Urban II had an opportunity to land tickets for the September 1 game in which Clay Buchholz no-hit the Orioles. He turned it down.

Just one week earlier, Urban had been laid off from his job working the overnight shift at the Target in nearby Watertown. Unemployed now, Urban was in belt-tightening mode. He would continue making his pilgrimages to Fenway Park to collect autographs, but, for now, games were out. He needed to find a job.

"I come from a family of workaholics," he said. "These days, who can afford not to work?"

11

A NEW BIG THREE

Danny Ainge has something up his sleeve,
and I think something special's gonna happen.

—Donnie Wahlberg

As Red Sox general manager Theo Epstein was busy tinkering with his roster in the weeks leading up to the postseason, and as Patriots coach Bill Belichick was putting his charges through the grunting and groaning that is typical of a blisteringly hot NFL training camp, Danny Ainge continued his pursuit of Kevin Garnett. But from the moment an unfortunate drop of Ping-Pong balls that night in Secaucus denied him the coveted first pick in the draft, he knew that acquiring Garnett was going to cost him Al Jefferson.

Ainge had already parted with one player of whom he was quite fond when he sent the talented young shooting guard Delonte West, who was about to turn twenty-four, to the Seattle Sonics as part of the Ray Allen trade. Now he would have to deal Jefferson, just twenty-two years old and coming off a season in which he had averaged sixteen points a game and was looked upon by fans and media as key to the future of the franchise.

Ainge recognized that West, with his generous assortment of body tattoos, and Jefferson, addressed affectionately as Big Al by just about everybody, were popular young players; he understood, too, that Celtics fans believed that the duo, working with veteran Paul Pierce, might one day lead the Celtics to a championship. The GM also knew that

West and Jefferson had done their part to take their respective games to a higher level.

"I understand the loyalty," Ainge would later say, recalling the emotional turmoil that went into trading West and Jefferson. "I understand the Boston mentality, the Boston thing, the loyalty and all that. But I'm a westerner. I'm different. It wasn't easy. I put my heart and soul into scouting and drafting and developing and nurturing Al Jefferson. So trading Al Jefferson, that was tough. And I loved Delonte West. He's one of my favorite players that I've ever drafted. I spent so much time talking to Delonte and helping him with life things.

"I really felt a bond with those two guys in particular. And it was really tough to make those trades. But it's part of the business."

Looking back on his dramatic reshaping of the Boston Celtics, Ainge believed that part of his resolve was born out of a 1988 Christmastime charity event he attended with Larry Bird, Kevin McHale, and Red Auerbach. As Ainge told it, "Larry was banged up. He had the sore Achilles tendon. Kevin was banged up. He had that screw put in his foot. And there was a lot of discussion going on—there were rumors Larry was going to be traded to Indiana for Steve Stipanovich and Herb Williams. And McHale was rumored to be going to Dallas for Detleff Schremp and Sam Perkins. And I was rumored to be traded to Utah for the number-one pick and Darrell Griffith."

Ainge remembered Auerbach saying, "I'm not trading you guys. I just wouldn't do that."

More than twenty years later, Ainge can still recall his response to Auerbach.

"I told Red I thought he was crazy," he said. "I said, 'I would trade Larry in a heartbeat. Because he's on his way down. I would trade Kevin and Schremp for Perkins as fast as you could do it, and I would trade me."

The reason for Ainge's candor was simple: "I could sense our team was fading."

About two months after this Christmas cheer, on February 23, 1989, Red Auerbach did trade Ainge—to the Sacramento Kings with Brad Lohaus in exchange for Ed Pinckney and Joe Kleine. Ainge would log six more seasons in the NBA; though he never played on another championship team, he made it to the NBA Finals in 1992 with the Portland Trail Blazers and in '93 with the Phoenix Suns. As for the team Ainge left behind, the 1988–89 Celtics were swept by Detroit in the first round of the playoffs; Bird and McHale played out the remainder of their careers in Boston, never making it beyond the second round of the playoffs.

"I was very fortunate to be traded and very excited to be traded, because I sensed that this was not the Celtics anymore," Ainge said. "Larry was not Larry. Kevin was not Kevin. Robert [Parish] was not Robert.

"I felt that that was the time when they needed to make those changes."

And here now was Ainge, bartering with his old teammate and buddy Kevin McHale to acquire Kevin Garnett. But not only did Ainge have to come to terms with McHale, he also had to convince Garnett to sign a contract extension that would keep him in Boston beyond one season.

At one point Ainge even visited Garnett at his Malibu home, where he was greeted by not one NBA player but two: Tyronn Lue, a journeyman NBA guard, was crashing for a while at Garnett's place after having undergone off-season knee surgery.

Ainge talked about the exciting possibility of Garnett, Ray Allen, and Paul Pierce playing on the same team. He talked about the emergence of young Rajon Rondo on the point and Kendrick Perkins in the paint. He talked about Boston. He talked about tradition. The Boston GM wasn't buying; he was selling.

After Ainge left, Lue quizzed Garnett about playing for the Celtics as the two NBA veterans sat by the pool.

"The Boston Celtics are your best opportunity to win a championship," Lue recalled telling Garnett. "They already have Paul Pierce. They went out and got Ray Allen. With you, they can win it all."

"But what's there to do in Boston?"

"Why are you asking that? You don't go out anyway. So why does it matter?"

"But it's cold in Boston."

"Well, it's cold in Minnesota, and you've been there for twelve years."

But Ainge was turning up the heat in Boston. He was working Garnett, and he was working McHale, to make this trade happen. And it
was not on impulse. Ainge had ticketed Ray Allen and Kevin Garnett
long before he actually tried to acquire them, watching them play a
hundred times for other teams, but, always, considering how they would
look in Boston uniforms.

This was exactly how Ainge wound up with Rajon Rondo: three seasons before he even drafted him—when Rondo was still *in high school*—
the newly named general manager of the Celtics was envisioning the
lightning-quick young guard in a Boston uniform. On February 7, 2004,
while his Celtics were in Philadelphia playing the 76ers, Ainge was
twenty-five miles away in Trenton, New Jersey, watching the PrimeTime
Shootout, which bills itself as the nation's top showcase for high school
basketball teams. Ainge made the trip to Trenton's Sovereign Bank
Arena to watch Oak Hill Academy's Josh Smith; he came home raving
about Rajon Rondo, who scored sixteen points in Oak Hill's 62–57 victory over Cardinal Dougherty of Philadelphia.

Ainge had also dispatched Jon Niednagel, an Ainge adviser known by
some as the Brain Doctor, to look at Smith. Niednagel, too, came back
with good reports on Rondo.

A native of Louisville, Rondo had already committed to the University of Kentucky. But he never fell off of Ainge's radar—even if he
seemed to be falling off the earth during his second year at Kentucky.

"Going into his sophomore year, we had [scouts] Ryan McDonough
and Chris Wallace watch him," Ainge recalled. "Ryan saw him play in
Dallas, and Chris saw him at a tournament in Argentina. He under-
achieved his sophomore year, based on what we thought he could do—
based on what the whole world thought he could do."

Ainge was aware that Rondo, young and immature, had spats with
Kentucky coach Tubby Smith. And though Rondo had dazzling speed
and great moves, Ainge questioned his shooting ability.

"His shot got worse," said Ainge. "His shot, mechanically, looked
worse than when he was a high school player. His shot worried people,
and his personality and his conflicts with his coach did not give him
ringing endorsements, and that's what was causing him to slip. But we

just could not as an organization forget what we had seen of him the three previous seasons of watching him. He was just too talented to give up on."

During a flurry of wheeling and dealing at the 2006 draft, Ainge acquired the twenty-first overall pick from the Phoenix Suns, which landed Rondo in Boston.

Three seasons. That's how long Danny Ainge had been following Rajon Rondo. It shouldn't have come as any great surprise, then, that the Boston GM had been tracking Kevin Garnett for just as long, if not longer.

On July 31, 2007, it all came together. The Celtics sent Ryan Gomes, Gerald Green, Theo Ratliff, Sebastian Telfair, two future first-round draft picks—and Al Jefferson—to the Timberwolves in exchange for Garnett. Beaming at his introductory press conference as he pulled on his number 5 jersey for the first time, the newest Celtic explained his initial reluctance about coming to Boston by telling the media throng, "When draft night went and Boston traded for Ray Allen, the whole situation changed for me. I actually thought about it, contemplated and thought about it. I really didn't speak publicly, really didn't say too much to my friends or any of that. Just by myself, I really tried to be comfortable with seeing myself in a Celtics jersey."[1]

The press conference to introduce Garnett was a happy, festive affair, though it lacked the aura of coronation that had been in place a decade earlier when Kentucky coach Rick Pitino took over as president and head coach of the Celtics. The Pitino presser was held on the parquet at what was then known as the FleetCenter, with the team's sixteen championship banners lowered to form a backdrop—as if Pitino had had anything to do with achieving them. By comparison, the Garnett press conference, held at the Legends bar/restaurant inside the Garden, was all about looking ahead, not pickpocketing the team's glorious past.

Ray Allen and an extremely happy Paul Pierce were brought in especially for the occasion, with Pierce telling the gathering, "This is like a dream come true for me. I feel like a rookie again."[2]

Pierce, who played his college ball at Kansas before being selected in the first round of the 1991 draft by the Celtics, was entering his tenth NBA season and was well on his way to finishing out his days in Boston as the Greatest Celtic to Never Win a Championship. He was already the team's seventh all-time leading scorer, but a quick read of the top ten revealed that everyone ahead of him (John Havlicek, Larry Bird, Robert Parish, Kevin McHale, Bob Cousy, Sam Jones) and those directly behind him (Bill Russell, Dave Cowens, JoJo White) understood the thrill of ending a season with the ultimate victory.

Pierce's days in Boston certainly had been star-crossed. When he was twenty-two years old and about to begin his third season with the Celtics, the Inglewood, California, native suffered eleven stab wounds, one of which was a half-inch from his heart, during a brawl at Buzz Club, a nightspot in Boston's Theater District. The fight broke out when Pierce, who was out on the town with Celtics teammate Tony Battie and Battie's brother Derrick, apparently said hello to a couple of women, whereupon a man approached him and said, "That's my sister." Pierce later told *Sports Illustrated* that his next words were "No disrespect."

"Next thing you know," he said, "all hell breaks loose."[3]

It's possible that Pierce would have been killed were it not for the leather jacket he was wearing. Though two men were later acquitted of armed assault with intent to murder, one of them, William Ragland, was convicted of assault and battery with a dangerous weapon. The other defendant was convicted of assault and battery. A third defendant was acquitted of all charges.

In 2005, when Pierce was ejected from Game 6 of the Celtics' playoff series against the Indiana Pacers, he ripped off his shirt and twirled it in the air as he sashayed to the visitors' locker room at Conseco Fieldhouse; he made an even bigger fool of himself at the postgame press conference, pretending to have a jaw injury and wearing a goofy makeshift bandage around his head. He sparred with Doc Rivers in the early going. There was talk that the Celtics would deal him away and then start over.

Yet here they all were: Ray Allen, Kevin Garnett, and a mature, settled-in, with-this-team-for-the-long-haul Paul Pierce.

The new Big Three.

Yet Ainge had apparently brought a wet blanket with him to the press conference, because he had some cautionary words for the assembled media and all their editors back at the desk who at that very moment were dreaming up their "New Big Three" headlines: "These guys will never be the Big Three until they win. And I think they know that."[4]

We think Ainge knew, even then, that that was a laughable statement. Either that, or his team's own marketing department didn't get the memo about how Pierce, Allen, and Garnett would have to, you know, *win* before they could be called the Big Three. The cover of the Celtics' media guide for the 2007–2008 season blasted the words THINK BIG over a posed photo of three men who had yet to win the big one: Ray Allen, Kevin Garnett, and Paul Pierce. And the Celtics had no problem sending the three players to Bristol, Connecticut, to appear in a commercial for ESPN's *SportsCenter* in which they trumpeted themselves as "the Three Amigos." The campaign was working: ticket sales for the 2007–2008 season were up some 60 percent.

And in a way nobody could have foreseen, that presented something of a problem to the Celtics. Kevin Garnett had already agreed to a contract extension with the Celtics, without which the trade could not have been made, but he also wanted to purchase two courtside seats for Celtics home games.

But the Celtics did not have any to sell him. Something needed to be done.

Martin J. "Marty" Joyce, the most vocal, over-the-top, in-your-face member of an odd, misshapen, courtside Celtic troika that included Donnie Wahlberg and Mike Rotondi, was born on January 6, 1964, in Boston's West Roxbury section, a pleasant, middle-class side of town.

His parents, too, were products of the city—Jack Joyce was from Mission Hill, and the former Marjorie Tynan from nearby Hyde Park. But go figure: they met in Albuquerque, New Mexico, at a time when each was doing a hitch in the Air Force. Later, they *got* hitched and settled in West Roxbury.

Marjorie Joyce went into teaching and spent thirty years in the Boston school system. "And mostly at the tough ones," Marty likes to say.

Jack Joyce somehow managed to raise a family while holding down various daytime office jobs and taking night courses in accounting at Northeastern University. In 1959, when the Boston Patriots joined the fledgling American Football League, Jack was among the first to sign up for season tickets.

But it was Marty's godfather, Richard Quinn, known to all as Quinnie, who was largely responsible for creating the hollering, finger-pointing, high-fiving, courtside zealot who has become as much a fixture at Celtics games as Pierce or Allen, Rondo or Garnett.

A bachelor and sports lover, Quinnie was a line worker for the telephone company during the day. Rather than join his pal Jack Joyce at night school, he chose to attend night games—lots of Red Sox and sometimes the Bruins, but most of all the Celtics. And on autumn Sunday afternoons, that's when he might hook up with Jack and go watch the Pats. It came down to this: if there were two teams, a scoreboard, and a hot dog involved, Quinnie was there.

When Marty was old enough, he started tagging along to the old Garden with Quinnie to watch Celtics games. Built in 1928, the original Boston Garden was cutting-edge at the time, a spectacular venue for boxing, hockey, and, later, basketball. What the place lacked in luxury suites, fancy restaurants, and exploding scoreboards, it made up for with its down-home, neighborhood feel—this because many of the seats were dazzlingly close to the action. But the Garden had a lot of poles, which translates to a lot of obstructed-view seats, which, given the price, was okay with Quinnie and Marty. On more than a few occasions, they were stashed under the overhang and behind a bunch of big galoots; every time there was an exciting play in the making, the big galoots would stand up and cheer, blocking the view for Quinnie and Marty. This was when Marty showed early promise as a salesman: he told the big galoots he'd fetch their beers for them if they stayed in their seats.

"That was back when they'd sell beer to kids," Marty notes.

In the early days of Larry Bird, Quinnie invested in season tickets. Nothing fancy, mind you. They were up in what locals called the Heavens, old-timey Garden slang for the nosebleed section. Or they'd be off in the corner, behind where organist John Kiley regaled the crowd during time-outs with "The Mexican Hat Dance" and selections from Broadway musicals, *Gypsy* apparently being a favorite of Kiley's.

Marty learned to *play* basketball at the West Roxbury YMCA, and he later scratched out a year on the varsity at Catholic Memorial High School in West Roxbury. He then attended "seven different schools," including the University of Massachusetts, after which he landed his first real job as an ad salesman at a Boston radio station. He moved on to the stock brokerage firm Smith Barney, where, he said, he made six hundred cold calls a day, and then to the investment bank Hambrecht & Quist. While he felt the new job would afford a better opportunity to deal directly with clients, the understanding was that he'd still be making cold calls. So he obtained the directory of a local company, picked up the phone, and dialed a number. In this case, it wasn't opportunity knocking, but rather opportunity answering the phone: as Marty tells the story, that first cold call resulted in a $100,000 stock order. When he moved on to the wealth management division at Deutsche Bank, the $100,000 man went with him.

As Marty began doing better and better at work, he did better and better at play. Where once it was ol' Quinnie who took his godson to Celtics games, now the godson took Quinnie to Celtics games. Better seats too. Soon he was buying more and more tickets—not just for himself and Quinnie but also for his bride, a gal from Somerville named Lisa Censullo. And soon he was buying season tickets—and discovering they came in handy when dealing with clients and would-be clients. As is his way, he grew to know various folks in the Celtics' ticket office, regaling them with stories about sitting in the Heavens with Quinnie. Marty was viewed as a good customer, and, well, how else to say it: good customers get good treatment. If a pair of courtside seats materialized for a particular game, someone would get on the phone and dial up Marty, see if maybe he was interested in coming down to the Garden that night and sitting with the swells.

Not that Joyce had to use his skills from the West Roxbury YMCA to muscle people out of the way. The Celtics staggered between mediocrity and futility through much of the '90s, and fan interest was nowhere near what it had been during the days of the original Big Three. But like any good stockbroker, Marty was buying low, his investment in season tickets lining him up for an opportunity to one day own a set of court-side seats. Assuming, of course, the Celtics would be worth watching again once that day arrived.

Ticket sales for the 1997–98 season skyrocketed when the Celtics reached into the college ranks and hired Rick Pitino as their head coach. Pitino had risen to the top echelon of college coaches, having led Kentucky to three Final Four appearances, including a national championship in 1996. But he was well known to New England sports fans long before that, and on several levels—as a player in the early 1970s at the University of Massachusetts, where his teammates included future Hall of Famer Julius Erving and future Boston College coach Al Skinner; as head coach at Boston University from 1978 to 1983; and as head coach at Providence College from 1985 to 1987. His 1986–87 Friars, a number-six seed in the Southeast Regional in the NCAA tourney, made the Final Four by rolling to an 88–73 upset over number-one seed Georgetown in the Elite Eight. The Friars lost to Syracuse in the national semifinal game, but getting that far was a coup nonetheless.

Pitino was not only named coach of the Celtics on May 8, 1997, but also given the title of president, which was appropriated from aging, semi-retired Red Auerbach just for the occasion. A collection of retired Celtics legends—including John Havlicek, Tommy Heinsohn, JoJo White, and recently deposed coach M. L. Carr—was on hand at the press conference. And Auerbach went along with the show. He even lit up a cigar.

Talk about times changing. When Auerbach was named head coach of the Celtics on April 28, 1950, the *Boston Herald* ran the story on an inside page, beside an advertisement for all-silk polka-dot ties that were on sale for ninety-nine cents at the Continental. In making the announcement that day in 1950, Celtics founder and president Walter A. Brown said, "Meet Red Auerbach. He tells me he always wanted to coach basketball in Boston. The opportunity has come. How long he holds the job depends on what he makes of the sport during the coming season."

So Red Auerbach, with no pomp, no circumstance, and a warning from the boss that if he didn't win he'd soon be looking for a new job, became one of the greatest coaches in sports history. And Pitino? The most lavish meet-our-coach press conference in Boston sports history turned out to be the opening trumpet blare to a disaster. The Celtics were coming off a 15–67 season and hoping to land the top pick in the NBA's draft lottery, which would bring them Tim Duncan of Wake Forest. Instead, Duncan went to the San Antonio Spurs, who would win four NBA championships over the next decade.

The Celtics continued to struggle during the Rick Pitino era. And not only had he swiped Auerbach's title, but he also jettisoned club employees he believed to be loyal to the Celtic legend, such as general manager Jan Volk, the only person in the organization with a keen understanding of how the National Basketball Association's complicated salary cap works. With Volk gone, Pitino made one clumsy personnel decision after another.

Marty Joyce is less kind: "Pitino was a nightmare. It was getting bad."

The reign of King Richard I lasted three and a half seasons, with Pitino finally stepping down on January 8, 2001; his record as coach of the Celtics was 102–146, a .411 winning percentage. He never coached the Celtics in a playoff game.

Pitino's demise as coach of the Celtics meant opportunity for Marty Joyce. He had remained loyal to the Celtics through these tough times, faithfully sending in his checks for four season tickets behind the Boston bench, and now the Celtics' ticket office was on the phone, telling Joyce that Pitino's exodus had created an opening of sorts. The ex-coach had owned two courtside seats, and now they were available.

"Look, I'm a maniac," Marty told the Celtics. "I can get the attention of players from the *tenth* row. I don't know what's going to happen once I'm down there."

The Celtics apparently didn't have a problem with this. Marty's first night as a courtside land baron was a Friday, April 6 game against the Los Angeles Lakers.

"And this is a story I always tell everyone," he said.

Just minutes after he and his wife settled into their pricey new courtside digs, the Lakers' Gigantor of a superstar, Shaquille O'Neal, won the opening tip, went around the Celtics' Vitaly Potapenko, and slammed home the first points of the game. Up from his seat leaped Marty, who hollered, "Hey, Shaq, you ain't all that!"

In Marty's telling of the story, Shaq stopped, looked at the bellowing Celtics fan, and said, "Yeah . . . I am."

The Lakers got the ball back, Shaq slammed home another basket, and then turned to Marty and said, "Now what do you think?"

And Marty Joyce said to himself, *I think we're never leaving these seats.*

Now he owned six season tickets—his two courtside seats and four seats farther back. Within a year he had an opportunity to purchase two more courtside seats, so he traded in two of the farther-back seats and bought two more on the floor. And two more after that. By the time Kevin Garnett arrived in Boston and teamed up with Paul Pierce and Ray Allen to transform the Celtics into a team worth the price of admission, Marty Joyce was in possession of six courtside seats.

And that's why, in a move that would have been shocking to Walter Brown, the original president of the Celtics, the team was now reaching out to Marty Joyce for a solution to the problem of procuring courtside seats for Kevin Garnett. In Walter Brown's day, it was a challenge just to get the telephone bill paid. The team might have been winning championships, but it wasn't always winning hearts.

And now the Celtics were actually *buying back* tickets from a fan.

In August 2007, shortly after the Garnett deal was announced, Shawn Sullivan, senior vice president of ticket sales, called Joyce and said, "We're trying to get two courtside tickets for Kevin, and we don't have anything."

"Well," said Marty, "you must have *some* way of getting them."

"We don't."

"Try. If you can't come up with anything, I'll be your last resort."

And then Joyce said it again: "But try hard. Because if I give up two courtside seats, I'm going to piss off a lot of people who have been sharing seats in the bad times."

Two days later, Sullivan called back.

"I could really use those two seats," he said.

It was not the first time a basketball team had turned to Marty Joyce in a time of crisis. When Joyce was a junior at Catholic Memorial, he had tried, and failed, to land a spot on the varsity basketball team. Not a particularly gifted athlete, his plan was to dazzle with hard work, determination, and, as he would display as a grown-up Celtics fan, one hell of a lot of spirit. Everyone was impressed. He didn't make the team.

Halfway through the season, as Marty tells the story, Gus Andrews, the Catholic Memorial coach, told his players, "That Joyce guy out-worked half the team when he was here. I should have kept him."

Gus Andrews reached out to Marty Joyce and put him on the team. Right?

"I'm not sure, but that's something I would have done," said Gus Andrews nearly three decades later. "I do remember Marty Joyce. The kid worked hard."

Now it was the Celtics who were reaching out to Marty Joyce.

Joyce gave two of his courtside seats to the Celtics, who sold them to Kevin Garnett. As it happened, just before the season began the NBA approved a request the Celtics had made to add two courtside seats next to the team bench. Those seats were offered to Marty Joyce. He now had two seats next to the bench that he usually made available to clients, two seats in the corner across from the visitors' bench, also for clients, and his two seats next to Mike Rotondi and Donnie Wahlberg.

He eventually traded the two seats next to the Celtics' bench for a different location on the floor.

"Most of the guys who sat in the seats next to the Celtics' bench didn't really like them," said Joyce. "There's a lot of commotion going on down there, a lot of stuff going. It was hard for them to enjoy the game."

For Marty Joyce, to sit next to the Celtics' bench would be tanta-mount to dragging the class clown up to the front of the room and plant-ing him in a seat beside the teacher's desk. No, Marty Joyce needed to be across the court, away from the players, away from Doc Rivers, where he could create his own buzz, his own niche.

Considering that local fans recognize him on the street . . . that he has jawed with Shaq . . . that NBA referees are aware of him . . . yes, absolutely, Marty Joyce has created his own buzz. What a tragedy it would be had Marty Joyce been reduced to sitting with his hands folded next to the Celtics' bench.

Kevin Garnett's unveiling as a member of the Celtics ended with a trip to Fenway Park. He had been invited by the Sox to throw out the first pitch prior to the team's August 1 game against the Baltimore Orioles, and the packed house of 36,649 erupted when the newest Celtic emerged from the first-base dugout.

He had a reunion of sorts with Red Sox slugger David Ortiz. They did not know each other very well, yet they had ties that extended to their days in the Twin Cities, Garnett playing for the Minnesota Timberwolves, Big Papi for the Minnesota Twins. More than a few onlookers made the observation that Garnett's arrival made yet another new Big Three: Players from Minnesota Who Now Star for Boston Sports Teams (the others being Ortiz and the Patriots' Randy Moss).

But as Garnett made the rounds in the Boston clubhouse that night, shaking hands with Ortiz, Coco Crisp, Curt Schilling, and die-hard Celtics fan Terry Francona, he was not the only newcomer in the room.

The Red Sox unveiled a new player of their own that day: to add some depth to their bullpen, they had acquired reliever Eric Gagne from the Texas Rangers in exchange for pitcher Kason Gabbard, outfielder David Murphy, and a minor leaguer. The move involved some intrigue. Worried that incumbent closer Jonathan Papelbon wouldn't like the idea of the team acquiring a veteran reliever with closing credentials on his résumé, a delegation of Theo Epstein, manager Terry Francona, pitching coach John Farrell, and bullpen coach Gary Tuck headed over to Papelbon's Back Bay apartment for an afternoon summit. The story, first reported by writer Michael Holley in *Red Sox Rule: Terry Francona and Boston's Rise to Dominance*, gets even stranger: because Papelbon had an apartment full of people at the time, the bullpen summit was moved downstairs to the boiler room. It was like something out of a Marx Brothers movie.

Papelbon was cool with the trade, so long as he was the closer and Gagne was a setup man. Deal. The next afternoon Eric Gagne was shaking hands with Kevin Garnett in the Red Sox clubhouse.

One of them would become a Boston legend. One of them would be just about run out of town.

12

SPYGATE

I n staking their claim as the first great NFL team of the twenty-first century, the New England Patriots developed a talent for turning any kind of slight, real or imagined, into a personal insult, something that could be posted on the bulletin board as a reminder to everyone in the locker room that there were doubters out there, disbelievers.

Back in January 2004, when the Patriots defeated Indianapolis in the AFC championship game, safety Rodney Harrison wanted it known that "we were really ticked off because nobody gave us any credit. Nobody gave us a chance to win this game."[1] The Patriots' playbook had as many of these types of quotes as defensive formations; here was a team that always perceived itself as the underdog, and so was determined to prove that *they* were wrong (exactly who *they* were being something of a mystery) in their preseason assessments.

It was a nice lounge act, and nobody could argue with the results. But in the run-up to the 2007 season, it had become impossible for the Patriots to whip out the no-respect card. They were stacked, and everybody knew it. In addition to acquiring some quality targets for Tom Brady in receivers Randy Moss and Wes Welker and signing Adalius Thomas from the Baltimore Ravens to add muscle to the linebacking corps, they also brought in Sammy Morris from the Miami Dolphins as a backup running back and Kyle Brady, a twelve-year NFL veteran with the New York Jets and Jacksonville Jaguars, to add depth at tight end.

Junior Seau, too, was back for another season. The veteran Hall of

Fame—bound linebacker had come out of semi-retirement a year earlier to play for the Patriots, but he seemed finished for good when, on November 26, 2006, he suffered a broken arm while making a tackle in the second quarter of a 17–13 victory over the Chicago Bears. Seau was a man with a wide range of interests, which included surfing. After deciding to stop kicking back at his San Diego home, he began taking lessons from a legend of the waves, sixty-three-year-old Donald Takayama, a five-time U.S. surfing champion. But to the surprise of many, Seau stowed his surfboard and returned for the 2007 season, and with yet another new hobby: he was now taking guitar lessons.

There were two big off-the-field stories during training camp. One of them involved Brady, who at one time was dating actress Bridget Moynahan but now was seeing Brazilian supermodel Gisele Bundchen. A ripe-for-the-gossip-pages soap opera started playing out earlier in the year once Moynahan announced that she was pregnant with the quarterback's baby; in late August, Brady missed a day of training camp and flew to Los Angeles to be on hand for the birth—a son named John Edward Thomas Moynahan—and then returned in time to throw two touchdown passes in the Pats' 24–7 preseason victory over the Carolina Panthers.

And then came an announcement involving veteran safety Rodney Harrison: on August 31, he was suspended for the first four games of the 2007 season for violating the league's policy on performance-enhancing substances. Following a meeting with NFL commissioner Roger Goodell, Harrison spoke with the media via a nighttime conference call, during which he said, "I haven't made excuses, nor will I make excuses. I made a mistake and I'm very sorry for that. . . . I don't condone my decision, my behavior. I'm very, very embarrassed by it. I'm disappointed in myself and to any young person, any high schooler, any college athlete, [to whom] I sent the wrong message with my actions. And I would ask and I would want to be the example for them to never jeopardize what they believe in and never jeopardize their health."[2]

Harrison was one of those players whose aggressive style of play—late hits, occasionally taunting opponents—results in being adored by the hometown fans and hated by just about everybody else. When in

2004 *Sports Illustrated* polled NFL players to determine the league's "dirtiest player," Harrison came out on top. Two years later, he again topped the list.

And Pats fans ate it up. He was also popular with the media for providing intelligent, peppy answers to almost any question. Yet the reality was that Harrison *was* making excuses. During that same conference call, he wanted it known that "not once did I ever use steroids," and that, while he did admit to Goodell that he had used a banned substance, his reason for doing so was "never to gain a competitive edge. Rather, my use was solely for accelerating the healing process of injuries I sustained while playing football."[3]

Compared with the next controversy to confront the Patriots, Harrison's suspension would become a mere footnote to the season.

The Patriots' 2007 opener was scheduled for Sunday, September 9, against the New York Jets at Giants Stadium. The Patriots and Jets had been fierce rivals since the days of the American Football League, their games becoming a scaled-down football extension of the Red Sox versus the Yankees. But what now was being referred to as the "Border War" had accelerated in recent years.

The Border War had its beginnings a decade earlier, when the Patriots were preparing to meet the Green Bay Packers in Super Bowl XXXI. The Patriots were coached by Bill Parcells, who had done more than anyone to restore respectability to the franchise when he arrived in Foxboro in 1993. Already a coaching legend, the man known as the Tuna had won two Super Bowls during his days with the New York Giants. When he took over the Patriots, he brought with him a powerful sideline presence and a talent for cajoling, inspiring, bullying—whatever it took—to get the most out of his players. He also had a good eye for hiring assistant coaches: one of them was Bill Belichick, who had been his defensive coordinator during the two Super Bowl runs with the Giants and in 1996 was added to the Patriots' staff after being fired as head coach of the Cleveland Browns.

Six days before the Super Bowl, a jarring story appeared in the sports pages of the *Boston Globe* under the byline of columnist Will McDonough: Parcells planned to leave the Patriots following the big game. The column also stated that Parcells "has been rumored to be the coaching choice of the New York Jets, who have made no secret of their desire to hire him."[4]

For the rest of the week, Parcells-to-the-Jets rumors were a daily theme; when the Patriots suffered a 35–21 loss to the Packers at the Louisiana Superdome on February 26, 1997, Parcells was criticized for spending too much time thinking about next year's Jets and not enough time thinking about this year's Packers.

At a Foxboro Stadium press conference five days later, Parcells cited his frustration over not having enough say in personnel decisions as his reason for wanting to leave the Patriots, uttering the now-famous comment, "If they want you to cook the dinner, at least they ought to let you shop for some of the groceries."[5]

But it wasn't going to be so easy for Parcells to pack up his shopping cart and move to New York. Then–NFL commissioner Paul Tagliabue ruled that Parcells's contract with the Patriots prevented him from coaching another team, whereupon owner Robert Kraft, holding his own Foxboro Stadium press conference immediately after his former coach had left the room, let it be known that any team interested in hiring the would-be grocery shopper had better be prepared to hand over a first-round draft pick.

Here the plot took a comical turn. The following week the Jets called a press conference at their practice facility on the campus of Hofstra University in Hempstead, New York, to announce that Bill Parcells was joining the team as a "consultant," the idea being that, since the Tuna wouldn't be doing any *coaching*, the Patriots were not entitled to compensation. The Jets also announced that their new head coach would be . . . Bill Belichick. Parcells did not attend the press conference, being just a consultant and all; instead, he spoke to the media through a speakerphone set up at the front of Weeb Ewbank Hall in Hempstead, while Belichick, looking stiff and awkward, sat idly by. It was an embarrassing affair, and Belichick was painted as a puppet. Or as columnist Bill Livingston of the *Cleveland Plain Dealer* put it, "Think of Parcells in the coming year, in which he will serve as the Jets' 'consultant,' as Edgar Bergen to Belichick's Charlie McCarthy."[6]

Less than a week later, Tagliabue stopped the insanity. The resolution was that the Jets sent four draft picks to the Patriots along with a $300,000 donation to the team's charitable foundation, and in return they got Parcells as their coach and Belichick as defensive coordinator. The hope, for the Jets, was that their eighty-two-year-old owner, Leon Hess, would live to see his team win the Super Bowl. It didn't happen. Parcells took a team that had been 1–15 in 1996 to a 12–4 record in 1998, but the Jets suffered a 23–10 loss to Denver in the AFC championship game. Hess died on May 7, 1999.

The Jets went 8–8 in 1999, after which Parcells decided to retire as head coach and assume a front-office role. Belichick was announced as the new head coach. Twenty-four hours later, again in Weeb Ewbank Hall, he stunned the Jets by saying he didn't want the job, thank you very much, scribbling on a note that he was "resigning as HC of the NYJ." Speaking with reporters, Belichick said, "There are a number of obvious uncertainties that would affect the head coach of the team. . . . I just don't feel at this time that I can lead the Jets with the 100 percent conviction that I need."[7]

Exit Belichick, enter Jets president Steve Gutman, who all but invited the assembled media to mull the possibility that Belichick had suffered a nervous breakdown by making this preposterous comment: "I think, I'm not a psychologist, but I think I just listened for an hour to a person who is in some turmoil and deserves our understanding and our consideration."[8]

A plethora of reasons would be suggested for why Belichick wanted out of Hempstead—the uncertain future of the Jets' ownership and the possibility that a better situation awaited him in New England being chief among them. But while there was merit to both of these theories, this is what everyone missed: it was time for Belichick to step out from behind the very large shadow cast by Bill Parcells. He had been the good soldier back when Parcells spoke to the media through a speakerphone. He would not, could not, do so again.

This theory didn't play well with the *New York Post*, whose back-page headline the next day said it all:

BELICHICKEN
Jets better off without quitter

A familiar scene played out again, only with the Jets and Patriots reversing roles: the Pats, who had fired Pete Carroll as head coach, wanted Belichick. And the Jets wanted compensation. On January 27, 2000, the Pats announced that they would send a collection of draft picks to the Jets—including their first selection in the 2000 draft—in order to hire Bill Belichick.

"The Border War is over," Parcells told reporters during a teleconference.[9]

Hardly.

When Belichick was assembling his Patriots coaching staff, he hired a young assistant whose background was strikingly similar to his own. Like Belichick, Eric Mangini was a graduate of Wesleyan University in Middletown, Connecticut. And just as Belichick began his career as a twenty-three-year-old, low-level assistant under Ted Marchibroda with the Baltimore Colts, Mangini, with a degree in political science from prestigious Wesleyan in his back pocket, took a low-level job with the Cleveland Browns when *he* was twenty-three. In 1995 he started out as a training camp ball boy and then landed an internship in the Browns' media relations department. One of his assignments was fetching pizza for the sportswriters covering the Browns.[10]

The Browns' coach at the time was Belichick, who met Mangini in, of all places, the copy room. Belichick always had a mentoring streak in him, no doubt an outgrowth of his own days as a hungry, young coaching wannabe, but also because he learned the game from his father, Steve Belichick, who spent thirty-three years of his life as an assistant football coach at the U.S. Naval Academy.

"The thing Bill loves about football, perhaps more than anything else, is the teaching of the game," said former NFL linebacker Steve DeOssie, who played two of his twelve seasons under New York Giants defensive coordinator Bill Belichick. "I saw it with his sons, I saw it with players, I saw it with coaches. He cherishes the process of the passing-down of information and all the traditions. It's the same thing his father did with him.

"I played for coaches who just gave you information," said DeOssie. "Bill wanted to teach it to you. There's a difference."

DeOssie, a Boston native who had moved on to a career in television and radio in his hometown, once invited Belichick to accompany him to Providence, Rhode Island, to watch his son Zak, who was playing football at Brown University.

"So Bill brought *his* sons with him," DeOssie said. "They kept asking him questions about the defense Brown was running. Listening to Bill talk, he was pointing out things that I hadn't even noticed. And I had been to every game."

It was in this spirit that Belichick eventually made Mangini a sort of protégé. In 1995, his last year in Cleveland, he added Mangini to his staff as a coaching assistant.

And then they went their separate ways for a few years. Belichick was fired at the end of the season, and Mangini remained with the Browns franchise when owner Art Modell moved it to Baltimore and renamed it the Ravens—and, continuing the remarkable intertwinings of Belichick and Mangini, hired Ted Marchibroda as his new coach. The same man for whom Belichick once worked on the Baltimore Colts, a proud, old-time NFL franchise that had long since relocated to Indianapolis, was now Mangini's boss on the newly christened Baltimore Ravens.

On February 14, 1997, with Bill Parcells finally having secured his new job as head coach of the Jets and Belichick stepping in as an assistant head coach, Mangini was named defensive assistant/quality control.

Three years later, Belichick brought Mangini to New England with him. The protégé spent five seasons as defensive backs coach, helping the Patriots to three Super Bowl championships as he established his credentials for bigger and better things. On February 12, 2005, one week after the Patriots defeated the Philadelphia Eagles in Super Bowl XXXIX, and four days after defensive coordinator Romeo Crennel exited New England to become head coach of the new Cleveland Browns, Mangini was promoted to defensive coordinator. Eleven years removed from his summer as a ball boy with the original Cleveland Browns, he was now one of Belichick's top assistants.

"I am thrilled to be with the Patriots," Mangini said at the time. "The

Kraft family and Bill Belichick have treated me tremendously. This team and our players are a special group and mean a great deal to me."[11]

The 2005 Patriots went 10–6 in the regular season and then rolled to a 28–3 playoff victory over Jacksonville. The Pats' season came to a crushing end, however, when they suffered a 27–13 loss to the Denver Broncos.

Three days later, Eric Mangini, one day shy of his thirty-fifth birthday, was introduced as head coach of the New York Jets at infamous Weeb Ewbank Hall.

Everybody said the right things. A statement released by the Patriots had Belichick calling Mangini "an outstanding coach and an even finer individual" and claiming that this was "truly an example of good things happening to a good, hardworking person." At his press conference, Mangini said that Belichick had encouraged him to take the Jets job and that "Bill and I are the best of friends."[12]

Whatever their relationship—and rumors abounded of a rift—Mangini was now head coach of a team Belichick had left on thunderously bad terms just six years earlier. And most reporters believed that Belichick truly did hate the Jets. Longtime *Globe* columnist Bob Ryan recalls a conversation he once had with the late writer David Halberstam, who had authored a critically acclaimed book on Belichick entitled *The Education of a Coach*. According to Ryan, who never wrote about the conversation, Halberstam told him that Belichick always referred to the Jets as "those fucking Jets."

During an interview for this book, Belichick was told of Halberstam's comment. He seemed amused.

"Most of the teams we play against are not talked about very favorably," he said. "When we were in Cleveland, it was the Steelers and the Bengals. Now it's the Jets and the Bills and the Dolphins. And I'm sure that's the way they feel about us. I'm sure that's the way the Red Sox feel about the Yankees, and probably the way the Yankees feel about the Red Sox."

When Belichick and Mangini met for the first time as opposing head coaches, on September 17, 2006, the Pats held on for a 24–17 victory. The game over, master and student met at midfield, where they executed a curious "handshake" that barely met the definition of the word. "Good game," said Belichick, and off he went.

In their next meeting, on November 12 at Gillette Stadium, the Jets won 17–14. In the aftermath of *this* game, Belichick pushed through a crowd of photographers, manhandling the *Globe*'s Jim Davis in the process, and planted a big, demonstrative hug on Mangini.

The next morning, Stacey James, the Patriots' vice president of media relations, telephoned Davis and told him to expect a call from Belichick. He was too late. Belichick had already called Davis and apologized for the shove. The shove made headlines; the apology barely made the bottom of the notebooks.

And now, as the rebuilt Patriots opened the 2007 season, they did so on September 9 at Giants Stadium against . . . the New York Jets. The Belichick-versus-Mangini story angle seemed to have run its course by now, as the media had fresh new subplots to focus on. One of them was rather somber: the previous spring, a twenty-four-year-old Patriots player named Marquise Hill, who had appeared in a total of thirteen games over three seasons and had hopes of making the '07 team, was killed in a jet-ski accident in Louisiana. The '07 opener against the Jets was the Pats' first regular-season game since Hill's death, and the players took the field wearing black "91" patches on their uniforms in memory of their fallen comrade. Back at Gillette Stadium, the Pats planned to keep Hill's locker in place for the remainder of the season.

The Patriots arrived at Giants Stadium without five-time All-Pro defensive lineman Richard Seymour, who was recovering from knee surgery, and without Harrison, serving his four-game suspension. But Pats fans were finally going to get their first look at Randy Moss, who had been kept out of the preseason as he recovered from a leg injury. Remember, Moss was an artist. Remember, Brady was a Hall of Fame–bound quarterback, with three Super Bowl championships on his résumé. Surely "Brady to Moss" was going to be a better story line than "Belichick versus Mangini."

It was no accident that Brady and Moss had adjoining lockers during training camp. By design, the incumbent quarterback and the new wide-out were given as many opportunities as possible to spend time together, the hope being that a measure of off-the-field bonding, including everything from deciphering the playbook to standard, everyday gossip, would lead to on-the-field chemistry.

Brady had already judged Moss's football abilities. The training-camp play in which Moss had injured his leg was a flea-flicker, and Brady remembered that he threw the ball "as far as I could throw it. When I let it go, I said to myself, *No way, it's way overthrown*. And he got to within about two inches of the football. Later, when I was watching the tape, I saw that he ran by the safety like the safety wasn't even moving."

In the locker room, they played endless rounds of poker on PlayStation, swapped stories, joked around. As Brady put it, "When you sit two feet next to someone all through training camp, you're going to get to know each other pretty well. We would just stay there and talk, and there's a lot of trust that develops in those situations.

"I found him to be a sensitive guy," Brady said. "He's a dog that barks but doesn't bite. He's been a star receiver everywhere he's gone. Since he's been little he's been the best athlete on every team he's ever been on. He got the most attention of anyone at his high school. When he was at Marshall, there was nobody better than him. He was a first-round draft pick when he came out. He's just had so much attention and responsibility his whole life, and he's very introverted and he doesn't let a lot of people in. And I think that's the way he likes it."

Belichick, looking back on the 2007 training camp, said, "If [Moss] hadn't missed a good part of the preseason, I'm pretty sure his teammates would have named him one of the captains, which they did in '08. That speaks to his whole presence and his whole attitude toward being on this team. And I don't think that's because anyone said anything to him or anybody threatened him, or if there was something in his contract. That's the way he is, and that's the way he's been."

Brady completed 22 of 28 passes for 297 yards and three touchdowns in the Patriots' easy 38–14 victory over the Jets in the 2007 season opener, including a 51-yarder to Moss, who raced into the end zone with three Jets in futile pursuit. Moss ended the game, his first in a Patriots uniform, with nine catches for 183 yards.

Brady's first touchdown of the season was an 11-yard strike to Wes

Red Sox manager Terry Francona (left) with third baseman Mike Lowell, spring training, 2007. Little did anyone know that the manager's fleece pullover would cause such a sensation during the season, with Major League Baseball's fashion police staging a surprise in-game inspection at Yankee Stadium. (*Matthew West/Boston Herald*)

tin Pedroia makes it clear who's number one r hitting a two-run homer against the Cleve- Indians in Game 7 of the 2007 ALCS. The ie second baseman kept a list in his head of ia members who doubted his ability to play in big leagues. (*Matthew West/Boston Herald*)

Curt Schilling, a postseason hero for the ages, salutes the Fenway Park masses after giving way to reliever Hideki Okajima in Game 2 of the 2007 World Series. It would be Schilling's last major league appearance. (*Matthew West/ Boston Herald*)

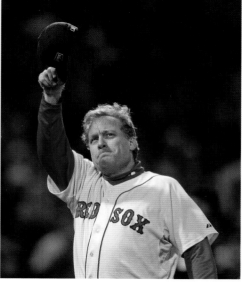

A little more than one year after being diagnosed with cancer, Red Sox left-hander Jon Lester g
teammate Kevin Youkilis following five and two-thirds shutout innings against the Colorado R
ies in Game 4 of the 2007 World Series. (*Matthew West/Boston Herald*)

"This guy ain't got shit on me," said Jonathan Papelbon to himself as he sat in a Fort Myers
and watched Pedro Martinez dazzle the St. Louis Cardinals in Game 3 of the 2004 World Se
Three years later, Papelbon (right) celebrates with teammate David Ortiz after striking out
Smith to complete Boston's four-game sweep of the Colorado Rockies in the 2007 World Se
(*Matthew West/Boston Herald*)

Red Sox fan extraordinaire Andrew J. Urban II (left) owns more than five thousand autographs, which he stores in Tupperware containers in his mother's basement. Here he greets Red Sox pitcher Manny Delcarmen during batting practice at Fenway Park. (*Matthew West/Boston Herald*)

ugh he didn't begin collecting autographs until vas fourteen, Andrew J. Urban II seemed des- d to hobnob with baseball players. In this ember 1979 photo, seven-year-old Andrew ts dapper Red Sox slugger Jim Rice at a local rmarket. (*Courtesy of Andrew J. Urban II*)

Tedy Bruschi exits the field at the RCA Dome in Indianapolis following the Patriots' 38–34 loss to the Colts in the 2006 AFC championship game. But the linebacker is not as dejected as this photograph suggests. Having recovered from a stroke and made it through an entire season with the Pats, Bruschi thought "Okay, I'm a football player again." (*Matthew West/Boston Herald*)

When the Patriots selected Michigan quarterback Tom Brady with the 199th overall pick in the 2000 draft, one Boston sportswriter assured readers that the selection "should not affect backup quarterbacks John Friesz or Michael Bishop." Within a few years, Brady was being compared with the greatest quarterbacks in NFL history. (*Matthew West/Boston Herald*)

More than mere athleticism, Randy Moss brought graceful artistry to the mix when he joined the Patriots for the 2007 season. (*Matthew West/ Boston Herald*)

Linebacker Junior Seau traded in a carefree life riding the waves when he came out of retirement to the Patriots. A year later, he celebrates New Engla 20–12 victory over the San Diego Chargers in the A championship game on January 20, 2008. (*Matt West/Boston Herald*)

reward for being named "Fans of the Year" by the Patriots, the Nantucket Gals —Jane Hardy, ine Dooley, and Joan Fisher (left to right) —were given an opportunity to attend Super Bowl I. By the time they arrived in Arizona, they worried that their late father, lifelong New York its fan Matt Jaeckle, had placed a curse on the Patriots. (*Courtesy of Joan Fisher*)

York Giants Michael Strahan (92) and Fred Robbins (98) celebrate after snuffing out a last-ditch England drive in Super Bowl XLII. Though one second remains in the game, Patriots coach Bill chick has seen enough and makes a beeline for the exit. (*Matthew West/Boston Herald*)

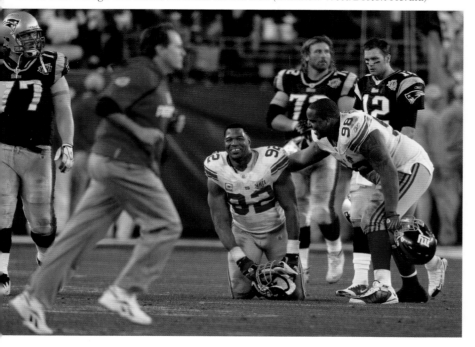

Singer/actor Donnie Wahlberg (center) [
stopped attending Celtics games until [
met Boston businessman Mike Roto[
(left). When stockbroker Marty Joyce (rig[
joined the act, the trio became insepar[
friends as well as courtside regulars at [
Banknorth Garden. (*Matthew West/Bos[
Herald*)

Point guard Rajon Rondo (left), in just his second NBA season, receives encouragement from Kevin Garnett (center) and Ray Allen in Game 7 of the Celtics' first-round playoff series against the Atlanta Hawks. (*Matthew West/Boston Herald*)

While taking piano lessons as a child, [
Allen learned the importance of practice [
sacrifice. Though these traits did not get h[
to Carnegie Hall, they did get him to the N[
Finals. (*Matthew West/Boston Herald*)

Paul Pierce (left) and Kevin Garnett are embraced by Doc Rivers as the Celtics close out the Lakers in Game 6 of the 2008 NBA Finals to win their first championship in twenty-two years. (*Matthew West/Boston Herald*)

nat's there to do in Boston?" Kevin Garnett asked his friend Tyronn Lue as he mulled a trade to the tics in 2007. There was plenty to do: by the end of the 2007–2008 season, Garnett was a member of ampionship team for the first time in his career. (*Matthew West/Boston Herald*)

Nine months after Doc Rivers showed Paul Pierce, Kevin Garnett, and Ray Allen what happ[ens] when a Boston team wins it all, the 2008 NBA champion Celtics ride the Duck Boats through Back Bay. Captain Paul Pierce can be seen on the last Duck Boat, holding aloft his trophy for b[eing] MVP of the NBA Finals. (*Matthew West/Boston Herald*)

As much as Danny Ainge loved Celtics patriarch Red Auerbach, he vowed not to hold on to his favorite players the way Red did. The result: Ainge's painful decision to include Al Jefferson and Delonte West in the trade that brought Kevin Garnett to Boston. (*Matthew West/Boston Herald*)

In September 2007, it cost Doc Rivers $75[0 of] his own money to rent a Duck Boat. Whe[n he] returned to the Duck Boats in June 2008[, he] rode for free. (*Matthew West/Boston Hera[ld]*)

Welker, a bullish little wideout who grew up in Oklahoma City, earned Oklahoma Player of the Year honors during his days at Heritage Hall High School, and, naturally, dreamed of heading a few miles south to Norman and a collegiate career at the University of Oklahoma. Never happened. Dismissed as too small, he wasn't even recruited. So Welker went to Texas Tech, became a star, and found a home in the NFL. When he joined the Patriots, it was just a matter of time before people began making favorable comparisons with the Red Sox' Dustin Pedroia: two guys, too small. And proving everybody wrong.

But the play of the game—indeed, one of the highlights of the season—was made by Ellis Hobbs, a twenty-three-year-old, third-year cornerback and kick return specialist. When the second half began, the Patriots leading 14–7, Hobbs took Mike Nugent's kick deep in his own end zone, eluded a tackle near the 20-yard line, and raced up the left sideline for a touchdown. It went into the books as a 108-yard kickoff return, at the time the longest in NFL history.[13]

"I didn't even think about kneeling that ball," Hobbs said after the game. "Like I said, I'm out there for a reason. This isn't college and this isn't high school. I'm out there to make plays."[14]

The reporters now sought out Randy Moss.

Running back Kevin Faulk, taking note of all this, was heard to quip, "You said he was a bum three months ago! That's what you all said!"

But to borrow a line from Samuel L. Jackson's Jules Winnfield character in *Pulp Fiction*, Randy Moss was Kool and the Gang about it all.

"I'm just enjoying the ride," he told reporters.[15]

The euphoria was short-lived. One day later, the NFL made a stunning announcement: it was conducting an investigation into a charge launched by the Jets that the Patriots had violated league rules by having a team employee use a video device to record the Jets' defensive signals. And it may not have been the first time the Patriots had done so. The *Herald* soon reported that during the previous season the Green Bay Packers had removed a Patriots employee who was using video equipment on the sideline during a Pats-Packers game at Lambeau Field. The Pats won that game 35–0.

Now the media had a good, old-fashioned feeding frenzy over this new story line, which came to be known as Spygate. And Belichick—and by extension, Mangini—were right in the middle of it. Mangini, remember, had worked in New England under Belichick for six seasons and, so the logic went, would have had intimate knowledge of the manner in which the Pats' coaching staff conducts its affairs.

Battle lines were quickly drawn. Pats fans argued that Belichick was doing something that was fairly common practice in the winning-isn't-everything-it's-the-only-thing NFL, and anyway, nothing gleaned from the videotape could be put to use in the game from which it was obtained. Mangini, in their view, was just an ungrateful, spiteful dime-dropper.

The other side argued, just as vociferously, that Belichick had been exposed as a fraud, a charlatan, a cheater, plain and simple. Mangini, entrusted with the fortunes of the New York Jets, had every right to cry foul. And besides, who was to say any such videotape couldn't be put to use in the very game in which it was obtained?

Throughout the NFL, the Patriots' rivals weighed in on the matter.

"Where there's smoke, there's fire," said Pittsburgh Steelers coach Mike Tomlin.[16] Michael Strahan of the New York Giants compared Belichick to former National Basketball Association referee Tim Don-aghy, who less than a month earlier had entered a guilty plea to charges of wire fraud and transmitting betting information following an FBI investigation into charges he had bet on games he'd officiated.[17] Har-kening back to the Pats' 2006 rout of Green Bay, Packers cornerback Al Harris said, "It almost looked like they knew what we were doing, you know?"[18]

The Patriots employee whose camera was confiscated was twenty-four-year-old Matt Estrella, a native of New Bedford, Massachusetts, who had started with the team as an intern in 2004 after earning a degree from Fitchburg State College in communications—with a con-centration in video production, according to the Patriots' media guide. But just as this latest low-level Belichick aide was being heaved into a media firestorm, the Pats issued a statement from their coach: "Earlier this week, I spoke with Commissioner Goodell about a videotaping pro-cedure during last Sunday's game and my interpretation of the rules.

"At this point, we have not been notified of the league's ruling. Although it remains a league matter, I want to apologize to everyone who has been affected, most of all ownership, staff, and players. Following the league's decision, I will have further comment."[19]

The NFL's investigation into the case was fast, and the outcome was furious. On September 13—just four days after the Pats-Jets game—it was announced that Belichick, personally, was being slapped with the largest fine allowed by league rules: $500,000. The team was fined $250,000. Dealing a more damaging blow to future New England seasons, the league also announced that the Patriots would have some time on their hands during the next year's NFL draft. If the Patriots qualified for the playoffs in 2007, they would lose their first-round pick in the draft. If they did not make the playoffs, they'd lose their second- and third-round picks. Given that the Patriots were considered a lock to make the playoffs, it was understood by all that they'd be losing their first-round pick in 2008.

It was the first time in history that the NFL had stripped a team of its first-round draft pick. True, the Patriots were still going to have *another* first-round pick in the 2008 draft, this because of an earlier trade with the San Francisco 49ers. But that was beside the point. The league had clobbered Belichick.

In a letter to the Patriots that left no room for niceties, Goodell wrote: "This episode represents a calculated and deliberate attempt to avoid longstanding rules designed to encourage fair play and promote honest competition on the playing field."

Goodell also made clear that this would be an ongoing investigation, as the league instructed the Patriots to hand over any videotapes, files, and notes that had anything to do with signals being given by opposing coaches during games.

Many Patriots fans believed Belichick had been railroaded by the NFL, or at the least, treated with needless harshness. The press box was less forgiving. The *Globe*'s Dan Shaughnessy compared Spygate with Watergate: "Belichick blew it when he flouted the rules and tried to rub it in against Eric Mangini and the Jets. It was absolutely unnecessary— truly Nixonian."[20]

Yet even among the media, there were those willing to point out that NFL coaches are a weird breed, willing to do just about anything to win a game. Belichick's real crime, they believed, was getting caught. As Gerry Callahan of the *Herald* put it, "Belichick was doing what he has always done, what he was hired to do, when he sent his camera boy onto the sidelines at Giants Stadium. He was looking for an edge, anything to help his team win a game, like he does every week, like every coach who hopes to last longer than a house plant does." According to Callahan, "Just as there is no crying in baseball, there is no conscience in football, at least not in NFL football."[21]

The *New York Post*, disseminator of the famous "Belichicken" headline from years past, had fresh new material to test its creative juices. It did not disappoint: for the remainder of the season, an asterisk was placed next to the New England Patriots in its NFL standings:

—Caught cheating

For those members of the Patriots who had played on Super Bowl winners, the stigma of being labeled cheaters was far more damaging than either the lost draft pick or the fines. Linebacker Tedy Bruschi, who broke in with the Patriots in 1996 when Belichick was on Bill Parcells's staff, recalled being bothered by how the coach "got beat up. It got very personal with a lot of people." But Bruschi was particularly angered by "people doubting our past championships, or people doubting our ability to win football games. It was a motivating factor for us, that people were thinking the only reason we won was because we had signals."

Belichick, in a statement released by the Patriots after the penalties were announced by the NFL, said:

> *I apologize to the Kraft family and every person directly or indirectly associated with the New England Patriots for the embarrassment, distraction and penalty my mistake caused. I also apologize to Patriots fans and would like to thank them for their support during the past few days and throughout my career.*
> *As the Commissioner acknowledged, our use of sideline video had no*

impact on the outcome of last week's game. We have never used sideline video to obtain a competitive advantage while the game was in progress. Part of my job as head coach is to ensure that our football operations are conducted in compliance of the league rules and all accepted interpretations of them. My interpretation of a rule in the Constitution and Bylaws was incorrect.

With tonight's resolution, I will not be offering any further comments on this matter. We are moving on with our preparations for Sunday's game.

But even in apologizing, Belichick was suggesting he had done nothing wrong, that he had merely made the "mistake" of "misinterpreting" the rules. And though he had said he would talk about the scandal after the NFL had made its ruling, now he was remaining faithful to the wording in his prepared statement: he would not be "offering any further comments."

Speaking at his regularly scheduled media briefing the day after the ruling was announced, Belichick made it clear he was focusing on the next game on the schedule, which would be the Patriots' September 16 home opener against the San Diego Chargers.

"Look, I understand there is interest out there," he said, referring to the ruling. "I understand there are a lot of stories, but everything is in the past. It's been decided."[22]

Belichick's reticence about the case leaped from the sports pages to the news side. Margery Eagan, a metro columnist with the *Herald*, weighed in with: "I'm no sports expert. But I know a coward when I see one. And a coward is what I saw scowling behind the podium Friday at the New England Patriots' press conference."[23]

But the coach found support in some important places, one of them being Patriots management: three days after the ruling, ESPN.com reported that Belichick had accepted a contract extension with the team. While it is believed that Belichick and the Patriots agreed to the deal before Spygate came to town, Kraft issued this statement: "I accept his apology and look forward to working with him as we move forward."

Belichick also found support from the team's fan base. The embattled coach received a thunderous ovation from the sellout Gillette Stadium crowd when the Patriots emerged from the tunnel to take on the Chargers. Oh, yes, the Chargers. Even had the cheating scandal not been added to the daily diet of football talk throughout New England leading to this matchup, the opposition provided a built-in subplot: during the previous postseason, one week before losing to Indianapolis in the AFC championship game, the Patriots had gone into Qualcomm Stadium and claimed a 24–21 victory over the Chargers.

The Chargers were shocked. They had qualified for the 2006 playoffs as the top seed in the American Football Conference, having gone 14–2 during the regular season, including an undefeated record at home. But their Super Bowl dreams quickly faded: after enjoying a first-round bye, they were eliminated by the Patriots. When the game was over, Chargers players claimed some Patriots players rubbed it in by doing a victory dance at the 50-yard-line . . . on their sacred team logo.

Keeping in mind that this game was played almost nine months before Spygate went to the top of the Hit Parade, consider what the Chargers' All-Pro running back LaDainian Tomlinson had to say about the manner in which the Patriots behaved: "I was very upset, just the way they show absolutely no class. Maybe it comes from their head coach."[24]

So there was that. Now the Chargers had Spygate to add to their array of bulletin board material going into their September 16 rematch at Gillette Stadium. And Tomlinson was perfectly willing to add his comments to what Mike Tomlin, Michael Strahan, Al Harris, and so many others around the NFL were saying about Belichick and the Patriots.

"I think the Patriots live by saying, 'If you're not cheating, you're not trying,'" Tomlinson told reporters in San Diego after Spygate broke. "You keep hearing different stories of people complaining about the stuff they do, so I'm not surprised."[25]

The Nantucket Gals—Joan Fisher, Jeanne Dooley, and Jane Hardy— were enraged over Spygate.

"I was mad *at the Jets*," recalled Jane Hardy. "I felt that every team in the league did sort of the same thing. And I thought the NFL was too harsh with the punishment. I thought they were playing to the media."

This was one football discussion about which the Nantucket Gals were in full agreement.

"It was way, way overdone," said Joan Fisher.

"It was all blown out of proportion by the media," said Jeanne Dooley. "And that's what the league was reacting to."

And of course, the Nantucket Gals were in attendance for the September 16 game against the Chargers. As Jeanne Dooley recalled, "We wouldn't have missed this one for anything."

They had been following the Patriots throughout the history of the franchise, and they had remained supportive during the bad times, which seemed endless. And, what, they were going to switch allegiances over something they considered to be trivial and overplayed?

The Nantucket Gals, remember, had done more than invest time and money in the Patriots over the years. They had also risked family harmony when they went against their father, grizzled old Giants fan Matt Jaeckle, by siding with the Patriots.

According to family lore, Joan was the first of the Nantucket Gals to stand up to Matt on this issue. A lifelong Nantucketer, she didn't think it made much sense to get all hot and bothered over a team from *New York City*. In the interest of trying new things, of forming her own grown-up opinions about life, she came to the conclusion that the Giants were so . . . so yesterday. But the Patriots! All new and shiny in the American Football League, the Pats were all about today! They represented the New Frontier of professional football, and she wanted in. And, heck, they were based right here in Massachusetts, she reasoned.

Sorry, Matt, came the news from Joan. Once a Giants fan from Nantucket, just like the old man, now she was a Patriots fan from Jump Street.

Jane and Jeanne followed their older sister into the world of the Patriots. At first, and for more than a decade, their support was limited to reading about the team in the old *Boston Record* and watching the games on television. Matt would submit a harrumph or two, and then return to what he considered *real* football, the Giants.

The Nantucket Gals never attended a Pats game in the early years, an era when the team was a collection of football vagabonds forced to latch on to whatever venue would have them. The Patriots played their first three seasons at what was then called Boston University Field, a rather generic-sounding name for what, really, was the remnants of

Braves Field. Imagine: on the same field where the Braves' Johnny Sain squared off against the Cleveland Indians' Bob Feller in Game 1 of the 1948 World Series, now the likes of Gino Cappelletti, Ron Burton, and Babe Parilli fought the good fight for the Boston Patriots. For the next six seasons, the team played its home games at Fenway Park, with portable wooden bleachers erected in front of the Green Monster. In 1969 the Pats spent a season at Boston College, playing their home games at Alumni Stadium. In 1970, in their first season in the National Football League following the NFL-AFL merger, the Pats played at Harvard Stadium. But Harvard had but one locker room available for most games, and it went to the visiting team. The Patriots would stay at a motel across from the Albert S. Teeven Traffic Circle at Fresh Pond in Cambridge the night before the game; following a morning breakfast, the players would put on their uniforms and then be transported to Harvard Stadium on a bus.

"And when the game was over," said Cappelletti, who starred with the Patriots for eleven seasons, "we would go under the stands and talk to the few reporters who were covering us, and then get on the bus and go back to the motel to take showers."

In 1971 the Patriots finally landed a home of their own, moving into a no-frills stadium located in the town of Foxborough (also spelled as Foxboro), about twenty-six miles south of Boston. Known by various names over the years—Schaefer Stadium (after a local beer), Sullivan Stadium (after Billy Sullivan, the team's original owner), Foxboro Stadium (after the town)—it remains one of the greatest deals in sports history. Without the new stadium, it's doubtful the Patriots could have remained in New England, but for the bargain-basement construction cost of just over $7.1 million, it was home to the Patriots for the next thirty-one seasons, until the team moved next door to the newly built Gillette Stadium.

It was to Schaefer/Sullivan/Foxboro Stadium that the Nantucket Gals first traveled to watch the Patriots in 1995. Tickets were easily obtained in those days, and they were cheap. The Gals could make a decision to attend a game on Saturday night, and by six-thirty the next morning they'd be on the ferry to Hyannis.

It wasn't until the Parcells era that they began purchasing season tickets, and even then it all happened sort of by accident. Joan had worked for years as a cashier at the Pacific National Bank on Main Street, and when she retired in 1995 her colleagues decided to throw a party in her honor. To that plan she submitted a firm thanks-but-no-thanks, for no other reason than that she had mixed emotions about leaving the bank. Retirement was fine, what with having more time for the grandchildren, her gardening, and, of course, the Patriots. But she also loved the bank, loved the people there. Retirement party? No. Absolutely not. The last time she left the bank, exiting the side of the old building to go out to the cobblestone street, she slammed the door.

So a party was out. But they were determined to at least give her a going-away present. A coworker placed a call to Joan's husband, Charlie, who owned Island Lumber over on Polpis Road. He had the perfect suggestion: "Get her season tickets to the Patriots," he said. "But you better get her two of them. She'll need someone to go with, and it won't be me."

When Jane and Jeanne heard about this, they decided that they, too, would purchase season tickets. They made arrangements to line up four adjoining seats, so that Joan and Jane and Jeanne could all sit together, with a fourth seat rotating among the grandchildren, or maybe a family friend.

The sisters quickly developed a routine, and they have remained faithful to it over the years, from the old, no-frills stadium on the edge of Route 1 to the new Gillette Stadium that opened out back of the old place in 2002. If the Patriots are playing a one o'clock game, they put Plan A into action: Out of bed at four-thirty in the morning, which gives them plenty of time to catch the *Eagle*, a car ferry that departs Steamboat Wharf in Nantucket at six-thirty. After arriving at Hyannis at eight-forty-five, the first order of business is coffee—either at the Café Dolce on Main Street in Hyannis or at the Dunkin Donuts on Route 132.

Joan always drives. There is no debate on this point. She is forever in a hurry and always a little fidgety until everyone is inside the stadium. She worries about the crowds, worries about the traffic. The very thought of missing the opening kickoff is repugnant to her, and, really, to Jeanne and Jane as well. But that doesn't prevent them from making a ritualistic, pregame stop at Primo's, a sub shop on Mechanic Street in Foxborough Center. Thank God for cell phones: now they are able to call in their order during the hour- to hour-and-a-half-long drive from Hyannis to Foxborough. They are partial to ham and provolone subs.

"They always amaze me," said Chris Dunn, who owns Primo's. "We get all these guys in here who leave their wives on Sunday to go watch football. And here are these very nice old ladies who leave their husbands on Sunday to go watch football. It's hard not to admire them."

They bring their own liquid refreshment, but don't quite grasp the concept of the designated driver. For while it is true that one of the sisters does not imbibe during these football excursions, as it happens, that sister is Jeanne, who, of course, never does the driving. While she is content to wash down her sub with a bottle of water or ginger ale, Joan, who *does* do the driving, enjoys a nice chardonnay, or maybe a merlot. Jane makes love to her gin and tonic, her toddies. "That's my antifreeze," she likes to say.

They consume their pregame meal in the parking lot outside the stadium, and then, as though a gong has gone off somewhere in the distance, they enter Gillette Stadium forty-five minutes before kickoff.

And—this is very important—they never leave before the game is over. Never. To them, only amateurs, no-nothings, tourists, leave before the game is over. They have long believed in the magic of the miraculous comeback, and, well, magical comebacks aren't much fun to talk about when you're driving down Route 1 as Tom Brady is driving down the field. Besides, it makes no sense to travel all this distance—Nantucket to Hyannis, Hyannis to the Café Dolce, the Café Dolce to Primo's, Primo's to Gillette Stadium—and then do something so déclassé as to sneak out early for no other reason than to beat the traffic.

"Some people like to do that," Jane likes to say. "But *we* are not some people."

When the game does end, and however it ends, they make a leisurely drive back to Hyannis. The ferry for Nantucket departs at eight o'clock.

That's Plan A.

Plan B is pretty much the same, except that it is put into place for a game that begins later in the day—say, a 4:00 PM start, or one of those nationally televised nighttime kickoffs. They still get out of bed at the same time, still catch the *Eagle* at 6:30 AM, still stop at Café Dolce, except that before hitting Primo's they check in at the clean, affordable Red Roof Inn in Mansfield, just south of Foxborough. They stay at the hotel overnight, returning to Nantucket the next morning.

The Patriots' 2007 home opener, on Sunday, September 16, was a nationally televised game with an 8:15 PM kickoff. For the Nantucket Gals, Plan B was in play.

They were back at Gillette, and back together: Joan and Jeanne and, now, baby Jane, who had missed the entire 2006 season because of her staph infection. She was so sick at one point that the people at Nantucket Hospital put her on a plane that transported her from the island to Hanscom Field outside Boston; from there, she was placed in an ambulance and rushed to Mass General for treatment.

Inside the stadium, the Nantucket Gals embraced. And then they shouted words of encouragement to Bill Belichick when the Patriots took the field against San Diego.

The 2006 playoff game between the Chargers and Patriots had been close. The 2007 regular-season rematch was not. The Patriots, no longer sending Matt Estrella and his video skills from Fitchburg State down to the sideline, rolled to a 38–14 victory over the Chargers. Tom Brady threw three touchdown passes, two of them to his new pal Randy Moss. Adalius Thomas, playing in his first home game as a member of the Patriots, intercepted a Philip Rivers pass and ran it back sixty-five yards for a touchdown.

Everyone had something to say when it was over, and the general sentiment boiled down to this: the Patriots were prepared to make a season-long statement to prove that they hadn't been winning with mirrors (or videotape) and that, whatever people were saying or thinking about them, they were better than everybody else.

"This might be the most satisfying win of all," said Tedy Bruschi. "I've never been in a situation where people were doubting us, our integrity. I care about that logo, as much as anyone in here. And I care about how we're perceived. What we do is win football games. What we did tonight speaks volumes about who we are."[26]

But the most telling commentary about the game was delivered by LaDainian Tomlinson, who was held to just forty-three yards rushing on eighteen carries in his team's humiliating loss to New England.

"This was a trap game for us," he lamented. "Everyone was calling them cheaters, and they said, 'Let's show everyone we're not cheaters.'"[27]

Bingo. For the rest of the season, the Patriots were hell-bent on proving they were not cheaters—or to put it another way, that they could do it without cheating. They never had to say so. The ease with which they were defeating their opponents said it all.

A week later, the Patriots scored thirty-eight points for the third consecutive game, this one a 38–7 victory over the Buffalo Bills at Gillette Stadium in which Wes Welker made it clear that, while it might be Moss who scored most of the touchdowns this season, it would be Welker, the gridiron Pedroia, who would set the table. He caught six passes for sixty-nine yards, one of them a twenty-six-yard completion that included a lateral to Moss, who added eleven more yards to the play. Welker also returned three punts for a total of seventy-two yards.

In week four, the Pats went to Cincinnati and crushed the Bengals, 34–13, on *Monday Night Football*. Brady tossed three more touchdown passes, two of them to Moss and one of them to veteran linebacker Mike Vrabel, an occasional offensive performer who once said his goal before retiring was to catch a touchdown pass for each of his three children. This was his ninth.

The Pats had now played four games without suspended safety Rodney Harrison and injured defensive lineman Richard Seymour, and during that span they had outscored their opponents by a combined 148–48.

Whenever a National Football League team rolls out of the gate with an impressive collection of victories, it's only a matter of time before fans and media begin talking about the 1972 Miami Dolphins. Playing in the era of the fourteen-game regular season, the '72 Dolphins made it through the entire campaign without a loss—fourteen regular-season victories, followed by playoff victories over Cleveland and

Pittsburgh and a 14–7 victory over the Washington Redskins in Super Bowl VII. Since then, no team has followed in the Dolphins' footsteps of going wire to wire without suffering a defeat.

That's why, when a team opens its season with seven or eight straight victories, reporters begin dialing up aging members of the '72 Dolphins—a Don Shula and a Mercury Morris here, a Larry Csonka and a Paul Warfield there—to ask their opinion about what's going on.

The 2007 season was different. The Patriots were 4–0, their quest for an undefeated season still in the embryonic stage, and already inquiring minds from the press box were chasing down the '72 Dolphins and saying, "What do you think?"

One of the first sportswriters to explore the possibility of the 2007 Patriots posting a 16–0 regular-season record was Michael Wilbon of the *Washington Post*. In a column on October 2, following the Pats' easy victory over the Bengals, he wrote, "There's a reason no NFL team has gone undefeated since 1972 when the Miami Dolphins did it—it's too hard. It requires not just greatness, but perfection. . . . Nobody, in fact, has ever gone 16–0 in the regular season and 3–0 in the postseason." Wilbon capped his article by stating that the Patriots are "good enough for people to start making the case and not get laughed out of the room. This is where their newfound ruthlessness might serve them really well."[28]

A few days later, in the October 7 *Boston Herald*, an article by John Tomase contained quotes from several members of the '72 Dolphins. One of them, former offensive lineman Bob Kuechenberg, couldn't believe he was being asked to discuss this topic so early in the season.

"You jumped it by six games," Kuechenberg told Tomase. "Talk to me in two months when we're in double digits, and then we'll make a little wager. If we make one now, I'm just taking your money."[29]

On the day the article appeared, the Patriots ran their record to 5–0 by crushing the Cleveland Browns, 34–17, with Rodney Harrison appearing in his first game of the season and Tom Brady throwing three touchdown passes.

At the homes of the '72 Dolphins, telephones were ringing with greater frequency.

13

CHEMISTRY CLASS

It's premature to say they're a top team.
Chemistry and depth breed success, and Boston has neither yet.
No matter what they say, making three stars work can be tricky.

—Anonymous NBA scout,
quoted in *ESPN: The Magazine*

Creating a solid chemistry on this Celtics team will be a
science experiment befitting Mr. Wizard.

—Mike McGraw,
Chicago Daily Herald

This might either be the start of another Boston dynasty
or the worst chemistry experiment in NBA history.

—Rich Hammond,
Los Angeles Daily News

These criticisms and caution flags—dozens of them appeared in newspapers and magazines and on websites across the country— were neither unfair nor unwarranted. Danny Ainge had made those two historic trades, bringing in Kevin Garnett and Ray Allen and teaming them up with Paul Pierce to give the Celtics an exciting new look, but there were no guarantees this modern-day Big Three would click.

Not everybody was a skeptic. Veteran Los Angeles Clippers point guard Sam Cassell, who could have no way of knowing that by the following March he would join the Celtics for the stretch drive and wind up with his third championship ring, told the *Washington Post*, "Kevin is the most unselfish ballplayer in the game of basketball. [He] is going to make the game easier for Ray and make it easier for Paul."[1]

But Garnett and Allen were not the only new members of the Celtics. Veterans Eddie House, James Posey, and Scot Pollard were all signed during the summer of 2007. Rookie hopefuls included Glen "Big Baby" Davis, Jackie Manuel, Brandon Wallace, and Gabe Pruitt, a pleasant, twenty-one-year-old stringbean from Los Angeles whose grandmother, a hard-core, lifelong Lakers fan, was still coming to grips with the fact that her beloved grandson was playing for, of all teams, the *Boston Celtics*.

Doc Rivers needed to find a way to make it all work. The Duck Boat ride with Pierce, Allen, and Garnett was a good first step, a rolling learning tool designed to reinforce the glory of winning a championship, but Rivers was still looking for something, anything, he could deploy as a teamwide concept. He needed another gimmick from the old-time radio serials.

Shortly before training camp began, the concept he was seeking was delivered to him by an old acquaintance from his days at Marquette—not a grizzled coach or a onetime teammate, but a woman who had been a resident assistant at O'Donnell Hall, which at the time was an all-girls dorm and, the story goes, a place not unfamiliar to the young Rivers.

In the spring of 1981, Stephanie Rossiter, born and raised in Omaha, was a sophomore at Marquette. She barely knew Rivers in those days, remembering only that he was a basketball star and, she would later say, "someone who had every right to be a big man on campus but never acted that way."

Now known as Stephanie Russell, the onetime RA at O'Donnell Hall returned to her alma mater as executive director for mission and identity. It was in that role that, during a warm summer day in 2007, she was reintroduced to Glenn "Doc" Rivers, class of '85. Rivers, one of Marquette's best-known graduates and a member of the school's board of trustees since 2005, had returned to Milwaukee for this latest board meeting, taking some time away from his pre–training camp preparation.

The meeting began at 8:00 AM. There was a lunch break at noon, whereupon members of the board of trustees, administrators (including Stephanie Russell), and selected students retreated to the president's dining room on the fifth floor of Alumni Memorial Union.

Russell, who was seated across from Rivers in the sun-splashed room, began talking about Marquette's South Africa Service Learning Program, which is run in partnership with the Desmond Tutu Peace Center. She noted that Archbishop Tutu had visited Marquette in 2003 to receive the Pere Marquette Discovery Award, the school's highest honor; during his visit, the archbishop spoke of *ubuntu*, a Bantu word from South Africa. In the *Encyclopedia of African Religion*, edited by Molefi Kete Asante and Ama Mazama, Tutu defines ubuntu this way: "My humanity is caught up, is inextricably bound up, in what is yours."[2]

The word has also been defined as: "I am because we are."

Rivers was immediately interested.

"Of all the things Archbishop Tutu left us during his visit," Russell told Rivers, "the most important and lasting was an understanding of ubuntu."

"Please tell me more," Rivers said, pushing a napkin across the table and asking Russell to jot down the word.

"It is saying to another person, in any context, that my happiness is tied up in your happiness," she said. "It's a very profound thing."

In subsequent retellings of this story, Rivers streamlined some of the details for the benefit of deadline- and space-challenged sportswriters, cutting directly to the chase by putting it out there that Russell had approached him at the meeting and said, "I have a word for you." Russell, though delighted that an otherwise casual lunchtime discussion would result in ubuntu playing a prominent role in the fortunes of the 2007–2008 Boston Celtics, said it was never her intention to introduce the word to her fellow Marquette alum and that it only came up after Rivers said he'd always wanted to visit South Africa.

But let's not quibble. By whatever means and intentions ubuntu was added to the lunchtime menu that day at Alumni Memorial Union, Rivers was fascinated. He continued to ask questions, the born coach in him knowing that he had found something that could turn his freshly assembled collection of strangers into a team. Rivers asked Russell if she would mind sending him an e-mail with any materials or Internet links for assistance in what was about to become a crash course in Ubuntu 101.

"As a coach, you're always looking," Rivers would later say. "You look all summer, or you hope it comes during the season at some point. You're looking for *something*—it doesn't have to be a word. It can be an action. And it hit me right away."

As he had planned, Rivers flew to Orlando, his off-season home, immediately after the meeting. Later that night—that is, very early the next morning—Rivers began doing his homework. By the time he finished, it was time for breakfast. He hadn't even gone to bed.

Now he posed a question to himself: having embraced ubuntu as a motivational technique—*My happiness is tied up in your happiness*—how was he going to present this to his team? He knew that simply walking out to the court and saying, "Gather 'round, I have a new word to share with you" was not going to cut it. He needed some kind of launching pad, a way of imparting this new wisdom in such a way that his players wouldn't just listen but would rally around this word and claim its philosophy as their own.

Rivers got on the phone, seeking out other coaches for advice. He spoke with the well-traveled Larry Brown, for whom Rivers had played briefly on the 1991–92 Los Angeles Clippers. He also sounded out Pat Riley, one of the game's coaching giants on many levels—victories as well as style being high on the list. The dashing, well-dressed Riley, who has coached five teams to NBA championships (the Lakers in 1982, 1985, 1987, and 1988 and the Miami Heat in 2006), also coached the New York Knicks for four successful seasons in the '90s, albeit without a championship. For three of those seasons, Doc Rivers was on his roster. And Rivers never forgot the experience, especially Riley's unique talent for motivating his charges.

"Riley's the best speaker I've ever heard in my life—in front of a team," Rivers would later say. "I've heard better speakers in front of hundreds of people, but in a team setting, I thought he was the best. Because the way he did it, you knew he was invested in what he was saying. The biggest secret Riley had as a coach, at least for me, was that you felt he had zero agendas except for winning."

Rivers didn't come right out and say, "Ubuntu! How do I teach it?" Instead, it was "I've got something. How should I present it? How can I teach this? What's the perfect moment? How can I get them to understand that I'm invested in this word myself?"

For all his respect for Riley, for all his respect for Brown, Rivers came away with no sage advice on how to make an obscure South African word part of the bright lexicon of winning in the modern-day NBA.

As of the night of September 27, 2007, with Media Day scheduled for the following morning, and with no new lightbulbs having gone off over his head, Rivers figured he'd do it the old-fashioned way: He'd simply tell them.

"I was just going to throw it out there and hopefully we'd all talk about it," he said.

On the morning of Media Day, Rivers, sitting in his office at the Celtics' training facility at HealthPoint, came up with a better idea: he would give his typical first-day-of-training-camp speech, ladling out the same old oratorical porridge about discipline and sacrifice and commitment that managers and coaches from Connie Mack to Bill Belichick have had on their menus for a hundred years, and then, at the end, his players beginning to fidget, ready now to empty out the ball rack and get down to the business of shooting baskets, he'd throw out an unexpected wrinkle. He would briefly mention ubuntu and its meaning, and then ask his rookies to step forward. Now would come the delivery: Rivers would give the newcomers the same homework assignment he had undertaken after returning home from Milwaukee a few weeks earlier.

The difference being that Glen Davis, Jackie Manuel, Brandon Wallace, and Gabe Pruitt wouldn't have to sit through a day-long Marquette board of trustees meeting.

For bookkeeping purposes, Friday, September 28, 2007, was the first day of training camp. But because the affair is also known as Media Day, not much training takes place. Instead, it is little more than a morning of photo ops and one-on-one interviews, a platform for everyone connected with the Celtics to wax enthusiastic about the upcoming season. The only players who did not take part in one-on-one interviews during this edition of Media Day were Pierce, Allen, and Garnett; instead, as if to hammer home the point that a new Big Three was in town, they were assembled for a media session that lasted some seventeen minutes.

Later, after the media cleared out, Rivers gathered his players at half-court. Waiting for exactly the right moment—think Tom Cruise in *A Few Good Men* asking Jack Nicholson if he ordered the Code Red—Rivers finally brought up the topic of ubuntu. And then he summoned Glen Davis, Jackie Manuel, Brandon Wallace, and Gabe Pruitt.

"That word will be very important to this team," the coach said. "And tomorrow, the rookies are going to give a presentation of that word. And then you'll understand what the true meaning of ubuntu is."

This was no photo op, and Rivers wasn't speaking into a microphone. It was, in a way, another ride on the Duck Boats.

The meeting over, Rivers brought the four rookies upstairs to his office. He provided some basic information about ubuntu, highlighting certain key points he expected them to cover in their presentation, and then he made it clear this was not a game.

"Guys, this is deadly serious," he said. "It's not a fucking rookie hazing. This is not a joke. I'm serious. This is as serious as your execution tomorrow on offense. When you guys do this, this is your final exam. I want this done professionally, seriously, and I want you to sell this word to the players."

He had some private words for his mischief-making Big Baby. This was a player who, after scoring twenty-six points to lead Louisiana State University to a 70–60 victory over Texas in the 2006 NCAA Tournament, vaulting the Tigers into the Final Four, danced around the court at the Georgia Dome while flinging a feathery gold boa over his head.

"Glen," he said, "I am not screwing around here. This is not the Glen Davis Show, or the Glen Davis Let's Have Fun Show."

"Okay," said Big Baby.

"I'm not kidding," Rivers repeated.

Davis, twenty-one, had played three years at LSU. Pruitt, also twenty-one, played three seasons at the University of Southern California. Wallace, twenty-two, played three seasons at South Carolina. Manuel, at twenty-four the oldest of the four, played four seasons at the University of North Carolina. And now they were all going back to school.

To Pruitt, the exercise was reminiscent, not of college, but of his days at Westchester High School in Los Angeles. He once had to stand in front of a classroom and do a presentation on global warming; as he recalled, he earned a B-minus for his efforts. This time he vowed to do better.

The four players, all hopeful of *playing* in the NBA, concluded that it would be a sound business practice to take Rivers at his word: this was to be an important presentation, not a lounge act. As their coach had done before them, they searched the Internet for information on ubuntu. They chatted on the phone, Big Baby calling Gabe, Gabe calling Jackie, Jackie calling Brandon, Brandon calling Big Baby. They decided to break up the presentation into four parts, each player taking a turn at the head of the class. Big Baby would speak a second time, delivering closing remarks.

The next morning the team assembled at center court at the Sports Authority Training Center at HealthPoint, a 140,000-square-foot facility that is as much a home to well-heeled suburbanites looking to shed those unwanted pounds as it is for the Boston Celtics. As late as the 1980s, when the original Big Three was still ruling the NBA, the Celtics trained at a no-frills gym at Hellenic College, located a couple of miles from Fenway Park in Brookline, hometown of Red Sox general manager Theo Epstein and Patriots owner Robert Kraft. Now the Celtics were far out in the burbs, in their spacious, state-of-the-art training facility, which the four rookies were about to turn into a classroom. Chemistry class.

Big Baby led off, offering a general explanation of ubuntu, its origins, and its meaning. Pruitt delivered a lecture on how people could use ubuntu in their everyday lives. Manuel and Wallace spoke of ubuntu in personal terms, explaining what it meant to them. And then, as per the plan, Big Baby wrapped it all up, instructing his audience that it was time for one and all to take ubuntu to their hearts and use it in the pursuit of a National Basketball Association championship.

"We had notes," Pruitt recalled, "but the best part about it was that we hardly looked at them. We were standing side by side, facing the entire team. I thought I'd be nervous, but it was a lot easier than the presentation on global warming. It was the material."

Big Baby, too, had memories of laboring through those awkward, uncomfortable class presentations back at University High School in Baton Rouge, Louisiana. Once, he had to deliver a report on the Holocaust.

"I took the same approach with ubuntu," he would later say. "It was like going to school and doing a research paper. After I had read up on it, I tried to tell everyone we had to do everything by that word."

Rivers was delighted. "They weren't just good, they were off-the-charts phenomenal," he said. "They all played a part, even quiet Gabe, who never talks. When those guys were finished, guys were clapping, patting them on the back. It was impressive."

And Davis was the headliner. Turns out the big kid, this Big Baby, had the capacity to reach deep within himself and pull the grown-up lever when decorum required him to do so. For instance, while he is often the life of the party, he isn't a party animal. Davis occasionally would appear at student gatherings at nearby Tufts University during his rookie season, to visit his girlfriend, who was a senior member of the Jumbos' women's basketball team, but students who met Big Baby were surprised to meet a hotshot professional athlete who didn't drink.

Given his nickname and his fun-loving nature, it might be years before Davis outgrows his reputation as an overstuffed child. More than a year after his ubuntu presentation, early in the 2008–2009 season, he would sit on the bench and literally cry after the tightly wound Garnett chewed out some of the bench players during a time-out huddle.

But on this day, the day of ubuntu, Big Baby was all man.

"I expected them to take it seriously because of the way they presented it," recalled Paul Pierce. "As for Glen, he can be pretty personable and serious when he has his stuff together. He really impressed me the way he talked about ubuntu. He helped imbed it on our team."

The basketball court used by the Celtics at HealthPoint was decorated with large banners commemorating each of the team's NBA championships, sixteen in all going into the 2007–2008 season. The Celtics claimed their first title in 1957, outlasting the St. Louis Hawks in a thrilling seven-game series and winning Game 7 in double overtime;

they won their last title in 1986, with series MVP Larry Bird leading the Green past the Houston Rockets in six games. It was now going on twenty-two years since the last banner, by far the longest championship drought in franchise history.

Some of the banners at HealthPoint were relics from the old Boston Garden: reproductions had been put in place at the new Garden because the originals were a tad too long and obstructed the view for fans seated in the balcony sections. Taking note of these banners hanging on the walls at Healthpoint, Rivers came up with another arguably corny motivational technique as the Celtics prepared for the 2007–2008 season. He had a small spotlight installed at the court, with its beam focused on the blank wall next to the 1986 championship banner. The message was clear: there was room on this wall for another banner, banner number seventeen.

In early November, with the Celtics three games into the 2007–2008 season, *Herald* basketball writer Steve Bulpett noticed the spotlight being suspiciously trained on the blank wall beside the 1986 banner and quizzed Rivers about what he suspected was no coincidence.

"I'm not going to say anything about the spotlight, but as far as expectations, they are what they are and I don't mind them," Rivers told Bulpett following a November 8 practice session. "I think a lot of people don't talk about expectations because they want to save their jobs. I've always thought that. They don't want to build hope, because if it doesn't come through, it looks like you did a bad job.

"Well, I don't work that way. I think there's nothing wrong with having hope and there's nothing wrong with going after something. And, hell, if you don't, it's disingenuous anyway, in my opinion."[3]

Rivers was pressing these ideas into service as fast as he could dream them up. The Duck Boat ride for the veterans. The ubuntu presentation for Jackie, Brandon, Gabe, and Big Baby. And the baby spotlight aimed at a blank wall where, it was hoped, banner number seventeen would reside one day.

Wasn't it all just shtick?

Celtics managing partner Wyc Grousbeck, a businessman, the man signing the checks, bought it, all of it.

"When it's done sincerely, it's not corny," he said of Rivers's motivational techniques. "This isn't splitting the atom or solving global warming. We are playing a game to entertain people. So there are emotional, corny aspects to it. Doc is a genuine coach, he's the kind of coach that I would have followed when I was an athlete back in college, and he—what he does, he doesn't do it for phony effect, he does it because he believes it. He believes that if those three guys got together and focused on being in a parade, we could get to a parade. And if they just did individualistic things and focused on themselves, we would never see a Duck Boat again."

Ray Allen, entering his twelfth NBA season, saw it this way: "Motivation comes in different forms. Through a long season you always need motivation. There's fatigue that sets in. You don't want guys to get complacent. You have those highs and lows, and you have to know how to reel yourself back and get focused. And that's what Doc was doing—he was putting the mechanisms in place to reel us back in."

As things happened, the 2007–2008 Celtics would be gifted, quite by accident, with one additional motivational technique. The previous February, during All-Star Game festivities in Las Vegas, the NBA announced that the Celtics would be among four teams to make a preseason trip to Europe from September 30 to October 10. The plan was for the Celtics to train for five days in Rome before playing an exhibition game against the Toronto Raptors. They would then move on to London to play Garnett's old team, the Minnesota Timberwolves. The event, billed as "NBA Europe Live," would also include the Memphis Grizzlies.

While such trips, in all sports, are often marketing windfalls for the teams, players and coaches regard them as a nuisance. A few years earlier, Patriots coach Bill Belichick privately groused over a plan for the team to travel to China for a preseason game against the Seattle Seahawks. The NFL eventually ash-canned the idea. But for the 2007–2008 Celtics, the European trip proved to be a training-camp bonding ritual: unable to slink back to their houses or apartments each day after practice, the players turned Rome into their own private fraternity mixer.

Allen recalled being in his hotel room, wide awake, at 1:00 AM. His body still on Boston time, he got up, dressed, and went downstairs to the lobby. There he found a gathering of teammates who'd migrated to the lobby for the same reason.

"Rome gave us a great forum to come together as a team," Allen said. "It *forced* us into bonding, more so than I think we would have if we were stateside."

They also did some goofy stuff. They visited the Coliseum and, naturally, dressed up as gladiators for the cameras. Pierce, Rondo, and Kendrick Perkins, having decided the bald look worked for Garnett and Ray Allen, buzzed their own heads. As part of a for-real rookie-hazing ritual, Glen Davis was made to dine on a plate of octopus. Garnett took the rookies out and bought them finely tailored suits, explaining to the *Herald,* "You've got to take care of the young boys. When I was younger, Sam Mitchell and Terry Porter were really strict on me about being professional and how you carry yourself."[4]

Mitchell, Garnett's onetime teammate on the Minnesota Timberwolves, was also in Rome at the time—in his role as head coach of the Toronto Raptors.

"I remember talking to him during the summer, and I was telling him how proud I was, and he was saying he has to do this, and he has to do that. In his mind, he didn't think he was quite good enough. And I guess that's what you have to have to be great. I said to him, 'Have you ever sat down for two minutes and thought about how far you've come from your rookie year to where you are now?' He said, 'I'll do it one day when I retire.'"

14

RETURN TO OCTOBER

With an 8–6 victory over the Tampa Bay Devil Rays on the night of September 22 at Tropicana Field, the Red Sox clinched a berth in Major League Baseball's upcoming postseason tournament. Yet the celebration was private, measured, the team enjoying a toast before the media was allowed inside the clubhouse. By the time the doors were opened and the reporters invited to step inside, the only visible evidence that any celebrating had taken place was a wastebasket in the center of the room containing empty champagne bottles and disposable glasses.

For while the Sox had nailed down the American League's wild-card berth at the very least, they were still waging a fight to clinch first place in the AL East. And capturing the East title was both strategic and symbolic for the Red Sox. Strategically, it would provide home-field advantage in the Division Series and, should they emerge with the AL's best overall record, home-field advantage in the American League Championship Series as well. Symbolically—and this appeared to mean more to Sox fans than to the team—the victory would place the Red Sox ahead of the Yankees in the standings, breaking New York's run of nine consecutive division titles.

But while Red Sox manager Terry Francona surely wanted to win the East, his larger task was to have his team healthy, rested, and sharp come playoff time. And the Red Sox were hurting. First baseman Kevin Youkilis had been hit on the right wrist by a Chien-Ming Wang pitch in a 10–1 victory over the Yankees on September 15 and missed seven games. Center fielder Coco Crisp missed a couple of games with stiffness in his lower back. Reliever Hideki Okajima needed some time off; having never made more than fifty-eight appearances in a season in Japan, he would make sixty-six appearances with the Red Sox in 2007, a franchise record for a rookie. Curt Schilling, the old, opinionated October warrior, had done two stints on the disabled list with shoulder tendinitis, his rehabilitation including three starts at Triple-A Pawtucket. It would not be revealed until after the season that, in September, Schilling received a cortisone shot in his ailing shoulder. "It was the only way," he explained later, "I was going to get through that period."

As for Manny Ramirez, this time he had an injury about which there was no debate: having played in 127 of the first 132 games of the season, he missed the next 24 games because of his strained left oblique. He didn't return to the lineup until the final week of the regular season.

And then there was reliever Eric Gagne. Though he had seemingly recovered from the various back, hip, and shoulder concerns that idled him earlier in the season with the Texas Rangers, he was nonetheless turning out to be a disaster with the Red Sox.

"We want to get him good consistent innings so we can get him on a roll," Francona told reporters in mid-September. "Then, if we start using him more, he's got a chance to make his pitches."[1]

The plan was for Gagne and Okajima to fill the gap between the starting pitchers and the inevitable nightly arrival of Papelbon. But it wasn't working out that way. Two days after Francona spoke those words, Gagne blew a save in a 4–3 loss to the Blue Jays.

It had been a season of calm for Red Sox fans. Thanks to their blistering start, which kept the Sox in first place virtually the entire season, there were few occasions on which players were booed. Newcomers Julio Lugo and J. D. Drew were by no stretch having good seasons, but each player emerged largely unscathed in the court of public opinion. Lugo did it with good humor: having gone through a 0-for-33 streak during the season that prompted Francona to drop him to ninth in the batting order, Lugo responded by saying, "I just don't want to bat tenth."[2] It was a good line, and it went over well with the fans. It didn't hurt any that he put together a fifteen-game hitting streak in July.

Drew's saving grace was that he got hot just as Sox fans were getting him in their sights: he hit .283 in August, followed by a .342 average and 18 RBI in September. He was also going through some issues at home, and the fans knew it. His seventeen-month-old son, Jack, was suffering from developmental displacement of his hips and underwent a six-hour operation in late July. The child had to be placed in a cast that extended from his chest to below his knees.

Sorting through his fan mail one day, Drew read several letters offering encouragement regarding his son's health crisis. He was particularly moved by a letter from a child who had undergone a similar procedure.

"I appreciated the fact that the fans understood my family's situation," Drew would later say. "It was really, really cool for me, for a kid to sit down and write a letter that says, 'Hey, I had this same kind of surgery and everything's fine now.' For people to relate to what Jack was going through, that was the one thing out of this, that Red Sox Nation was so supportive."

That left Gagne. He had built no season-long goodwill with the fans and had said nothing witty and disarming. To his credit, he was remarkably candid about his failures. When Francona tried to fluff off one particularly bad outing in Baltimore by explaining that the reliever was making the difficult transition from closer to setup man, Gagne said, "It's just an excuse. Three outs. You've got to get three outs. It doesn't matter what inning. I'm not doing my job right now. The last four games have been horrible. So I better step it up now and do my job and get people out. There's no excuse. The whole setting up thing, it's just . . . it's just bullcrap."[3]

Despite the initial reservations Papelbon may have had about Gagne joining the team, the two relief pitchers became good friends. And while Papelbon saw very little in the way of good relief pitching from Gagne, he saw something else.

"He was the most stand-up guy I ever met," Papelbon recalled. "Granted, he didn't pitch good when he was here . . . [but] he was the first one to say, 'You know what? I fucking sucked.' And that, to me, takes a lot. That's not an easy thing to do. Where you have other guys in this clubhouse that if that happened to them they'd shimmy out to the back. So, to me, that takes a lot."

Lots of guys were hurting, Okajima was tired, Gagne was lousy. And as late as September 23, the Red Sox had just a one-and-a-half-game lead over the Yankees.

But then, just like that, the suspense went away. The Sox came home and won two straight over the Oakland A's. On September 28, Matsuzaka worked eight strong innings in Boston's 5–2 victory over Minnesota. It was the Dice Man's last regular-season start, and his final rookie record went into the books at 15–12. With the win, the Sox had clinched at least a tie for first in the AL East; all eyes then turned to that night's Orioles-Yankees game, which was still in progress. The Orioles tied it in the bottom of the ninth in uproarious fashion, Jay Payton tripling home three runs, and they won it in the tenth with another dose of moxie: Melvin Mora dropped a bases-loaded bunt, plating Tike Redman with the deciding run in a 10–9 victory over the Yankees.

At Fenway, few fans had gone home after the Sox' victory over the Twins. One hour and seventeen minutes after the Sox game ended, the old park's new JumboTron showed Mora beating out his bunt and Redman beating a path to the plate, and Fenway erupted all over again. The Sox were AL East champions for the first time since 1995, and they would have home-field advantage for the Division Series.

Save for one memorable occurrence, the Sox' division-clinching celebration was the usual pageant of players dousing one another with champagne, making goofy comments to television people, and, as always, declaring that nobody thought they could do it. But Papelbon went out to the field and, wearing a pair of black spandex shorts and swimming goggles, began dancing a jig in front of the pitcher's mound. His Charles Riverdance was to become the 2007 baseball equivalent of Red Auerbach lighting up his cigar when victory was at hand for the Celtics.

The resting Red Sox dropped their season finale to the Twins. Their final record was 96–66. Josh Beckett, with his 20–7 record, was a candidate for the Cy Young Award. The Red Sox had three strong candidates for Rookie of the Year in Dustin Pedroia, whose .317 batting average made his April struggles a dim memory; Daisuke Matsuzaka, with his 15–12 record; and Hideki Okajima, who was 3–2 with a 2.14 earned run average in 66 relief outings. Ramirez didn't have much of a season for a man of his renown, hitting .296 with 20 home runs and 88

RBI; however, he was going into the postseason hot, with 7 hits in 18 at-bats since returning from his oblique injury. And while Ortiz didn't match his club record 54 home runs from 2006, Big Papi still socked 35 homers in '07 and hit a career-high .332. Mike Lowell had chosen an opportune time to have his finest season: the free-agent-to-be hit .324 with 21 home runs and 120 RBI. Kevin Youkilis, who spent most of 2004 and '05 shuttling back and forth between Boston and Pawtucket, now was on the cusp of stardom, enjoying a 2007 season in which he hit .288 with 18 home runs and 83 RBI. His defensive brilliance at first base earned him a Gold Glove Award.

The Red Sox also had a good bench. Back in April, when Pedroia was struggling, reserve infielder Alex Cora never took the bait when reporters asked whether he thought he should be playing more. Though he hit only .246, Cora performed deftly at second (thirty starts) and shortstop (twenty-two starts) and managed to make his major league debut at first base. Having finally abandoned their hopes that Wily Mo Pena could be a right-handed offensive threat off the bench, the Red Sox traded the outfielder to the Washington Nationals in mid-August. They replaced him with switch-hitting journeyman Bobby Kielty, who, while lacking Pena's awesome power, was a better overall player. Backup catcher Doug Mirabelli was nearing the end of the line but was kept around because of his ability to catch Tim Wakefield's knuckleball.

Francona and first-year pitching coach John Farrell loved their starting rotation, and they were able to set up their pitching for the upcoming Division Series as they saw fit. The Sox would be playing the American League West champion Los Angeles Angels of Anaheim in the Division Series, and Beckett, of course, would get the start in Game 1, followed by Matsuzaka in Game 2. The series would then shift to Anaheim for Game 3 and the postseason return of Schilling, one of modern-day baseball's great October dramatists. Beyond his bloody-sock heroics of three years earlier, he was the owner of an 8–2 postseason record, including a 3–1 mark and 2.11 ERA in six World Series starts. His power eroding, his aching shoulder calmed by cortisone, Schilling was now more of a finesse pitcher who substituted wisdom and guile for a fastball that no longer crackled as it once did.

*   *   *

The Division Series came and went in a blur. On October 3 at Fenway Park, Beckett overwhelmed the tattered, injured Angels in the opener, pitching a complete-game, four-hit shutout. Youkilis gave the Red Sox all the offense they would need when he hit a first-inning homer off Angels starter John Lackey, and Ortiz drove in a pair of runs.

Matsuzaka lasted only four and two-thirds innings in Game 2, allowing three runs, but the bullpen foursome of Javier Lopez, Manny Delcarmen, Okajima, and, in the end, Papelbon held the Angels hitless over the last four and a third innings. Trailing 3–2 in the fifth, the Red Sox tied the game with some help from an unexpected source: a fan in the front row of the box seats. With runners on the corners, one out, Ramirez hit a foul pop near the box seats between home plate and first base, and Angels catcher Jeff Mathis seemed poised to make the catch. But as he extended his mitt into the stands at box 37 in search of the ball, seventeen-year-old Danny Vinik was just a little faster, reaching up and making the catch, denying Mathis. Ramirez proceeded to walk, and Mike Lowell hit a sacrifice fly to bring home the tying run. As Red Sox fans celebrated, celebrated Red Sox fan Stephen King reached out and congratulated Vinik, who just happened to be the son of a Red Sox limited partner.

The play illustrated just how different were the Red Sox from their long-suffering cousins from the Midwest, the Chicago Cubs. In Game 6 of the 2003 National League Championship Series, the Cubbies were five outs away from eliminating the Florida Marlins when one of their own fans, Steve Bartman, reached out for a foul ball being pursued by Cubs left fielder Moises Alou. The Cubs were ahead 3–0 at the time. By the time the inning was over, the Marlins had eight runs across. Florida won the game, and the series, and then beat the Yankees in the World Series behind the pitching of Josh Beckett. And the Cubs, absent a World Series championship since 1908, braced for yet another cold, lonely winter . . . only this time squawking about one of their own, the pitiable Steve Bartman.

As for Danny Vinik, he was stamped an instant rock star after the Red Sox emerged with a 6–3 victory over the Angels. The game was tied 3–3 in the bottom of the ninth when Manny Ramirez, the beneficiary of Vinik's unlikely heroics, clobbered a pitch from Angels closer extraordinaire Francisco Rodriguez for a three-run, game-winning homer, the ball easily clearing the Green Monster seats atop the left-field wall and landing across Lansdowne Street. It was Manny's twenty-first career postseason home run, and it left him one shy of the Yankees' Bernie Williams for the major league record. Baseball purists were, and are, quick to point out that these totals have been padded by Major League Baseball's added tiers of playoff rounds, noting that, say, Mickey Mantle was limited to playing in the World Series when he hit his eighteen career postseason home runs. But that was of no concern to Manny, who told reporters, "It feels great, man. It's been a long time since I did anything special like that. But I haven't been right all year round. But I guess, you know, when you don't feel good and you still get hits, that's when you know you are a bad man."[4]

The series moved to Anaheim for Game 3. The Red Sox needed only to have packed an overnight bag, rolling to a 9–1, series-clinching victory over the Angels. Schilling worked seven shutout innings, spacing six hits and allowing only one walk. In the fourth inning, back-to-back home runs by Ortiz and Ramirez off Angels starter Jered Weaver gave Schilling all the offense he'd need.

Going into the postseason, there were fans, and sportswriters, rooting for a Red Sox–Yankees showdown in the American League Championship Series. Their two previous postseason meetings had been historic, what with Sox manager Grady Little leaving in a tiring Pedro Martinez in Game 6 of the 2003 ALCS and, of course, the mother of all comebacks in 2004.

As it would happen, there would be plenty of drama in the 2007 American League Championship Series. But none of it would be provided by the Yankees, who were taken out by the Cleveland Indians in the Division Series.

Had the Yankees been a little tougher and extended the Division Series to an all-or-nothing Game 5, the Indians would have started their ace, six-foot-seven, 290-pound lefthander C. C. Sabathia. Instead, the Indians had a rested and ready Sabathia for Game 1 of the ALCS at

Fenway Park, thereby setting up a Sabathia-Beckett showdown.

On paper, it was a classic. Sabathia, like Beckett, was coming off his career season, having gone 19–7 with a 3.21 earned run average in thirty-four starts. Sabathia-Beckett may have lacked the sexiness and name recognition of the Pedro Martinez–Roger Clemens "fight-of-the-century" postseason showdowns of the past, but no matter: they were the two top pitchers in the American League. Voting for the AL's Cy Young Award had already been conducted, and the consensus was that it would be a two-man race, Sabathia and Beckett, when the results were announced in November.*

But the showdown was anything but. While Beckett was taking his game to a significantly higher level in the postseason, Sabathia was going in a different direction. Having won a so-so outing in his Division Series start against the Yankees, he was shelled by the Red Sox in Game 1 of the ALCS, allowing eight runs in four and a third innings. Beckett allowed two runs in six innings. The Red Sox rolled to a 10–3 victory.

Schilling took the mound in Game 2, looking to burnish his reputation as one of the game's great postseason pitchers. He didn't have it on this night, lasting only four and two-thirds innings and allowing five runs. Nor was Indians starter Fausto Carmona any great shakes, allowing four runs in four innings. Rafael Perez relieved Carmona and gave up back-to-back home runs to Ramirez and Lowell, with Manny's shot making history: it was his twenty-third postseason home run, moving him past Bernie Williams and into first place on the all-time list.

Yet by the time it was over, Schilling and Carmona, Perez and Ramirez, were all footnotes.

With the game tied 6–6, Papelbon worked a scoreless ninth. In the bottom of the inning, Pedroia reached on a two-out single, and Ellsbury, running for him, stole second. Up came Youkilis, who waged one of those classic on-the-edge-of-your-seat battles with Indians reliever Rafael Betancourt, fouling off pitch . . . after pitch . . . after pitch, six

---

* Sabathia won the Cy Young Award in balloting conducted by the Baseball Writers' Association of America. He had 119 points, including 19 first-place votes. Beckett placed second with 86 points, including 8 first-place votes.

fouls in a row. Betancourt threw eleven pitches in the showdown, all of them fastballs; Youkilis nailed number eleven, hitting a hard, sinking liner to center field. Grady Sizemore, one of the game's fast-rising young stars, made a sliding, game-saving catch.

Papelbon came out for the tenth and again kept the Indians off the board. The Red Sox went down 1-2-3 in the bottom of the inning. Now it was the eleventh inning, and Francona, having already gone through Manny Delcarmen, Hideki Okajima, Mike Timlin, and Papelbon, placed a call for Eric Gagne. He struck out Casey Blake, but then things got ugly. Gagne gave up a single to Sizemore and then walked Asdrubal Cabrera. On came situational lefty Javier Lopez to face onetime Red Sox hero Trot Nixon, now a spare part on the Indians; Nixon lined a single to center to bring home Sizemore, and a wild pitch by Lopez brought home Cabrera. Jon Lester was summoned from the bullpen and didn't fare any better; by the time the inning was over, the Indians had scored seven runs. The Indians won in a rout, 13–6.

The series now moved to Cleveland, and Jacobs Field was packed and electric for Game 3. It had been forty-nine years since the Indians last won a World Series, and the press was quick to remind the locals that Boston had done its part to make it all happen: in 1948 the Indians won a one-game playoff against the Red Sox to win the American League pennant and then defeated the late, rarely great Boston Braves in the World Series.

Matsuzaka, making his second postseason start, again failed to last five innings. He allowed all four Cleveland runs in a 4–2 loss to the Indians; after the game, he sat before his locker, his head buried in his hands. He would occasionally look up, stare into his locker, and then shake his head.

Deadline-challenged reporters kept creeping ever closer to Matsuzaka's locker, seeking a comment or two about what had happened. The crowd kept building, and building, and finally Red Sox media relations director John Blake swept in, screamed at the media to give the players some room, and punctuated his request by manhandling a black leather couch and pushing it several feet toward the middle of the clubhouse. Blake, a native of the Boston area, had joined the Red Sox in 2006 after starting his baseball career with the Baltimore Orioles and then putting in more than two decades with the Texas Rangers. He was a man known for fierce and sometimes amusing displays of temper; grizzled, old-time baseball writers barely even noticed, while newcomers often didn't know what to make of it all. Blake had been remarkably tame during his time with the Red Sox, but suddenly, out of nowhere, it was classic Blake. Old-timers snickered. Young'ns retreated.

At 11:46 PM, one hour and eight minutes after the game ended, reporters were told that Matsuzaka had issued a statement through his interpreter, Masa Hoshino.

"I allowed them to score first and I wasn't able to hang on after giving up the lead," Hoshino said, reading the statement. "I wanted to do everything I could today to win, and hand it over to [Game 4 starter Tim] Wakefield in a good way."[5]

Game 4 was a matchup of two soft-throwing veterans, Boston's Tim Wakefield and his funky knuckleball versus Cleveland's Paul Byrd and his double-pump windup that seemed right out of the old Movietone newsreels. The two men matched zeroes through four innings, the deadlock ending in the bottom of the fifth inning when Casey Blake led off with a home run off Wakefield. After that, everything fell apart for the Red Sox. A single here, a hit batsman there, a dropped infield pop-up. Wakefield didn't make it out of the inning. The Indians scored seven runs, five of them being charged to the old knuckleballer.

The Sox rebounded the next inning with consecutive home runs by Youkilis, Ortiz, and Ramirez, with Ramirez's homer traveling 451 feet to center field. Ramirez reacted to the home run in an odd fashion, standing at home plate, thrusting his hands into the air as though he'd just hit a walk-off, game-winning blast. His teammates were not amused, and some of their frustration made it into print: "I've got to ask him about the hands up in a 7–2 [game]," said Mike Lowell. "I don't really understand that one, but that's him."[6]

The Red Sox were now one loss away from being eliminated by the plucky, bargain-basement Indians. But optimists were quick to point out that the 2004 Red Sox had rebounded from a three-games-to-none ALCS deficit against the Yankees, and those optimists included Ortiz,

Ramirez, Schilling, Youkilis, Timlin, Varitek, Wakefield, and backup catcher Doug Mirabelli—all veterans of the greatest postseason comeback in baseball history.

Papelbon, whose contribution to the 2004 Red Sox was watching the World Series at the Ale House in Fort Myers, returned to the team's hotel after Game 4 and hooked up with his buddy Eric Gagne. No way was he going to let a 3–1 series deficit ruin his night. The two ballplayers connected with their wives and some friends and began pounding Gray Goose vodka, having decided that all was right in the world so long as there was another game to be played.

For Tim Wakefield, though, the evening wasn't so pleasant. His shoulder had been bothering him for weeks; now it was killing him. When he woke up in the morning, he could barely lift the blanket off his chest. When he got into the shower, he tried, and failed, to run his right hand through his hair.

Cleveland was bracing for the World Series. "The next step for Boston? Extermination," wrote John Horton in the *Cleveland Plain Dealer*. "The Tribe is a win away from zapping Boston out of the American League Championship Series. Do that and a mile-high World Series date awaits with the Colorado Rockies."[7]

Grayson Pitman, an Indians fan from Mansfield, Ohio, was quoted as saying in the *Plain Dealer*, "We smell blood. We're not going back. They've got nothing."[8]

Not exactly. What the Red Sox had was a pitcher named Josh Beckett, who had already breezed through two postseason starts, including a Game 1 victory over the Indians. But as if Game 5 needed an added measure of intrigue, Indians management provided it in their curious decision to import country singer Danielle Peck to sing the national anthem. Given that Peck and Beckett had dated in 2006, conspiracy buffs immediately wondered aloud: were the Indians bringing in the singer to somehow psych out Boston's starting pitcher? Absolutely not, said the Indians. "An incredible coincidence," said Bob DiBiasio, an Indians vice president.[9]

Beckett, deep into his October zone by now, was neither amused nor upset that an old flame was going to be showing up. In a game in which all the pressure was supposed to be on his team—facing elimination, playing on the road before a packed, festive, World Series–anticipant crowd—Beckett submitted yet another outstanding performance. In pitching the Red Sox to a 7–1 victory over the Indians, he allowed one run in eight innings and registered eleven strikeouts.

Fans and media hoping for some sparks to fly between Beckett and the lovely Danielle Peck had to settle for sparks between Beckett and Indians outfielder Kenny Lofton. When Lofton thought he had looked at ball four while facing Beckett in the fifth inning—the pitch was called a strike—he flipped his bat to the ground, thus inspiring some yelling from Beckett. The two players had engaged in a similar boys-will-be-boys episode in 2005 when Lofton was with the Phillies and Beckett with the Marlins. Now, in Game 5 of the 2007 American League Championship Series, Lofton moved toward the mound, which resulted in the obligatory emptying of the benches and lots of standing around, after which both teams returned to the business of playing baseball.

Beckett's postgame press conferences were becoming uncomfortable affairs for Major League Baseball officials, with the pitcher decorating his answers to questions with the occasional cuss word. Today's was no exception. Naturally, he was asked about Danielle Peck's appearance. Naturally, Beckett had something colorful to say.

"I don't get paid to make those fucking decisions," he said. "She's a friend of mine. That doesn't bother me at all. Thanks for flying one of my friends to the game so she could watch it for free."[10]

The series returned to Fenway Park for Game 6 and, the Sox hoped, Game 7. And there *were* two games, each of them an embarrassing mismatch. The Red Sox rolled to a 12–2 victory in Game 6, with old Curt Schilling regaining his classic postseason form and limiting the Indians to two runs in seven innings. While the offensive star was right fielder J. D. Drew, who hit a first-inning grand slam off Indians starter Fausto Carmona, Boston's center fielder also generated some buzz: Jacoby Ellsbury was finally in the starting lineup. Though he had played terrifically in September, hitting .361 with 17 RBI, Ellsbury was reduced to pinch-running or going in as a late-inning defensive replacement for Ramirez in left field, with Coco Crisp getting all the starts in center field. But Crisp had only two hits in ten at-bats in the Division Series, and through the first five games of the ALCS had just three hits in twenty-one at-bats.

Now it was Crisp who was the late-inning defensive replacement, and he played his role with memorable aplomb when Game 7 came down to the final out. Matsuzaka started for the Red Sox and did the one thing he was supposed to do: keep the Red Sox in the game. He worked five innings, allowing two runs, and left with a 3–2 lead. It turned out to be enough, with a little help from the Indians. With one out in the seventh, Kenny Lofton on second base, Franklin Gutierrez hit a hard grounder inside the third-base bag that caromed off the wall along the grandstand and into shallow left field. Lofton should have scored easily, but he was held up by third-base coach Joel Skinner. Casey Blake then hit into a 5-4-3 double play, and the Indians still trailed by a run.

But their season was over. Dustin Pedroia provided the Red Sox some insurance when he hit a two-run homer into the Monster seats in the bottom of the inning, and the Sox busted the game open with a six-run eighth.

In the top of the ninth, with Red Sox fans on the cusp of celebrating their team's second trip to the World Series in four seasons, Crisp grabbed his glove and trotted out to center field. Ellsbury moved over to left field to replace Ramirez. Papelbon, who had pitched the eighth, came back out for the ninth.

With the Indians down to their last out, Casey Blake rifled a shot to the 420-foot sign in center field, the deepest part of the old ballpark. Rarely do balls get hit to this neck of the Fenway woods; when they do get hit there, rarer still is it for the ball to be caught. During the magical summer of 1967, pinch hitter Norm Sieburn helped win a game for the Red Sox by hitting a triple to the 420-foot sign, a clutch hit that old-timers are still talking about.

Crisp, the starter turned fill-in, raced after the ball. Running at a full gallop, he extended his glove and the ball disappeared into his fine leather just as the outfielder crashed into the bullpen wall. He fell to the ground in a heap, but still holding the ball, and the American League pennant, in his glove.

Fenway went crazy all over again. Crisp, limping back to the infield to join the celebration, said, "When we had our backs against the wall, we didn't let our guard down," in his case speaking literally as well as figuratively.[11]

The Red Sox had rebounded from a 3–1 series deficit against the Indians, wrapping it up in an 11–2 laugher. They had outscored the Indians 30–5 in the last three games of the series. Beckett, 2–0 with a 1.93 ERA in two starts, was series MVP. Ramirez hit .409 with 10 RBI. Kevin Youkilis, scorching everything thrown to him, hit .500 with 7 RBI. Mike Lowell, J. D. Drew, and Dustin Pedroia all hit over .300.

Earlier in the week, Papelbon had promised to "dance all night long" if the Red Sox won the pennant. The game now over, the series in the bag, Papelbon dusted off his Charles Riverdance as Fenway roared.

15

A FALL CLASSIC WITH A CLASSIC ENDING

Albert L. "Dapper" O'Neil, a throwback Boston politician who made his first foray into the political arena under the guidance of legendary Boston mayor James Michael Curley in the late 1950s, had a ready quip whenever anyone asked him about his latest race for the City Council.

"They won't count my votes," O'Neil would say. "They'll weigh 'em."

Everybody understood the joke. The Dap's campaigns for City Council were as blustery as they were efficient, about affirmation as much as reelection. As he implied, the race was no race at all. His assessment of the situation was usually correct.

And so it was with the 2007 World Series. The Red Sox went into the Fall Classic as overwhelming favorites to defeat the Colorado Rockies, and they won the first three games with men-against-boys dispatch. Josh Beckett, who had actually warmed up during Game 7 of the ALCS in the event that Terry Francona needed his staff ace to help out in relief against the Indians, was pitching on five days of rest in the Series opener at Fenway Park, and he did to the Rockies what he had done to the Angels and Indians: as the Irish would say, he shillelaghed them.

The Red Sox hung a 13–1 beating on the Rockies in Game 1, with Beckett allowing one run in seven innings. He struck out nine Rockies, including a rat-a-tat-tat first inning in which he struck out Willy Taveras, Kaz Matsui, and Matt Holliday on fifteen pitches.

Leading off in the home half of the inning was Pedroia, whose first visit to baseball's postseason was turning out to be precisely like his first season in the big leagues: after getting off to a slow start, now he was rifling everything that was thrown his way. He hit .154 in the Division Series . . . then .345 in the ALCS, and now, in his first World Series at-bat, he rocketed the second offering from Colorado starter Jeff Francis over the Green Monster for a home run.

The Rockies were so overwhelmed that in the fifth inning reliever Ryan Speier set a World Series record when he issued three consecutive bases-loaded walks. They had won fourteen of their last fifteen regular-season games in order to qualify for the postseason and then swept through the Division Series and National League Championship Series in seven straight games; now, against the Red Sox in the World Series, they looked more like the expansion Colorado Rockies of 1993.

Beckett was now 4–0 in four postseason starts, allowing four earned runs in thirty innings. Throw in the deciding game of the 2003 World Series against the Yankees and Beckett was 5–0 with a 0.93 earned run average in his last five postseason starts.

He was, then, stepping into Curt Schilling's shoes as the game's next great postseason pitcher, except that Schilling happened to still be around to improve on his own October résumé. Starting for the Red Sox in Game 2, the forty-year-old right-hander worked five and a third innings, allowing one run, in Boston's 2–1 victory over the Rockies and then stood in the dugout cheering as Okajima and Papelbon combined for three and two-thirds innings of shutout relief to secure Boston's victory.

Schilling had walked off the mound in the sixth inning with arms stretched high, doffing his cap, the message being that this might be the last time the Fenway masses saw him in a Red Sox uniform. It was.

"In the postseason you look at everything differently," Schilling recalled. "You just want to win. And we won that game. But I wanted to be the guy on the mound when it was over, raising his arms in the air, not going to the dugout in the sixth inning. But Okie came in and pitched great, and then Pap did his thing. That was the story. It didn't hit me until later that I got the win. I mean, I guess I knew it. But I had come out so early that it didn't feel like it."

It was also the game in which one of Boston's coaches, Brad Mills, stepped out of the shadows and into the national spotlight. Mills, Francona's bench coach, had a relationship with the Boston manager that began years earlier when they were teammates at the University of Arizona. More than just being a coach, he was best buddy, confidant, and chief of staff for Francona. And now, in the eighth inning of Game 2 of the World Series, he recalled an item in the team's scouting report of the Rockies that would help nail down Boston's victory.

Papelbon had relieved Okajima with one out in the inning and given up an infield single to Holliday. With the tying run on base, up to the plate stepped the Rockies' cleanup hitter, Todd Helton.

As is the case with most relief pitchers, Papelbon does not throw much to first base and thus is not known for his pickoff move. His job is to throw one hard inning, occasionally two hard innings, and then go home. Tinkering with base runners isn't part of the arrangement. But Mills, who had read in the scouting report that the Rockies sometimes take generous leads off first base, flashed a "throw-over" sign to catcher Jason Varitek . . . who relayed the signal to Papelbon . . . who turned and fired a throw across to first baseman Kevin Youkilis . . . who slapped the tag down on Holliday. First-base umpire Ted Barrett made the out call.

After the game, Francona, Varitek, Papelbon, and Schilling all credited the team's scouts for submitting valuable information about the Rockies' base-running habits, reserving special praise for Mills, who noticed Holliday's lead and flashed the throw-over. The result: Mills, a career lieutenant and thus someone who was seldom called on to speak with gatherings of reporters, was besieged with questions. The next night, on MSNBC's *Countdown*, host Keith Olbermann included Francona, Papelbon, and Mills in his rundown of "Goofballs and Good Guys," with the Boston trio anointed "our top three best persons in the world."

Now the World Series shifted to Denver's Coors Field for Game 3. Matsuzaka was scheduled to pitch for the Red Sox. Pitching for the Rockies would be right-hander Josh Fogg, who was born in Lynn, Massachusetts, in 1976 but was only two weeks old when his family relocated to Florida. His father, Charles Fogg, grew up a Red Sox fan and played third base at Lynn English High School; in a game against Lynn's

St. Mary's High School in 1962, he was on the opposite bench from future Sox star Tony Conigliaro.

Game 3 of the World Series was scheduled to begin at 5:35 PM local time on October 27. Dustin Pedroia planned to be at Coors Field many hours before that. A clubhouse rat by nature, the rookie second baseman often arrived at the ballpark before any of his teammates, and for no particular reason other than to hang out, maybe play some cribbage with third baseman Mike Lowell and manager Francona.

On this day, getting into the ballpark proved problematic, leading to an episode that over time would take on a life of its own and become part of the growing legend of Dustin Pedroia. As first reported several months later in Mike Lowell's book on his 2007 season with the Red Sox, *Deep Drive: A Long Journey to Finding the Champion Within*, it seems that Pedroia was stopped by a Coors Field security guard as he tried to enter the ballpark. The guard chose not to believe that the baby-faced, not-terribly-athletic-looking, twenty-four-year-old was a member of the Red Sox. After producing an ID card failed to convince the security guard of his status as a real, live big league ballplayer, Pedroia reached deep within himself and called upon some of the I-can-lick-any-man-in-the-bar bravado that has been a part of him since his first day at Arizona State.

"Why don't you ask Jeff Francis who I am?" snarled Pedroia, referring to the Rockies pitcher against whom he had homered in Game 1 of the World Series, as he triumphantly walked through the gate.

Pedroia's verbal joust with the Coors Field security guard became a sort of calling card. Whenever anyone on the Red Sox was asked to discuss the second baseman's feisty nature, the best, and easiest, response was to begin by saying, "Well, you heard what happened at Coors Field, right?"

Nearly a year later, veteran baseball writer Bob Nightengale of *USA Today* submitted his take on Pedroia, filing a story under the headline "Little Engine That Hit .327; Banty Pedroia Continues to Defy Doubters." When it was time to truck out the obligatory Coors Field story, Nightengale chose Terry Francona as his narrator:

He says, "You don't know who I am? You don't know who I am?"
Francona says. "Ask Jeff f—— Francis who the f—— I am. I'm the
guy who hit a bomb and just ended their f—— season."[1]

These are the kind of stories that, over time, sprout wings and travel
to wondrous places. Did Babe Ruth really call his shot in the 1932 World
Series? Did legendary Boston Celtics announcer Johnny Most, while
slumming as a hockey announcer one night in the 1960s, really react to
a shot on net by saying, "It hit the fucking post?"

But this story really did happen. Moreover, Francona's saucy descrip-
tion of the events of Saturday afternoon, October 27, 2007, is not far
from the truth.

"The security guard was hammering me," Pedroia recalled. "I thought
maybe someone put him up to it. But he really wouldn't let me in the
stadium. I showed him my ID card, and he still wouldn't let me in. And
I'm like, 'Dude, did you watch the games?' And he says, 'No, I didn't
watch the games.' He's really yelling at me. It's like he wanted to fight or
something. So I said, 'Dude, go ask Jeff Francis who I am,' and I started
walking."

Though the Rockies do not question the accuracy of Pedroia's story,
they have never revealed the identity of the security guard in question.
"We have a lot of entrances and we move a lot of people around," said
Jay Alves, the Rockies' vice president of communications. "It could have
been any number of people."

Whoever it was, chances are he knew who Pedroia was by the time
Game 3 was over, the Red Sox claiming a 10–5 victory in a game that
took four hours and nineteen minutes to complete—the longest nine-
inning game in World Series history. Pedroia had three hits, including
a two-run double to right in the eighth inning. Boston's other rookies in
the lineup also acquitted themselves well: Jacoby Ellsbury became the
third rookie in World Series history to have four hits in a game and only
the second player to have two doubles in an inning, and Matsuzaka,
in addition to earning the win, allowing two runs in five and a third
innings, also drove in a run with a third-inning single to left.

Leading the way for Boston's veterans was Mike Lowell, who lined a two-run single to center in a six-run third inning. Four years earlier, with the Florida Marlins, Lowell suffered a broken hand late in the season and barely made it back in time for the postseason; he struggled, though, getting just nine hits (two of them being home runs) in forty-six at-bats in the Marlins' march to a World Series title. Now he was wrecking postseason pitching, hitting a combined .333 in the first two rounds of the playoffs and going 4-for-11 with three RBI in the first three games of the World Series.

In winning Games 1 and 2 in Boston, and then Game 3 at Denver's Coors Field, the Red Sox outscored the Rockies by a margin that bore a striking resemblance to halftime at a typical 2007 Patriots game: 25–7. (The analogy is remarkably close to reality: on the very night the Red Sox won the World Series, the Patriots, back east at Gillette Stadium, had run up a 24–0 halftime lead over the Washington Redskins en route to a 52–7 victory.)

When the Red Sox arrived at Coors Field for Game 4, they did so with their champagne on ice, their postgame victory speeches prepared. Clubhouse assistants were already in possession of long sheets of plastic to protect the players' lockers from the anticipated postgame bedlam, and a wooden platform was at the ready, needing only to be maneuvered into place for live television coverage of the championship presentation. Back home in Boston, plans were already under way for yet another rolling rally after the Red Sox took care of business against the upstart Rockies.

The Red Sox were one victory away from their second World Series championship in four years, but, as Manny Ramirez cautioned reporters, "We don't want to eat the cake before your birthday."[2]

On the day before Game 1 of the World Series, the Red Sox summoned the media to the Players Club, a function room located beyond Fenway Park's right-field bleachers in an old brick building that for decades had housed an industrial laundry company.

Now it was a part of the ever-expanding Fenway Park, and it was here, on a cloudy Tuesday afternoon, that Tim Wakefield, close to tears, sat at a table and announced he was not going to be on the Red Sox'

World Series roster. Not only had his shoulder not recovered from his start against the Indians in Game 4 of the American League Championship Series, but doctors were telling him that he needed to shut it down for the season, right now, or risk a more serious injury.

Having joined the Red Sox in May 1995, Wakefield had the longest tenure of any player on the team. As of the end of the 2007 season, he had won 154 games as a member of the Red Sox, behind only Cy Young and Roger Clemens in franchise history, and he had won 17 games in '07. Now he was done. Now he was an emotional wreck.

"I don't think it's fair to the 24 guys that are in that clubhouse, and I don't think it's fair to the organization, and I don't think it's fair to me, lastly, that I go out there and injure myself and [not be] available for the next year or the year after that," he told reporters. He spoke for just a few minutes, and then left the room and climbed into a golf cart and was driven back to the Boston clubhouse.[3]

To replace Wakefield on the roster the Red Sox chose Kyle Snyder, a thirty-year-old right-hander and onetime first-round draft pick by the Kansas City Royals whose major league dreams had been cruelly derailed by a six-year litany of arm injuries. The Royals finally gave up on him in June 2006, and he was picked up by the Red Sox. In 2007 he earned a spot in the Boston bullpen in spring training and finally logged his first full season in the big leagues.

The larger story was who would replace Wakefield in the World Series starting rotation. Had he been healthy, Wakefield probably would have been on the mound for Game 2 and, if necessary, Game 6. Now Francona shuffled the deck: following Game 1 starter Josh Beckett would be Schilling in Game 2, with Matsuzaka in Game 3.

Starting for the Red Sox in Game 4 would be Jon Lester. A little more than one year after being diagnosed with cancer, and seven months from beginning his comeback via a one-inning stint against the Minnesota Twins in a March 5 spring training "B" game, twenty-three-year-old Jon Lester was now going to start the game that could clinch a World Series championship for the Red Sox.

It became the subplot, the hook, the story line, that had been missing from this World Series. Not that it mattered much to the millions of fans who claim citizenship in a make-believe hardball fantasyland called Red Sox Nation, but the Sox had become so methodical in their dismantling of the Rockies that, for those baseball fans not sashaying around in Big Papi T-shirts and homemade versions of Curt Schilling's bloody sock, the World Series lacked intrigue, drama, controversy.

This did not escape the attention of the national media. Jim Caple of ESPN.com, harrumphing that he was witnessing "the worst postseason in baseball history," professed a longing for the old days: "Remember when the old Red Sox used to play those epic World Series, the sort that made grown men cry? I know the old Sox always wound up losing, but damn, those were entertaining series. I miss them. These new Sox are like the old Yankees. They just bludgeon teams."[4]

Wrote Mike Vaccaro in the *New York Post*: "There is nothing romantic and nothing charming about what the Sox are doing right now. They are taking what 15 minutes ago was among the most scorching-hot teams in baseball history and making them look like September's version of the New York Mets."[5]

It wasn't like this in 2004. When the Red Sox rallied from a 3–0 deficit to take down the Yankees in the American League Championship Series, and then, when they swept the St. Louis Cardinals in the World Series, there were so many subplots that by the following spring Charles Steinberg, vice president of public affairs for the Red Sox, estimated that more than twenty Sox-related books were in the works. And why not? In becoming the first team in baseball history to win a seven-game series after losing the first three games, the Red Sox had finally conquered their longtime nemeses from the Bronx. Talk about score-settling: this was the team that sold Babe Ruth to the Yankees . . . the team that dropped the final two games of the 1949 season to the Yankees to lose the American League pennant . . . the team that lost a heartbreaking one-game playoff to the Yankees in 1978 on Bucky Dent's home run off Mike Torrez . . . the team that lost the ALCS to the Yankees in five games in 1999 . . . the team that lost the 2003 ALCS to the Yankees when manager Grady Little left Pedro Martinez on the mound in the eighth inning of Game 7. The Red Sox not only defeated the Yankees in the 2004 ALCS—they humiliated them.

Look at it another way: when the Red Sox won the World Series in

2004, it was an event not just for the ages but for the aged. Suddenly, ninety-five-year-old Red Sox fans were being hunted down and asked to sit in front of the television cameras and please tell us: what was more exciting, watching Babe Ruth pitch the Red Sox to a 1–0 victory over the Chicago Cubs in Game 1 of the 1918 World Series . . . or watching Pedro Martinez pitch the Red Sox to a 4–1 victory over the Cardinals in Game 3 of the 2004 World Series?

Even *dead* Red Sox fans were being invited to participate in the 2004 hoo-ha. At cemeteries throughout New England, people brought pennants, caps, programs, and plastic batting helmets to leave at the graves of friends and family members who'd always dreamed of seeing the Sox win the World Series, except that, well, what are you going to do.

But baseball's great moments cannot be scripted. Either events that take place in a World Series game are going to make history or they are not going to make history. And if it *is* history—Carlton Fisk hitting the foul pole in Game 6 in 1975, or Bill Mazeroski taking the Yankees' Ralph Terry out of the yard in the bottom of the ninth inning of Game 7 of the 1960 World Series at Pittsburgh's Forbes Field—we remember it, memorize it, pass the information on to the children.

And if it's *not* history?

When was the last time you heard anybody talk about the 1983 World Series? The Orioles beat the Phillies in five. And that was pretty much that.

That's where the 2007 World Series was headed. The Red Sox were going to beat the Rockies in four . . . and to anyone outside Red Sox Nation that would be pretty much that.

But then the Rockies came to bat in the bottom of the first inning of Game 4 of the World Series, this after the Red Sox had taken a 1–0 lead. As the Rockies' Kaz Matsui stepped up to the plate, Jon Lester stood on the mound, holding a freshly rubbed baseball in his left hand, ready to make his first career postseason start.

Though the Red Sox were never so crass as to put it this way, they were playing with house money in Game 4: even if Lester struggled—and he hadn't started a game since September 26 against the Oakland A's—Josh Beckett would be on the mound in Game 5.

It will never be known if the Rockies could have solved Beckett in

Game 5, because they were unable to solve Lester in Game 4. The kid didn't mow down the Rockies with breathtaking stuff; what he did was pitch efficiently and methodically, showing a willingness to let opposing hitters put the ball in play. The first batter he faced, Matsui, hit a little pop fly right in front of the mound, and Lester gloved it himself. And then he struck out the next batter, Troy Tulowitzki.

He would pitch into the sixth inning, leaving the game after issuing a two-out walk to Garrett Atkins. Manny Delcarmen took over and struck out Ryan Spilborghs to end the inning, whereupon Lester's World Series line went into the books as: five and two-thirds innings pitched, three hits, no runs, three walks, three strikeouts.

But the Red Sox still had to win the game. Their lead was a don't-go-away 2–0, the second run coming across in the top of the fifth when Varitek singled home Lowell, who had doubled to left. They added still another run when Lowell led off the seventh with a home run off Rockies starter Aaron Cook.

And now, with Lester looking on from the dugout, a towel draped over his head, the Rockies finally got on the board in the bottom of the seventh when Brad Hawpe blasted a too-fat fastball by Delcarmen for a home run. Out came Delcarmen. In came forty-one-year-old Mike Timlin. Now, to best appreciate Timlin's World Series credentials, consider that Delcarmen, a native of Boston who grew up rooting for the Red Sox and was drafted by the team in 2000 after a stellar career at West Roxbury High School, was just twenty-five years old when he faced the Rockies in the '07 Series. Lester was twenty-three. Lester and Delcarmen came into the game with a *combined* 131 regular-season major league appearances. Timlin came into the game with 1,011 regular-season major league appearances, the tenth most in history. He also brought with him a glittering postseason résumé: he pitched on the Toronto Blue Jays' back-to-back World Series–winning teams in 1992 and '93, recording the final out of the '92 Series against the Atlanta Braves when he fielded Otis Nixon's bunt attempt and made the putout at first base. Plus, he was a member of the Red Sox' 2004 World Series team.

Lester, tall and scrawny and placid, looked like a model from an old Norman Rockwell painting, all dressed up in his Sunday best and sitting next to his dad on the running board of the family car in "Breaking Home Ties." Delcarmen looked like he could still be hanging out with his old high school buddies during Boston Park League games at Dorchester's Casey Field, which, in fact, he occasionally did on off nights during the 2007 season. But Timlin? It's not so much that Timlin looked *old* but that he looked weathered; he had the walk and the talk and the attitude that one would expect from a guy who broke into the big leagues in 1991. And so, perhaps knowing he'd have more than three months to rest his aging arm before giving it another go in spring training 2008, Timlin got all nasty with the Rockies. He struck out Matsui. He struck out Tulowitzki. On to the eighth inning.

The Red Sox needed an insurance run, and they got one from Bobby Kielty, the late-season replacement for the departed Wily Mo Pena. Pinch-hitting for Timlin in the top of the eighth, and making his first career World Series appearance, Kielty, a California native whose New England blood tie is that his grandfather had been a postal worker in Fitchburg, Massachusetts, back in the day, rifled the first pitch he saw from reliever Brian Fuentes to left field for a home run. The Red Sox now led 4–1.

It turned out to be the run that won the World Series for the Red Sox. Hideki Okajima opened the eighth inning for the Red Sox and, after getting Matt Holliday on a grounder to second, gave up a single to left by Todd Helton. Next up was Atkins, who awakened the Coors Field masses with a two-run homer, making it, again, a one-run game. When Francona came out to make a pitching change—naturally, the game's last five outs would be placed in the hands of Jonathan Papelbon—it meant that both the first and last pitches thrown by Okajima in 2007 had been hit for home runs. Six months earlier, on Opening Day in Kansas City, the first pitch to leave his fingers left the yard, powered by the Royals' John Buck.

Papelbon pitched first to Ryan Spilborghs. Grounder to short. Next up was Brad Hawpe. He flied to center. After going eighty-six years without winning a World Series, the Red Sox were now three outs away from their second championship in four seasons.

After the Red Sox went out in order in the top of the ninth, workers began the frantic transformation of the visiting clubhouse at Coors Field into the staging for a post–World Series celebration. But there were still those three outs.

Make that just *two* outs, this after Rockies catcher Yorvit Torrealba grounded out to second leading off the bottom of the ninth inning.

Jamey Carroll, a veteran all-purpose player with nine career home runs in 1,509 at-bats, was the next batter. He had entered the game in the eighth inning as a defensive replacement and now, like Kielty, would be making his first World Series at-bat.

And he damn near made history. Carroll jumped on a Papelbon fastball and hit a screaming line drive to left, the ball still climbing as it neared the left-field fence.

One inning earlier, Francona had made a defensive change of his own, one that he had made in Games 1 and 3 of the World Series and that, as such, didn't raise any eyebrows: he removed Manny Ramirez from the game, shifted Ellsbury to left field, and sent in Coco Crisp to play center. The Red Sox thus had speedy, defensively sound players in both left and center fields, with the older, slower, erratic Ramirez on the bench.

The ball Carroll hit could not have been caught by Ramirez. But Ellsbury had a chance, and he knew it. He raced toward the left-field fence, leaped into the air, and came down with the ball.

Two down.

Seth Smith, a twenty-five-year-old outfielder who had made his major league debut with the Rockies during the 2007 season, was sent up by manager Clint Hurdle to pinch-hit for reliever Manny Corpas. Smith had batted just eight times during the regular season; this would be his sixth at-bat of the postseason, his second in the World Series.

He had no chance against Papelbon. When he struck out to end it, Papelbon reacted by heaving his glove high into the air and then leaping into the waiting embrace of his catcher, Varitek, who had been in a similar position in St. Louis in 2004, only with Keith Foulke on the mound. But while it was a second World Series triumph for Varitek, the man he was hugging, Papelbon, was backing up all that smack from the Ale House in October 2004:

This guy ain't got shit on me. I can do this.

And one can only wonder if, on the night Papelbon mowed down the Rockies, some minor leaguer was kicking up some verbal dirt at the Ale House, talking *his* brand of smack about being on the mound in the World Series.

When the Red Sox won it all in 2004, it was said to be a once-in-a-lifetime experience. But when they won it again in 2007, this time with a dazzling collection of young players joining a cast of high-priced veterans, the Red Sox suddenly looked like a team capable of making yet more World Series appearances in the coming seasons. Papelbon. Ellsbury. Pedroia. Delcarmen.

And Jon Lester.

When it ended, he somehow managed to sort through the hundreds of revelers on the field and find his parents. He finally made it into the champagne-soaked bedlam of the Boston clubhouse, but not before several of his teammates had already spoken on his behalf. Schilling called Lester's performance the "gutsiest" he had ever seen. Timlin, putting a biblical spin on it, said, "This is going to sound funny, but God blessed Jon Lester when He gave him cancer. He gave him the opportunity to show everybody what you can do when you don't feel you can make it. I think it's a great opportunity he has."[6]

John W. Henry, the principal owner of the Red Sox, said, "When I think about where we were a year ago, and where *he* was, it's just amazing."[7]

The Red Sox were in disarray at the end of the 2006 season, and Lester was in the hospital. Now the Red Sox were champions, and the young lefty from a place called Puyallup, having defeated cancer, had no difficulty defeating the Rockies. The Red Sox had their storybook ending after all: even in sweeping the Rockies, they did so in a manner that made the last game memorable. For the rest of their lives, connoisseurs of baseball would remember and applaud Lester's graceful journey from diagnosis to treatment to rehabilitation to spring training to the minor leagues . . . to the clinching game of the World Series.

The Red Sox scored twenty-nine runs in the Series, the third-highest total in history for a four-game series. Bobby Kielty, whose home run proved to be the game-winner, said, "This went from one of the roughest years I've ever had to one of the greatest years I've ever had."[8] Curt Schilling, with three postseason victories in 2007, improving his

204 Wicked Good Year

postseason record to 11–2, improved his chances for the Hall of Fame. Mike Lowell, having hit .415 in the four games, was named MVP of the 2007 World Series. Terry Francona went into the books as the only manager in World Series history to win his first eight games. General manager Theo Epstein, still a couple of months from his thirty-fourth birthday, was now the architect of not one but *two* World Series championship teams.

But the real winner was Jon Lester.

"I knew with my competitiveness I'd be back pitching," he said. "I just didn't know that it would turn out this way."[9]

Andrew J. Urban II watched the Red Sox win the World Series while sipping mugs of Pepsi at Jillian's, a mega-bar and entertainment complex on Ipswich Street out behind Fenway Park.

Urban's mother and stepfather always spend the month of October at a time-share they own in Aruba, and he usually joins them. This year was different. Still looking for a new job, he couldn't justify taking a month off to sit in the sun, doing nothing. Plus, the Red Sox were in the playoffs. He had been watching the games on television, but on the night of Game 4 of the World Series, with the Red Sox on the cusp of registering a sweep of the Colorado Rockies, he didn't want to be home alone. So he took his familiar public transportation route to Fenway Park—the 70-A bus to Watertown Square, followed by a ride on the 57 bus into Kenmore Square, and a stroll over the bridge to Fenway Park. Only this time he took a left at Lansdowne Street behind the Green Monster and made his way to Jillian's.

Urban was thrilled when Papelbon fired that final World Series–clinching fastball past Seth Smith. But he didn't stay around long. Knowing that the area around Fenway Park and Kenmore Square would soon be crawling with celebratory Red Sox fans, many of them beer-drenched students from nearby Northeastern University and Boston University looking to escape the confines of their dorm rooms, Urban pulled his Red Sox cap down over his eyes and made his way to Kenmore Square in search of the 57 bus back to Watertown Square.

And it all worked out for Andrew J. Urban II: in December he landed a job at a nearby Toys 'R Us, stocking shelves on the overnight shift. It was supposed to be just for the Christmas rush, but they liked Urban and kept him on.

As had by now become a Boston tradition, a rolling rally commemorating the Red Sox' latest World Series championship was scheduled for Monday afternoon. Thousands of Red Sox fans lined the parade route to applaud the newly crowned champs, and in a way, Sox fans from a hundred years ago were also in attendance: in 2004 a popular, Boston-based rock band called the Dropkick Murphys had dusted off "Tessie," a nearly forgotten ballad from the early twentieth century that 'Nuf Ced McGreevey's Royal Rooters crooned with abandon during the inaugural 1903 World Series in which the then–Boston Americans toppled the Pittsburgh Pirates. With some new lyrics contributed by *Herald* sportswriter Jeff Horrigan, "Tessie" had become a staple of the Fenway jukebox, right up there with the ritualistic late-inning blasting of Neil Diamond's "Sweet Caroline." The old had become the new.

The 2007 rolling rally had some added twists. Sox fans were in a lather over World Series MVP Mike Lowell, whose contract was up, so naturally, "Sign Mike Lowell!" chants were heard all along the parade route. And it wouldn't have been a show without some dancing, and it was provided by Jonathan Papelbon, who was only too happy to provide several encores of his now-famous Charles Riverdance.

Red Sox pitchers Curt Schilling, Josh Beckett, and Tim Wakefield were assigned to the same Duck Boat. When they arrived, toting with them their families and a collection of friends, Schilling was the first to climb aboard. He was greeted by the driver, who threw a bear hug on the veteran pitcher and said, "Thank you for everything you've done for the Red Sox the last four years."

It was Charlie Perry, aka Admiral Amnesia.

And the Duck Boat on which Schilling, Beckett, and Wakefield rode, with Schilling's wife Shonda providing Fluffernutter sandwiches for all the kids, was none other than *Haymarket Hannah*.

Some two months earlier, Admiral Amnesia had welcomed Doc Rivers and his newly assembled Big Three of Paul Pierce, Kevin Garnett, and

Ray Allen aboard *Haymarket Hannah* and given them a taste of what a rolling rally would be like for the Celtics. Now he was taking part in the real thing with the Red Sox.

On this occasion, Admiral Amnesia did not ask the three Red Sox pitchers to say, "Quack, quack, quack!"

Instead, he yelled out, "Duck!"

"After the rolling rally was over, I was driving them back along Memorial Drive in Cambridge, and they were still standing and waving," Charlie Perry recalled. "All of a sudden we came up on this huge branch that was extending out over the street. I yelled, 'Duck!' Nobody knew that day how close I came to taking out three-fifths of the Red Sox' starting rotation."

16

REMATCH IN INDIANAPOLIS

T he weekend of October 27–28 goes into the books as one of the busiest, newsiest two days in Boston sports history. Anytime the Red Sox win the World Series is naturally going to make for a memorable, scrapbook-of-the-mind news cycle, especially when the Jon Lester, Jonathan Papelbon, and Mike Lowell plot lines are added to the mix, but the sports flashes on this particular weekend were not all about baseball. And the news was not all good.

On Saturday afternoon, October 27, as the Boston Red Sox were arriving at Coors Field for Game 3 of the World Series—this being the day Dustin Pedroia was famously dissed by a ballpark security guard— the Boston Bruins were back east, taking on the Philadelphia Flyers in a matinee at TD Banknorth Garden.

The 2007–2008 Bruins were off to an impressive start. Banished to the road for the first five games of the season because the Ringling Brothers Barnum & Bailey Circus was ensconced at the Garden, the Bruins rebounded from a 4–1 opening night loss at Dallas to win five of their next six games, including a 4–1 home victory over the Tampa Bay Lightning once the elephants and the clowns were gone and the Garden was re-fit for hockey. When the B's hosted the Flyers at the Garden on the afternoon of the twenty-seventh—some fifteen hours after the Celtics wrapped up their preseason schedule with a 114–89 victory over the Cleveland Cavaliers and one day before the Patriots hung a 52–7 beating on the Washington Redskins—they had won six of their first nine games. And with the new-look Bruins desperately trying to win back the trust of a fan base that had not experienced a Stanley Cup celebration since 1972, getting off to a fast start was a good way of getting the word out that things had changed, pucks-wise, down on Causeway Street.

With just under four minutes remaining in the first period, center Patrice Bergeron, just twenty-two years old but already in his third NHL season, skated behind the Philadelphia net in pursuit of a loose puck. As Bruins fans looked on in horror, he received a vicious hit from behind by Flyers defenseman Randy Jones and went into the glass hard, collapsing to the ice in an awkward heap. The Garden was now eerily quiet as Bergeron lay on his back, breathing heavily, his arms and legs extended as though he were a small child doing a snow angel. As medical staff took to the ice to attend to the stricken hockey player, Bruins fans in attendance and watching on television couldn't help but think of Travis Roy, a freshman hockey player at Boston University whose collegiate career lasted exactly eleven seconds. Roy, taking his first-ever shift with the Terriers in an October 20, 1995, game against the University of North Dakota, missed a check and went head-first into the boards, falling to the ground, motionless. Paralyzed from the shoulders down, Roy never played hockey again; he has gone on to a career as a motivational speaker, and a rather gifted one at that. He vows to walk again one day.

Bergeron was rushed to Massachusetts General Hospital, located barely a mile from the Garden. His parents had been in attendance for the game, and now his mother was riding in the ambulance with him, holding her son's hand.

Later in the day, following the Bruins' 2–1 loss to the Flyers, some encouraging news was announced: though Bergeron suffered a concussion and broken nose, initial X-rays and a CT scan revealed no neck or spinal cord injuries.

It would be twelve days before Bergeron spoke to the media. And it was actually his decision to do so. He had received hundreds of text messages, phone calls, and e-mails from anxious friends, and while his long-term prognosis was good, he was in no condition to sit up in his bed and get back in touch with everybody. As a native of Quebec City, Quebec, he knew, too, that the French-speaking as well as English-speaking media would be interested in news of his recovery. With the Bruins scheduled to host the Montreal Canadiens on November 8, Bergeron asked the team to arrange an afternoon media availability, during which he hoped to allay fears about the severity of the injury.

There would be no one-on-one interviews, no live television chats, no call-ins to the local radio shows. The ground rules were made clear: Bergeron, who is bilingual, would answer five minutes of questions in English, followed by five minutes of questions in French.

Locked up in an uncomfortable-looking neck brace, Bergeron took slow, measured steps when he arrived in the room, and as he lowered himself into a chair he did so with the unsteadiness of an elderly man finding a seat on a moving subway train.

What he said, and how he appeared, made for two entirely different discussions. "Obviously I would be lying if I said I look good right now," Bergeron told the gathering. But, he said, "there has been improvement from last week. I look at that as a positive and look forward to getting better."[1]

He would miss the entire season.

While the Bergeron press conference was a major news and sports event in Boston, the game in which he suffered the injury was caught up in the whirl of World Series frenzy and the Patriots' ongoing quest for an undefeated season.

Consider: Bergeron gets hit on Saturday afternoon . . . the Red Sox win Game 3 of the World Series on Saturday night . . . the Patriots roll to their stop-the-insanity 52–7 pounding of the Redskins on Sunday afternoon . . . the Red Sox complete their four-game World Series sweep of the Colorado Rockies on Sunday night.

With their easy victory over Washington, the Patriots were now 8–0—halfway to an undefeated regular season. It was also the third straight game in which they had scored forty or more points, and Brady was ripping more pages out of the NFL record book each time he walked on the field. When he threw five touchdown passes in the Pats' 48–27 victory over the Dallas Cowboys on October 14, he became the first quarterback in NFL history to have three or more TD passes in each of the first six games of the season. A week later, he threw *six* touchdown passes (five of them in the first half) in a 49–28 victory over the Miami Dolphins, giving him twenty-seven for the season—three more than he had during the entire 2006 season, pre-Moss, pre-Welker.

But the Washington game was sick. Before we get to the details, recall the weepy commentary of San Diego Chargers running back LaDainian Tomlinson after his team's 38–14 loss to the Patriots in week two: "This was a trap game for us. Everyone was calling them cheaters, and they said, 'Let's show everyone we're not cheaters.'"

Against the Redskins, the Patriots felt a need to add a couple of exclamation points to that statement.

So, *how* sick was it? It was as though the Patriots, in an attempt to make the game more interesting, tossed out the playbook and kept trying new ways to move the ball. Though Brady did throw his obligatory three touchdown passes, he twice ran the ball into the end zone, the first time he had done so in a single game. Linebacker Mike Vrabel made another visit to the offense, and, naturally, he scored another touchdown, the tenth of his career. On defense, he submitted perhaps the best game of his career: fifteen tackles (eleven of them solo) and three strip sacks that were recovered by the Patriots, one of them scooped up by linebacker Rosevelt Colvin, who ran the ball eleven yards into the end zone for his first career touchdown.

The Patriots did not let up. In the fourth quarter, leading 38–0, they went for first down on a fourth-and-1. With a 45–0 lead, and with Matt Cassel now at quarterback, they went for first down on fourth-and-2 from the Washington 37-yard line, with Cassel hitting Jabar Gaffney for a twenty-one-yard completion. Two plays later, Cassel ran the ball into the end zone for *his* first career touchdown.

After the game, Belichick was asked if it occurred to him that his team might have been piling on.

"What do you want us to do, kick a field goal?" Belichick said. "It's 38–0. It's fourth down. We're just out there playing."[2]

The Redskins' Joe Gibbs, like Belichick a man with three Super Bowl championships on his coaching résumé, did not take the bait.

"I have no problem with anything they did," he said after the game. "Nothing. No problems from me."[3]

The running-it-up story line had a short run because, from the moment the Patriots finished off the Redskins, there appeared on the horizon an exciting new story line. The Pats' next opponents were the Indianapolis Colts. Throughout the 2007 season, and increasingly so as the Patriots kept piling up the victories, fans and media talked about the November 4 Pats-Colts game, which would take place at the RCA Dome in downtown Indianapolis. It was going to be a rematch of the previous season's AFC title game, in which the Pats suffered a shocking 38–34 defeat when Peyton Manning, whose team trailed 21–3 in the first half, guided the Colts to a thrilling comeback and sent the New England front office scrambling for new talent. (Hello, Adalius Thomas, Randy Moss, Wes Welker. . . .)

But week after week, game after game, the Patriots generally refused to talk about the game, sticking with their Belichick-mandated, all-we-care-about-is-the-next-game-on-the-schedule mantra. Even Rosevelt Colvin, who grew up in Indianapolis—as a teenager, he was a popcorn vendor at Colts games and attended Broad Ripple High School, whose alumni include nighttime talk-show host David Letterman—showed little interest in talking about the Colts before it was time to do so.

Now the first eight games of the schedule were in the books. Now it was time for the Patriots to talk about the Colts. *Now.*

And what a matchup it was going to be. After beating the Pats in the '06 AFC title game and then taking out the Chicago Bears in the Super Bowl, the Colts kept right on winning: they'd be taking a 7–0 record into their November 4 date with the Pats, thus making the game part rematch, part battle of the unbeatens. As soon as the previous Sunday's games were over, the Colts-Pats matchup was already being hyped as one of the biggest regular-season games in NFL history, and not without justification: the league cracked open some dusty old stat books and discovered that this was going to be the deepest into a pro football season that two undefeated teams had met since November 13, 1921, when the Buffalo All-Americans (6–0) took on the Akron Pros (7–0) in an American Professional Football Association showdown that ended in a 0–0 tie.

Rematch. Battle of the unbeatens. And this: good versus evil. This was the third layer of hype for the game, and it was a big hit. The Colts represented Good. Their coach, Tony Dungy, was well liked by the sportswriters because he provided thoughtful answers to their questions during his daily press briefings and, when the lights went out, remained pleasant and approachable. Put another way, Tony Dungy showed that it was indeed possible to be a successful NFL coach without living up to all the old stereotypes about sideline-skulking zealots who spend twenty hours a day watching tape and the remaining four hours napping on a cot in the trainer's room.

As for Peyton Manning, he had long since been determined by Madison Avenue to be a solid-gold, take-it-to-the-bank pitchman, as evidenced by the fact that it was impossible to watch television on any given Sunday without seeing the Colts quarterback hawking everything from credit cards and cell phones to satellite television and thirst quenchers. ESPN brought in the entire Manning family to do a spot for *SportsCenter*. Viewers loved it.

The Patriots, naturally, played the role of Evil. ESPN.com's Gregg Easterbrook, who was among the multitudes who explored the good-versus-evil angle, minced no words in a piece suggesting that something more than football was on the writer's mind:

> *Argument for the New England Patriots as scoundrels in the service of that which is baleful: Dishonesty, cheating, arrogance, hubris, endless complaining even in success. The Patriots have three Super Bowl rings, but that jewelry is tarnished by their cheating scandal. They run up the score to humiliate opponents . . . thus mocking sportsmanship. Their coach snaps and snarls in public, seeming to feel contempt for the American public that has brought him wealth and celebrity. Victory seems to give Bill Belichick no joy.*[4]

And so on. The Patriots would have had to appropriate every last bulletin board from the inventory at Staples for all the material they had.

But as the buildup continued, with constant references to the 2006 AFC title game, not every member of the Patriots found it necessary to look upon that day with sadness and a wish for vengeance.

For one member of the Patriots in particular, there was some triumph to be found in that 2006 loss to the Colts.

Tedy Bruschi was never supposed to play football again. In the early hours of February 16, 2005, just ten days after the Patriots defeated the Philadelphia Eagles in Super Bowl XXXIX, and just three days after he participated in the Pro Bowl, he was awakened by a headache. He felt numbness in his left arm and leg. He was weak, unsteady on his feet.

His wife, Heidi, was now on the phone summoning an ambulance. Soon Bruschi was being transported from the couple's home south of Boston to Mass General, where an army of medical specialists began performing all kinds of tests on the six-foot-one, 247-pound linebacker, who in nine NFL seasons had played in 151 out of a possible 159 games, including four Super Bowls.

And then came the news: Tedy Bruschi, thirty-one years old at the time, had suffered a stroke.

The story of Bruschi's comeback—how he returned to the Patriots in the seventh game of the 2005 season after much soul-searching, countless consultations with doctors, and many a roundtable discussion with his family—has become the stuff of Boston sports legend. He eventually agreed to do a book about the comeback. And Bruschi minced no words: he not only described his stroke and rehabilitation in vivid detail but also discussed earlier chapters in his life, including issues with alcohol abuse during his wild days as a University of Arizona Wildcat.

"I felt like I didn't have anything to be ashamed of," Bruschi said in an interview for this book. "It was who I am. It was how I got to be who I am today. And I didn't want to write a book and have people read it and say there wasn't anything in it, that there was nothing [they] didn't already know. For them to understand why I would possibly want to come back from a stroke and play professional football, they would have to know who I am, how I was brought up, how I looked at things, how I looked at challenges in my life."

The book, *Never Give Up: My Stroke, My Recovery, and My Return to the NFL*, is indeed remarkable in its candor. It ends with the conclusion of the 2006 season, Bruschi's second season back, with the Pats losing the AFC championship game to the Indianapolis Colts at the RCA Dome.

"There are nights when I still think about it, when I can't get to sleep because I'm thinking about what could have been," he says in the book. "It's tough, but it also adds motivation for the 2007 season."[5]

It wasn't the stroke and its aftermath that introduced Bruschi to straight talk. A month before he was stricken, while doing an interview at his home with *Globe* columnist Jackie MacMullan, he started talking about his problems with alcohol. MacMullan, in fact, had no plans to bring up the topic when she arrived at the Bruschi home in suburban North Attleboro.

"We started talking about college, and I think the question might have been, 'Were you reckless in college?' or something like that," Bruschi said. "I started answering the question, and a thought just popped into my mind, and then it was, 'Let me tell you how things really were.'"

Bruschi remembered looking at his wife, who was sitting in on the interview. But instead of shooting him a honey-can-I-see-you-in-the-other-room look, Heidi remained silent.

"It wasn't like I had just quit drinking the other day," Bruschi said, recalling the interview with MacMullan. "I was comfortable with people knowing."

After MacMullan left, Tedy and Heidi stared at each other for a moment. No words were spoken. Bruschi described it as an "okay-what-are-we-eating-for-dinner kind of thing."

The point here is this: ask Bruschi the right question at the right time, and there is a chance he will provide a remarkably candid answer. Which brings us to the Patriots' loss to Indianapolis in the 2006 AFC championship game.

Was he upset the Patriots lost? Of course. But that's only from a football perspective. From the perspective of where Bruschi was in his life, it was impossible for him to be anything other than happy. Not only had he made it through the season without any health scares, he had led the team in tackles while playing with a broken wrist, an injury he suffered during training camp. In his mind, he was back—back all the way.

When he made his initial comeback in 2005, getting ten tackles in the Pats' 21–16 victory over the Buffalo Bills, his head was still filled with doubts that perhaps he was making a mistake, that maybe he should just stay home and be done with football. Those doubts remained with him throughout the 2005 season, including the Pats' 27–13 playoff loss to Denver.

"If there was a story line regarding the whole comeback that maybe people don't know about, it's that after that first season, from the Buffalo game all the way to the loss in Denver, I was going through the motions as a football player," he said. "Emotionally, I didn't know if I was all together.

"I wasn't 100 percent sure at points during that season if this was safe," he said. "Can you understand where I was, and then, to be chopped down at the knees like that? Know what I mean? To realize that, man, am I an old man? I mean, man, *am I an old man?* Is there something wrong with me? And then, to get the confidence needed to be an NFL linebacker, it was a tough process.

"I was an emotional wreck that entire season. Coming to the *end* of that season, in Denver, when we lost, that was when I had the biggest decision on my mind, [whether] I wanted to continue or not. It was, okay, now you've done it. You came back. All right. Now it's: do you want to come back and play *again?*"

A year later, when the Patriots' season ended with that loss in Indianapolis, the consolation prize for Bruschi was that he had erased the doubts.

Okay, I'm a football player again, he remembers thinking.

"The way I felt was, shit, man, you can't win 'em all, you can't win 'em all," he said. "Finally Indy beats us in the AFC championship game, and you know what? We almost won that game, and, to me, that was the Super Bowl, man. I think either team on the field at that point was going to beat Chicago.

"Football-wise, we got here, we lost, I feel terrible. But you can't win 'em all. That was Peyton's year, and I felt happy for him. That's what I told Peyton. There's a shot of me and Peyton after the game where I'm whispering something in his ear.

"I made sure I found him. I put my hand with my broken wrist and the cast and everything, I put it around the back of his head, and I held him tight, and I said, 'Man, you deserve this. Enjoy this today, now go out there and win your championship. You did a great job.'

"We had beaten up on him for his entire career. You know? And he had just beat us in the most meaningful game our teams could have played, since we can't meet in the Super Bowl.

"Leading the team in tackles with a broken wrist, yeah, at that point in my career I felt like I was back and excited to continue on to that next season."

Now, in November 2007, Bruschi was heading back to the RCA Dome. This time, he wasn't interested in silver linings.

Professional sporting events often fall woefully short of delivering on all the hype. Not so with the rematch between the undefeated Pats and the undefeated Colts. After rolling through the first eight games of the season, easily beating their opponents—and, as some saw it, humiliating said opponents by running up the score—the Patriots defeated the Indianapolis Colts the old-fashioned way: they came from behind.

With the Patriots trailing 20–10, and only 9:47 remaining in the game, the Brady-Moss tandem went to work. A short pass over the middle to Moss on second-and-10 was good for fifteen yards, and two plays later Brady looked to his left and threw a bomb that was collected by Moss for fifty-five yards. Four plays after that, Brady hit Welker in the end zone with a three-yard strike. The Pats now trailed 20–17.

Welker set up the Pats' next drive when he returned a punt twenty-three yards to the New England 49. From there, Brady needed only three plays: a five-yard pass to Moss, a thirty-three-yard pass down the left side to Donte Stallworth, and a thirteen-yard pass to Kevin Faulk.

The Colts got the ball back with 3:15 remaining, but the drive came to a screeching stop when Manning was sacked from behind by the Patriots' Jarvis Green. The ball popped loose and into the waiting arms of former RCA Dome popcorn vendor Rosevelt Colvin, clinching the Patriots' 24–20 victory.

"It was probably the first game all year that we really had to play the entire game," Colvin told the *Herald*. "You've got to credit the Colts for that. They're a good football team. For the guys to continue to make plays in the situation we were in builds character, and the next time we're in that situation, it will be a little easier."[6]

The win kept the Patriots undefeated, sure. But it also was the first time the Brady-to-Moss tandem had been put to the test in a tight, come-from-behind situation, and the results were spectacular. Brady's numbers were garden variety—21-for-32 for 255 yards, with three touchdowns and two interceptions—but Moss was up to the challenge, catching nine passes for 145 yards and a touchdown. It was his twelfth of the season, tying him with Stanley Morgan, who caught twelve touchdown passes for the Pats in 1979, for the franchise record.

It was the ninth game of the season. And the man's *artistry* was on display too: he made one of his patented leaping, breathtaking, jaw-dropping, one-handed catches, this one in the third quarter for a seventeen-yard gain.

"He's a beast," said Donte Stallworth. "That was insane."[7]

What a difference from the last time the Patriots had been in this building.

And, yes, what a difference for Tedy Bruschi.

"Some victories *do* feel better than others," he said that day. "This was one of those that you'll remember."[8]

The Pats enjoyed a bye week following their victory over the Colts, and then returned to the rock pile and submitted their biggest offensive output of the season: a 56–10 victory over the Buffalo Bills at Ralph Wilson Stadium. Once again, Moss was a beast . . . insane . . . spectacular: ten catches for 128 yards and four touchdowns, all of them in the first half. He was now the owner of the Pats' single-season record for touchdown receptions, and with six games still on the schedule. Brady, playing just three quarters, was 31-of-39 for 373 yards and *five* touchdowns, giving him thirty-eight for the season.

The Pats' next three games provided some splendid examples of the lunacy of betting on professional football. They *should* have easily defeated the so-so Philadelphia Eagles and the going-nowhere Baltimore Ravens, and they *should* have had a relatively close game with the perennially tough Pittsburgh Steelers.

Instead, they were lucky to escape with victories over the Eagles and Ravens. And though their game with the Steelers was tight well into the third quarter, it ended with a 34–13 New England victory.

They trailed the Eagles 28–24 in the fourth quarter of their November 25 showdown, but Laurence Maroney scored a four-yard touchdown with 7:20 remaining. Even then, the Pats needed an Asante Samuel interception in the end zone with eighteen seconds remaining to seal the victory. Samuel had thus finished what he began: on the third play of the game, he had intercepted a pass from Eagles quarterback A. J. Feeley and ran it back forty yards for a touchdown.

The victory was not without a price: Rosevelt Colvin suffered a foot injury during the game. Two days later, he was placed on injured reserve, the NFL's way of saying he was out for the year.

The Patriots should have lost the Baltimore game. Trailing 24–20 with 1:48 remaining, the Pats appeared done when Brady was stuffed on fourth-and-1 at the Baltimore 30 . . . except that, just before the play, Ravens defensive coordinator Rex Ryan called for a time-out. The play was run again, with Heath Evans stopped short of the first down, except this time the Patriots' Russ Hochstein was penalized for a false start before the play. The Patriots now had a *third* chance, this time on fourth-and-5, and Brady ran the ball twelve yards for a first down. He finally tossed an eight-yard pass to Jabar Gaffney with forty-four seconds remaining, and now the Ravens got the ball back trailing 27–24. One more bit of drama remained: Ravens quarterback Kyle Boller threw a fifty-two-yard Hail Mary to Mark Clayton, but the Baltimore wideout was dragged down at the 3-yard line as time ran out. The Patriots were now the sixth team in league history to start a season 12–0.

The Patriots' 34–13 victory over the Steelers was a Brady-Moss special. Was it ever. Brady: 32-for-46 for 399 yards and four touchdowns. Moss: seven catches for 135 yards and two touchdowns. He now had nineteen touchdowns on the season, three shy of the league record set by Jerry Rice in 1987.

In the third quarter, the Patriots leading 17–13, Brady took the snap on first-and-10 from his own 44, looked to his right, and tossed what at first glance was a screen pass to Moss. It was actually a lateral, with

Moss scooping the ball up, turning, and then throwing it back to Brady. The rest was easy: Brady tossed the ball to a wide-open Gaffney for a fifty-six-yard touchdown completion.

It was but one play in the late stages of a sixteen-game season, yet it remains important on many levels. One of them being this: in any discussion about Bill Belichick being robotic and joyless, it should be noted that the Brady-to-Moss-to-Brady-to-Gaffney play brings out the high school sophomore in the New England coach.

Speaking about that play nearly two years later, Belichick said, "If there's one play that sums up the entire season, it would be the double pass. We practiced that play going one way, and then we changed it, and then we flipped it back to the way we ended up running it, with Moss on the right, throwing it back to Brady on the left. We probably ran that play I would say twenty times in practice over a period of a couple of weeks. It took us a while to get it right, and then when we ran it in the game it was pretty well executed. It wasn't just something that happened. It was something that the players worked on to make it happen, and then at the critical time when we called it, *the one time of the year for one play,* they hit it pretty good."

So now the Patriots had another date with the Jets, this one at Gillette Stadium on December 16. Given the fallout over Spygate, and with the 13–0 Patriots still being branded by some as no more than a talented collection of cheaters, it was clear that the good old days of the Border War had returned. Pats fans were determined to make sure Jets coach Eric Mangini knew exactly what they thought of him. The Nantucket Gals, during the ride from Hyannis to the Café Dolce, from the Café Dolce to Primo's, from Primo's to the Gillette Stadium parking lot, talked more about Mangini than they did about the Patriots—the first time they could remember investing so much time and discussion to the opposition. As far as they were concerned, "In Bill We Trust" now had a flip side to it: "In Mangini We See a Snake."

Dubbing the game the "Spy Bowl," Gary Myers of the *New York Daily News* wrote that Mangini is "a hated figure in New England, perceived as a snitch and traitor." Because of this, "the Patriots don't want to win today by 40. They want to win by 80."[9]

They had to settle for winning by ten. On a freezing, windy, rainy day at Gillette Stadium—conditions often said to favor the underdog—the Patriots came out of the cold with a 20–10 victory. They scored only one offensive touchdown, Maroney going in from one yard out late in the first half after Kelley Washington blocked a punt by the Jets' Ben Graham to give New England a first down at the New York 8-yard line. On a day not suitable for the Brady aerial game—the quarterback was 14-for-27 for 140 yards and for the first time all season did not throw a touchdown pass—Maroney had career highs in carries (26) and yards (104).

The game-after-the-game was at midfield, as Belichick and Mangini moved toward each other for the Handshake. But this little football tradition had long since stopped being a barometer of the animosity between the two men; they politely shook hands, with Belichick throwing in a "Great game . . . awesome."[10]

The Patriots' next opponents, in their final home game of the regular season, were the 1–13 Miami Dolphins. Even when one takes into account that these Dolphins were out to prevent the Patriots from wiping the undefeated '72 Dolphins out of the history books, it was a game with about as much drama and suspense as a schoolboy scrimmage. The Patriots were too good. The Dolphins were, well, too bad: they came out of it with a 28–7 loss that could have been much worse. Whatever critics may have thought about the Patriots running it up in previous games, this time the Pats took a 28–0 lead at halftime and coasted.

With three more touchdown passes, Brady was now one shy of Peyton Manning's single-season record of forty-nine. Moss had two more touchdown receptions, leaving *him* one shy of Jerry Rice's single-season record of twenty-two.

And the Patriots, at 15–0, were one win away from an undefeated regular season.

17

PURSUING BANNER 17

An official National Basketball Association backboard measures six feet across and three and a half feet vertically, and is transparent, thus enabling fans behind the net to see if a shot is going around the rim and in . . . or not. At the lower left-hand corner of each backboard is affixed the NBA logo, showing a red-and-blue background framing a silhouette figure in white, deftly moving with the basketball in his left hand.

As all basketball purists know, the silhouette figure in the NBA logo was modeled after Jerry West, the Hall of Fame guard who played his entire fourteen-year career with the Los Angeles Lakers. If a player takes a particularly bad shot, completely missing the rim and clanging the ball off the backboard—the equivalent of a shortstop throwing the ball into the first-base dugout—it's not uncommon for some wiseass to remark that said shot "almost took Jerry West's head off."

And after all the press conferences, after all the hoopla, after all the Big Three photo ops, after all the sportswriters had dutifully revisited their preseason prognostications, this is precisely what happened: taking his first shot in a regular-season game as a member of the rebuilt, reborn, we-are-no-longer-to-be-trifled-with Boston Celtics, Kevin Garnett almost took Jerry West's head off.

It was opening night at the Garden, November 2, 2007, the Washington Wizards providing the opposition. The crowd roared when Garnett launched his first shot as a Celtic, and then the crowd gasped when it smacked loudly off the glass backboard, bruising Mr. West. Here's your new Big Three, Celtics fans: not only did Garnett miss his first shot of the season, but so, too, did Allen and Pierce.

But it was opening night jitters, nothing more. By the time this festive and at times emotional evening was over, the Celtics had themselves a 103–83 victory over the Wizards, sending everyone home happy. And the Big Three was, well, big: Garnett, overcoming the shot he had clanged off the backboard, had twenty-two points, twenty rebounds, and five assists. Pierce, no longer the only star on his team, had a game-high twenty-eight points. And Ray Allen contributed seventeen points.

It was Pierce who summed up the evening with a nod to the accomplishments of the Red Sox and Patriots, saying, "As professional athletes, I think we respect the other sports also. I'm a fan of the Red Sox. I'm also a fan of the Patriots. But we got our own mark to make. Those guys have made their own mark. They've won championships."[1]

If Doc Rivers was privately nudging his players toward a connection with the Red Sox and Patriots through his pre–training camp ride on the Duck Boats, now Paul Pierce was standing before the world and announcing that, yes, absolutely, the Celtics were out to do what the Sox and Pats had done, which was bring championships to Boston.

But in no way was opening night an homage to the Sox and Pats, even if the crowd included Jacoby Ellsbury, Tim Wakefield, and Boston native Manny Delcarmen of the Red Sox and Jarvis Green and Laurence Maroney of the Patriots. In terms of tradition, remember, the Celtics have won more championships than the Red Sox, Patriots, and Bruins *combined*, and so opening night was designed to remind everyone what this basketball team has contributed to Boston sports history over the years.

Red Auerbach had died a little more than a year earlier, just three days before the start of the 2006–2007 season. Now, before this new season began, the Celtics wanted not only to honor their patriarch but also to incorporate his memory into the hoped-for drama that was to unfold. They did so during a pregame ceremony in which the famous surface on which the Celtics play was renamed the Red Auerbach Parquet, with the honoree's signature burned into the floor. Rivers, speaking with reporters in a hallway outside the locker room before the ceremony, said, "Anytime you're part of anything involved with Red, it's special." If it hadn't been for Auerbach, he noted, "they wouldn't be talking about bringing things back to the glory days."[2]

It was a wonderful gesture, and well timed. Auerbach, who devoted fifty-seven years to the Celtics as coach, general manager, and president, had been instrumental in every one of the team's sixteen championships. And here now was a new edition of the Celtics hoping to do what Auerbach had done so often: win it all.

True, Auerbach would have privately chuckled at how corporate the modern-day Celtics had become. Danny Ainge now had four full-time assistants, and Doc Rivers had five. Standing at the ready behind the bench were a trainer, a physical therapist, a massage therapist, and a strength and conditioning coach. When Auerbach was coach *and* general manager, his only assistants were his secretary, the tireless Mary Faherty; a jack-of-all-trades PR man named Howie McHugh; and McHugh's cat, No-Cut, who roamed the Celtics' offices with a grand smugness. The all-purpose trainer was Buddy LeRoux, who performed a similar role for the Red Sox.*

Part of Auerbach's genius lay in his ability to make others believe they had pulled one over on him. It was a practice that extended to all aspects of his life. Glenn Ordway, a member of the Celtics' radio broadcast team throughout the '80s, likes to tell the story about how he and others in the organization would pilfer cigars that were kept in a box placed conveniently on Auerbach's desk. Years later, Ordway said, Auerbach confided to friends that he'd purposely place his old, stale cigars in the box, knowing they'd be swiped. That way, went Auerbach's reasoning, these same people wouldn't feel a need to ask him for the primo cigars he kept hidden away in the drawer.

Auerbach may have been years ahead of his competitors when it came to assembling a roster, but he remained, to the end, an old-school old soul. With Auerbach, it was all about the basketball; in his day, fans

---

* LeRoux, who dabbled in real estate and other side ventures, emerged as a part owner of the Red Sox in 1978.

came to the original Boston Garden to watch Russell and the Cooz, Havlicek and the Jones boys. During time-outs, venerable Garden organist John Kiley would bang out such show tunes as "Everything's Coming Up Roses" and "Cabaret." Fans requiring additional entertainment were best served by trekking a few miles away to the Colonial Theater or, before it was steamrolled to make way for Government Center, to Scollay Square to catch the burlesque shows.

By the twenty-first century, the Celtics, like all NBA teams, had turned in-game presentation into a cross between a Fourth of July fireworks extravaganza and the Ringling Brothers Barnum & Bailey Circus. The Celtics employed a mascot, Lucky, who was decked out like a leprechaun as he performed a variety of gymnastics stunts during stoppages in play. Garden cameras would zoom in on unsuspecting fans and then match them up with pictures of look-alike celebrities, the results being shown, to great amusement, on the JumboTron high above center court.

Another gimmick, one that began to attain an almost cultlike following, was the nightly playing of a video from a 1977 *American Bandstand* program in which a collection of young people were shown dancing to the Bee Gees' classic "You Should Be Dancing." The video became yet another modern-day equivalent to Red Auerbach lighting up his cigar: it was only played when victory for the Celtics was at hand. Fans would watch and wait for the video to show a dancing, bearded young man sporting brown bell-bottoms and a skintight T-shirt with the word GINO emblazoned across his chest, at which time the Garden would roar. Ginomania was born.

The new-look Celtics also had . . . cheerleaders. They had actually debuted a year earlier and were billed as the Celtics Dancers, with thirty-two-year-old Marina Ortega, imported from Los Angeles, as director. She had previously led similar groups in the employ of the Los Angeles Lakers, the San Francisco 49ers, the Indiana Pacers, and the Tampa Bay Buccaneers; now, with a new season beginning, she spruced up the second edition of the Celtics Dancers, twenty-one of them in all, with new hairstyles from a local salon.

Red Auerbach, who died just days before the 2006 debut of the Celtics Dancers, was said to have been famously opposed to cheerleaders strutting their stuff during NBA games. "I was going to win him over," said Ortega, who never got a chance to meet Auerbach. "I had done a lot of reading about him. And I was going to say to him, 'Mr. Auerbach, I know that you're a very competitive person, and that you did everything you could to make your team the best in the NBA. And I want you to know that I am also a very competitive person, and I'm going to do everything I can to make the team the best in the NBA.'"

But Wyc Grousbeck offers a twist on the widely held belief that Auerbach went to his grave hating the idea of cheerleaders dancing on his parquet. Out of respect, the new owners of the Celtics ran most issues past the team's president emeritus; when they told him about the cheerleaders, Auerbach replied, "I'd prefer if we didn't have them."

"I know," said Grousbeck.

"But tell me this," said Auerbach. "Can you make money off them?"

"Yes, there are sponsors, and we can make money off them."

"Good, you gotta do it."

Looking back on the conversation, says Grousbeck, "Red was all about paying the bills, and everyone knows how he scrambled over the years to pay the bills. So he was fine with the cheerleaders, just for the record, but reluctantly."

And so went opening night for the 2007–2008 Celtics—new do's for the Celtics Dancers . . . Lucky the Leprechaun leaping off a trampoline and slam-dunking undersized basketballs . . . a dedication of the parquet in memory of Red . . . members of the Red Sox and Patriots shouting their approval . . . a victory cigar in the form of the bearded fellow in the Gino T-shirt . . . and, best of all, a smashing debut of the new Big Three.

"Obviously we've raised the hopes, not only for us, but for the fans," Doc Rivers told reporters after the game. "Last year, I think there was really a nice love affair with our players and the fans, and they were looking forward to the future. Now, they're looking at the now. Hope is a great thing."[3]

The next day the Celtics traveled to Toronto for a Sunday afternoon game against the Raptors.

At 4:00 AM, Rivers's phone rang.

"It's Gar," said the voice at the other end of the line. And Rivers began crying. Without his brother saying so much as a word, Rivers knew that his father, Grady Alexander Rivers, had died.

"People who travel for a living will understand this," Rivers would later say. "And it's something that will haunt me forever. I was going to go home the week before. I went home once when he was out of the hospital. Then he went back in. . . . We had a stretch coming up where I could sneak home for a day. But I said no, I'm just going to stay here, I can go home next week. And my brother, my mom, and the rest of the family got to see him before he passed. And I didn't. And that really bothers me. For the rest of them, who got a chance to talk to him, they got a chance to say what they needed to say."

Later that morning, Rivers gathered his assistant coaches and told them he was going home to Chicago for his father's funeral. He gave the offensive sheet to Armond Hill, the defensive sheet to Tom Thibodeau. And then he delivered the news to his players; he closed by saying, "Don't take your family and your friends for granted."

A couple of days later, following his father's funeral, Rivers's mother, Bettye, asked him, "What time are you going to leave for the game?"

"I'm not going to the game," he said. "I'm going to stay here."

"You're absolutely going," she said. "You think your dad would want you sitting around here eating food? That's exactly what he didn't stand for. You're supposed to be doing your job."

Grady Rivers had been more than a father to young Glenn Rivers. He was also one of his first coaches—in baseball. But while Rivers's heart—and athletic skills—directed him to basketball, his coaching skills came from the baseball diamond, from his father.

Rivers's mother had struck a chord with the comment about how his father would not want him sitting around. "Moms, they really do know best," he would later say. "She knew I needed to be around the team."

Jimmy Haber, an old friend of Rivers's, had chartered a plane to attend the funeral, and he would be flying back to New Jersey, and it so happened that the Celtics were scheduled to be playing the New Jersey Nets on that November 10 evening at the Meadowlands. Rivers hitched a ride on the flight to Jersey and then hired a Town Car to take him to his team, arriving one hour and fifteen minutes before game-time.

"I don't know if I can do this," he told his coaches. Yet he did.

Between the day his father died and the day of the funeral, Rivers had managed to return to Boston to coach the Celtics to easy victories over Denver and Atlanta. Counting a 98–95 overtime victory in the Toronto game, with Ray Allen scoring thirty-three points—including a three-pointer with three seconds remaining in overtime to break a tie—the Celtics were 4–0 on the young season.

Make it 5–0: the Celtics topped the Nets 112–101. While the Big Three combined for seventy-three points, the Celtics also displayed some depth, what with Eddie House scoring thirteen points and Big Baby Davis contributing six points and eight rebounds in just seventeen minutes, this at a time when the game was still close.

"Long day for me," Rivers told reporters after the game. "I needed this probably more than anybody."[4]

Donnie Wahlberg might never have returned to active, being-there status as a Celtics fan were it not for his fast friend Mike Rotondi, the well-heeled season-ticket-holder who picked him up at his mother's house that night in 2003 and reacquainted him with the parquet.

And Mike Rotondi might never have been in a position to swing those expensive, coveted courtside seats at the Garden had not a Boston-area wholesale lock company gone out of business in 1970.

Rotondi, like Wahlberg and like Marty Joyce, came from modest circumstances. His father, Tony Rotondi, was a product of the Depression who spent most of his early years bouncing around from job to job, usually in the hardware business, but always with the hope that one day he'd be able to open a store of his own. His dream was realized in the late '50s when he scraped together enough money to buy Boyle & Chase Inc., a paint and wallpaper store at 1281 Hyde Park Avenue in Boston's Hyde Park section.

Tony had found his calling: he was his own boss, and he was a local businessman, even if the business happened to be tiny and out of the way. And it turned out that Mike Rotondi, too, loved the business. When he graduated from high school in 1964, he went directly to his father and said he wanted to work not for him but *with* him.

It was impossible for customers not to like Mike Rotondi. For what he may have lacked in academic credentials he made up for with the gifts of soft eyes, a warm smile, and a smooth, calming voice. Behind all that was a man with an engaging personality and a ready wit; even when he punctuated his prose with cuss words, which was often, it all seemed okay coming out of the mouth of Mike Rotondi. People liked him. Put the entire package together, and he had attributes that came in handy when working behind the counter at a father-and-son hardware store.

But as much as Rotondi enjoyed retail, Boyle & Chase wasn't exactly establishing a new business plan in the neighborhood hardware game. By early 1970, Rotondi, six years out of high school, was bored helping to run a business whose stock consisted mainly of paint and wallpaper, with a small inventory of tools, nails, locks, and other items on the side.

On a winter Saturday in 1970, everything changed. It was cold that day, and snowing, not very inviting for folks to step out and buy wallpaper. Rotondi father and Rotondi son opened the store at seventy-thirty in the morning, and by three in the afternoon they had done about $45 in retail business.

And then a man named William R. McMenimon entered the store. A World War II veteran who had served as a tank commander in the Philippines, McMenimon had settled into life as a locksmith and, on the side, seeking a diversion, he used the GI Bill to take flying lessons. He was now calling himself the Flying Locksmith.

On this day, however, the Flying Locksmith was grounded. A local wholesale lock supplier had just gone out of business, which was bad news if you were a locksmith with a whole lot of appointments on your schedule, snow or no snow.

"I saw in the yellow pages that you have an ad," the Flying Locksmith told the Rotondi men. "And I need some locks."

It was true that Boyle & Chase had an ad in the local yellow pages. But as Rotondi recalled, "You could have covered that ad with a dime."

The Flying Locksmith not only needed locks, he needed them on the fly. Specifically, he needed the A51PD Plymouth, manufactured by Schlage. He had seen the dime-size ad, and here he was, coming out of the snow and into the sparseness of Boyle & Chase.

"Yes, I have that lock," said Rotondi.

"I'll take a case of them," the Flying Locksmith said.

"A case?" asked Rotondi. "I don't even know what to charge you for a case. I don't know what kind of discount you're supposed to get for an order that big."

The Flying Locksmith placed $240 in cash on the table and asked if that would be enough.

"Deal," said Rotondi, who quickly did some ciphering in his head and came up with the following: from seven-thirty in the morning until three in the afternoon, he and his father had done $45 in retail. From 3:00 PM to 3:05 PM, they had done $240 in wholesale.

At 3:06 PM, the Rotondi family was in the lock business.

"We began with a question: could we in a million years fill the void in the lock business?" Rotondi recalled. Father and son each came up with $5,000—which was pretty much all they had—to get the business running. They kept the name Boyle & Chase. The first year, working 365 days, they grossed $50,000. The next year $100,000.

"If someone called and needed ten locks, I'd get in the car and drive over there and bring them there myself," Rotondi recalled. "We tried to dazzle them with service. Hell, I didn't have anything else to do all day. I had nothing to lose at that point in my life. I went out on the road, and I got a customer here, a customer there, and then this customer recommended me to that customer, and that's how it all started."

Boyle & Chase, which now sells everything from door closers and exit devices to security systems and decorative hardware, has since relocated south of Boston to the town of Hingham, where Mike Rotondi and his wife, Trish, have a home.

It was the late '70s, and business was booming. And Rotondi, seeking diversions of his own but apparently having no interest in becoming the Flying Lock Wholesaler, began going to Celtics games—and at a time when the team wasn't particularly popular. He bought some season tickets, and he occasionally landed courtside seats the old-fashioned, hardscrabble way: he'd just wander down to the floor and grab whatever was available. It was the nonbasketball equivalent of no harm, no foul, and Rotondi didn't have a problem with it.

As his business was expanding—by now he had more than eighty employees—Rotondi decided it was time to expand his interest in the Celtics. He wanted his own courtside seats. Once again, the timing could not have been better: he made his commitment at precisely the same time Larry Bird was breaking in with the Celtics.

One day Rotondi picked up the paper and read the news that a local gangster had run into some bad luck: the FBI had raided his house. The gangster went on the lam, leaving behind, among other possessions, his four courtside seats at the Garden.

Before long, Rotondi got a call from the Celtics' ticket office: they wanted to know whether he was interested in four on the floor.

"You bet your ass I am," he said.

Rotondi settled in nicely as a courtside swell. Television footage from the Bird-McHale-Parish era shows occasional glimpses of him seated courtside. He even had a chance encounter with Donnie Wahlberg years before they became friends. Invited to a Celtics game at the height of his New Kids on the Block fame and seated courtside next to Rotondi and his wife, the teen heartthrob said, "Hey, mister, I'll give you anything in the world for these tickets. I'll sing at your kid's party."

Rotondi's first encounter with Marty Joyce wasn't so pleasant. A pecking order had been in place where courtside seats were involved, the understanding being that anytime a subscriber dropped out an opportunity presented itself for others to move closer to center court. This practice became particularly prevalent when the Celtics moved from the old Garden into what was then called the FleetCenter, with tickets doubling in price from $125 to $250 per game. Rotondi moved up four seats. When the cost went to $500 a ticket, Rotondi moved up again, this time to seats 5, 6, 7, and 8.

At the beginning of the 2002–2003 season, with courtside tickets now going for $1,000 a pop, Rotondi was surprised to see strangers at seats 3 and 4. He didn't much like these people: they were loud and arrogant, he thought, and spent too much time talking on their cell phones and not enough time watching the game.

"They were assholes," Rotondi said.

The next game, different people showed up . . . but the same *kind* of people. Loud, arrogant, disrespectful.

"That's why I never put my tickets up for sale to strangers," Rotondi said. "If I can't go to a game, I make sure they go to people I know."

Game three: *nobody* showed up.

"That drove me out of my fucking mind," Rotondi said.

Game four: not so bad.

Game five: "Probably the worst yet," Rotondi said. "I almost got into a fight with them, telling them to sit down."

When Rotondi showed up for the sixth game, he looked to seats 3 and 4 and spotted a man and a woman. As Rotondi was settling in, the man bounced out of his chair, extended a hand, and said, "Hi, I'm Marty Joyce."

When the game started, Joyce said, "Tell me if I jump in front of you or anything."

"Don't worry, I will," Rotondi harrumphed.

During a time-out, Rotondi leaned over to Joyce and said, "You seem to be a pretty nice guy, as opposed to the assholes who were here for the other games. Whose seats are these?"

"They're mine," Joyce said.

Rotondi, incredulous, said, "Where the fuck did you get these? You've never been in the front row before."

And Joyce told him how he had owned season tickets for several years, how he had been bouncing all over the building, and how, as the Celtics were in the last year of the ownership of Paul Gaston, with old employees stepping out, new ones coming in, he happened to know one of the employees who was stepping out. And who, on the way out the door, set up Joyce with choice courtside seats. Stockbroker Joyce had been using the tickets from the earlier games as perks for clients. Now he was here for himself, enjoying his new seats, and . . .

"Why, does it bother you?" Joyce said.

"Yeah, you're fucking right it bothers me," Rotondi said. "It's wrong."

Nothing was said between Rotondi and Joyce for the remainder of the game. Come the next game, Rotondi could tell that Joyce was reaching out to him, trying to make peace.

For some reason Rotondi liked the guy. He also knew nothing was going to change. Marty Joyce was now the owner of seats 3 and 4, and that was that.

"I'm going to make a deal with you," Rotondi said. "If you use the tickets, that's fine. But if you put one more set of assholes in here, I'm going to the front office. End of conversation."

"Agreed," said Joyce, and they shook hands.

Actually, it was just the beginning of the conversation. They made small talk. Turns out they both grew up in Hyde Park. Turns out they both graduated from Catholic Memorial.

Joyce kept his word: never again did he give his floor seats to assholes.

"We became best friends," said Rotondi. "He's the funniest bastard in the world, and I love him with all my heart."

And it didn't bother Rotondi that Marty Joyce became the loudest, most over-the-top fan at TD Banknorth Garden, treating members of the Celtics as though they were old buddies from Catholic Memorial, berating officials, taunting opponents.

"Well, there's that," says Rotondi. "But he's a real Celtics fan. He's not there to be seen. He's there to watch the game. That's the difference."

The Celtics suffered their first loss of the 2007–2008 season on November 18. They fell behind by twenty points against the Orlando Magic at Amway Arena, and though they clawed back to a fourth-quarter lead on consecutive three-pointers by James Posey and House, they were unable to continue the pace. Magic 104, Celtics 102.

"We're not perfect," explained Garnett. "We didn't think we were going to go 82–0. But we are a team of character. We do play hard. We do play together—just not perfect."[5]

They won their next three games, including a 107–94 victory over the Lakers at TD Banknorth Garden on November 23 that was looked upon by nostalgic Celtics fans as a preview of the NBA Finals, complete with those wonderful old "Beat L.A.!" chants. Lakers superstar Kobe Bryant did a better job summing up the Celtics than any of the sportswriters in attendance when he quipped, "Since I've been in the league, they've sucked. Now they're kicking our butts."[6]

But now came some additional early-season tests. The first test: could the Celtics find a way to win on nights when they simply didn't have it? The test took place in Charlotte, North Carolina, against the Bobcats, who were playing without top scorer Gerald Wallace. The Celtics were sluggish all night—particularly Ray Allen, who had missed eleven of his fourteen previous shots as the game clock ticked down to 4.7 seconds remaining. With Boston trailing by two points, Eddie House tipped a pass by the Bobcats' Jason Richardson, and Pierce grabbed the loose ball and fed it to Allen at the top of the key. Cold all night, now he was on fire, hitting a three-pointer at the buzzer to give the Celtics a 96–95 victory.

And there were tests that, like the Celtics' victory over the Lakers, were against teams that loomed as possible playoff opponents. On November 27, the Celtics traveled to Cleveland for their first meeting of the season with the Cavaliers, whose top player, LeBron James, had a nickname—King James—that was so much more than just good marketing. Still a month away from his twenty-third birthday, the Akron, Ohio, native was already in his fifth NBA season; a phenomenally gifted basketball player, James had the look and the mannerisms of an old soul, a throwback to another time. To see him sitting regally at his locker after games, his feet dropped into a bucket of water, suggested a man who'd been in the league for fifteen seasons. On top of that, James was a polished and interesting postgame speaker, having learned to deal with media hordes during his days as a burgeoning superstar at St. Vincent–St. Mary High School in Akron.

He was, in short, a present-tense legend. And the present-tense legend played up to his reputation on this night against the Celtics, scoring thirty-eight points, eleven of them in overtime, as the Cavaliers emerged with a 109–104 victory. The Cavs showed a Big Three of their own, what with Drew Gooden scoring what for him was a season-high twenty-four points and seven-foot-three Lithuanian center Zydrunas Ilgauskas adding fifteen points. But the Celtics helped make things easy for the Cavs with a litany of mistakes, including two missed free throws by the usually reliable Ray Allen when the game was tied 92–92 late in the fourth quarter. "The Celtics sweat just like everyone else," the *Herald*'s Mark Murphy observed. "They are just as prone to throwing the ball away, missing crunch-time free throws and leaving the wrong shooter open."[7]

The Celtics bounced back with a nationally televised 104–59 trouncing of the New York Knicks, the beginning of a nine-game winning streak that included an 80–70 victory over the Cavaliers in a rematch at TD Banknorth Garden. Since King James was out with a sprained finger, the game did not qualify as a test.

But a test *did* await the Celtics on December 19 when the Detroit Pistons pulled into Boston. One of the best teams in the NBA, the Pistons were 18–6 when they arrived at the Garden. They were also one of the best-*known* teams in the league, led by veteran point guard Chauncey Billups, a onetime Celtics draft pick traded away in haste by then-coach Rick Pitino in 1997. The buildup for this game was huge, and the Celtics seemed to have everything going for them—they were undefeated at home, and Ray Allen was back in the lineup after missing two games with an ankle sprain. But the buildup also included this harmless but foreshadowing comment from Allen: "We have to be even more attentive to small little details."[8]

And that's precisely what doomed the Celtics in this particular test: not paying attention to small little details.

In the game's final seconds, the score tied 85–85, Paul Pierce failed to connect on a shot from the left baseline, and the Pistons' Rasheed Wallace pulled down the rebound. The Pistons called a time-out with 1.7 seconds remaining.

Rivers gathered his players and made an emphatic point, over and over. "Chauncey Billups pump-fakes! Chauncey Billups pump-fakes!" he said, and then the time-out ended and the game resumed. The Pistons delivered the ball to Billups. He pumped. He faked. And he drew a foul on the Celtics' Tony Allen with one-tenth of a second remaining. Billups went to the foul line and made both free throws, and the Pistons departed the Garden with an 87–85 victory.

The Celtics had lost at home for the first time all season. Rivers, meeting with reporters, repeated the warning he had given to his players. *Chauncey Billups pump-fakes! Chauncey Billups pump fakes!* He noted that he liked the way the Celtics had played in the first half, but quickly added, "I wasn't real happy with our execution in the second half at all."[9]

The Celtics were hardly derailed. They staged a nine-game winning streak, culminating with a 92–85 victory over the Pistons in early January at Auburn Hills, Michigan, in which Big Baby Davis came off the bench and led the Celtics with twenty points, sixteen of them in the fourth quarter. It was the first game of the season in which Pierce, Allen, or Garnett did not lead the Celts in scoring. Doc Rivers, mindful of the Celtics' loss to the Pistons a couple of weeks earlier in Boston, said, "Our players needed this. We needed to return the favor."[10]

The nine-game winning streak was impressive in other ways. It included a western trip in which the Celtics won games against Sacramento, Seattle, Utah, and the Los Angeles Lakers; the victory over the Sonics was their twenty-fourth of the young season—matching their win total for the entire 2006–2007 campaign.

"It's a great feeling to be on the other end of the spectrum like that," said Allen, who was making a triumphant return to Seattle, where he'd played five seasons before being traded to Boston. "Everyone in this locker room has been on the opposite side."[11]

18

16–0 . . . AND BEYOND

Long before there was any serious talk about the Patriots going undefeated in the regular season, the Nantucket Gals had already looked ahead to the last game on the 2007 schedule, and for reasons that had nothing to do with the possible history-making ramifications.

The Patriots would be closing out the season where they began, at Giants Stadium. Only, instead of game sixteen being yet another round of the Pats-versus-Jets Border War, with more point-counterpoint about handshakes, hidden cameras, and the wrath of Roger Goodell, this time the Patriots' opponent would be the team for whom Giants Stadium was built in the first place.

And so, as the 2007 New England Patriots cruised through the season, moving ever closer to what the Miami Dolphins had accomplished in 1972, the Nantucket Gals started talking about the final game on the schedule, and how it would bring them into conflict with their late father, old Matt Jaeckle, whose passion was the New York football Giants.

Not a problem, they all said. They had long since made their peace with Matt, even if, now, the Gals began to make wisecracks that it would be just like their father to put some kind of hex on the Patriots.

"It's not that he hated the Patriots," said Joan Fisher. "It's just that he loved the Giants so much."

The game was played on Saturday night, December 29, and was the first in league history to be televised simultaneously on three networks—NBC, CBS, and the ambitious, still-unsteady-on-its-feet NFL Network. It was that rare sporting event that had moved far beyond the interests of mere fans, hard-core or otherwise; it had become a sort of regular-season Super Bowl, the kind of whiz-bang television extravaganza that inspires people to call the neighbors and throw a party. As far away as Buenos Aires, Argentina, an American sports bar called Shoeless Joe's Alamo picked up the game on satellite and charged patrons a cover to come inside. The place was packed, with Argentines and American tourists alike standing elbow to elbow for a chance to witness history.

A victory by the Patriots would elevate their record to 16–0, a perch believed to be unattainable in an era of so-called parity, when it's no great shock if one of the league's lesser lights knocks off a powerhouse. Steve Sabol, president of NFL Films, told Eric McHugh of the *Patriot Ledger* of Quincy, Massachusetts, that he would absolutely be pulling for the Patriots because, he said, "when you're working as an historian and you've been following the game for 45 years and you have a chance to see something that hasn't happened before and may never happen again, [you want it to come true]. Our job is to record it for history. I'm not afraid to say we're rooting for them to do it."[1]

Beyond history, part of the interest lay in the ongoing good-versus-evil drama, only this time with the role of Good being played by an unlikely choice: a team from . . . *New York!* Why not? The Giants' quarterback was Eli Manning, Peyton's baby brother, and as we have seen, America loves the Mannings. If the Patriots represented Evil, then who better to deny them their place in history—and presumably ruin Steve Sabol's day—than one of the Manning boys?

The Giants had been erratic all season. They opened with two straight losses, followed by six straight victories, and were just 4–3 in the seven games leading up to the New England showdown. But the Giants had already clinched a playoff berth: regardless of how the game turned out, win or lose, history or no history, they would be the fifth seed in the National Football Conference playoffs, with a wild-card game against Tampa Bay already in their date book. The Patriots, too, went into the sixteenth and final game of the regular season knowing that the outcome was not going to alter their playoff prospects: they already had clinched the best record in the American Football Conference, meaning a first-round bye followed by two home games if they made it as far as the AFC championship game.

"Honestly, we never talked about 16–0 until the Giants game," recalled Belichick. "We talked about whoever the next team was, Buffalo, Miami, Pittsburgh, Indianapolis, whoever was on the schedule. When we got to the Giants game, that's when we said we have a chance to have an undefeated season here, and we can finally talk about it because it's the next game. But even then, we didn't make a big deal out of it. We were focused more on beating the Giants than being 16–0, if that makes any sense."

As Jim Donaldson of the *Providence Journal* put it, "If the Patriots lose tonight, it's not the end of the world. It's not even the end of the season. Which is why tonight's match-up in the Meadowlands is not as big a deal as a lot of people are trying to make it out to be. Put simply: Would you rather go 15–1 and win the Super Bowl, or 16–0 and lose in the playoffs?"[2]

So, from a postseason perspective, the Giants had nothing to lose and the Patriots had nothing to lose.

And then the game began, and the two teams played as though they had everything to lose. The Giants played the Patriots tough, leading by twelve points in the second half, but New England roared back for a history-making 38–35 victory that included no small amount of individual history for Brady and Moss.

With 11:06 remaining in the fourth quarter, the Patriots now trailing 28–23, Brady went to the air and found Moss wide open at the 20. Problem was, Moss dropped the ball. So Brady threw *another* bomb, and this one was a sixty-five-yard touchdown completion. With that one pass, two significant NFL records were set: it was Brady's fiftieth touchdown pass of the season, one more than Peyton Manning had in 2004 when he set the record for touchdown passes in a season, and it was Moss's twenty-third touchdown reception . . . one more than Jerry Rice had when *he* set the record with twenty-two TD receptions in just twelve games in the strike-shortened '87 campaign.

Maroney gave the Patriots some insurance when he followed the touchdown with a two-point conversion. The Pats got the ball back when Ellis Hobbs intercepted a Manning pass at the New England 48, and soon Maroney was in the end zone again on a five-yard run. The Giants scored one last time, Manning leading the New Yorkers down the field and finishing the drive with a three-yard pass to Plaxico Burress, but there wasn't enough time left for a comeback. Mike Vrabel recovered the Giants' onside kick with 1:03 remaining; with thirty-five seconds left, Tom Brady took a knee. And then everyone counted down the last seconds to history.

The New England Patriots were 16–0, their first victory coming at the expense of the New York Jets, who cried foul, and the last victory coming at the expense of the New York Giants, who collectively said, "Good game," and then prepared for the playoffs.

The Nantucket Gals, watching the game on television, rejoiced.

And being good Catholics and regular communicants at Our Lady of the Isle Church, they were confident that their dear, late father, old Matt Jaeckle, was also watching the game.

And was not happy about the outcome. Not at all.

When the American Football League and National Football League merged in 1970, one of the fringe benefits for hard-core, old-timey Giants fans living in New England was the occasional opportunity to see their beloved team pay a visit to the Patriots.

The Pats' inaugural season in the NFL included a home date with the Giants, with the New Yorkers registering a 16–0 shutout on October 18, 1970, at Harvard Stadium. Attendance that day was 39,091, at the time the second-largest crowd ever to see a Patriots home game.

A year later, when the Patriots moved into their new home in Foxborough, their first steps onto the field were for an August 15, 1971, preseason game against the Giants. It was to become a preseason tradition through much of the decade, with the Pats hosting the Giants again from 1972 through 1976.

But for all his passion for the New York football Giants, Matt Jaeckle never saw the team play in person. Not once in his adult life did the

Nantucket farmer gather his buddies and make a boys-will-be-boys foot-ball pilgrimage to New York, and Matt never did what in the years ahead would become a ritual for his three daughters: take the ferry from the island to Hyannis and then drive to Foxborough.

"My father would rather have stayed at home and watched the Giants on television with some of his friends," said Joan Fisher. "He very rarely left the island. That's just the way he was."

Matt followed his favorite team in the newspapers, each morning walking down to Roger's, a small shop on Main Street that carried the Boston papers, and picking up a copy of the *Record-American*, whose editors understood they had readers who wanted a daily dose of the Giants. He kept a bobble-head doll of Giants great Sam Huff on top of his television, the little figurine standing guard as Matt sat on the edge of his green leather recliner, either cheering or complaining, depending on how the game was progressing.

"You didn't go near Matt's TV set," said Ralph Hardy, Jane's husband. "Friday night was for the fights, and Sunday was for the Giants. He eventually got a big outside antenna. When the reception was bad, he'd take a hose and go up to the roof and spray the salt off the antenna."

In the late '50s and early '60s, when the Giants were an elite NFL team, Matt had a bounce in his step. When the Giants were bad, as was the case for a good chunk of the 1960s, including a 1–12–1 record in 1966, Matt did more than complain. He took action, firing off an angry letter to Wellington Mara, the owner of the Giants, stating in no uncertain terms what he would do if only he were in charge. It is not known if Mara ever replied.

Old Matt had other passions. A small, wiry pepper pot of a man, he loved to hunt, and in those days game was plentiful on Nantucket. He'd go off for hours in search of duck, geese, and pheasant. "Sometimes," said Joan, pausing just a beat for comedic effect, "he'd even hunt in season."

And then there was the Nantucket High School football team, which Matt loved as much as he did the Giants. He attended every home game at Burnham Dell Field and was particularly proud during the years his own grandsons played for the Whalers. But while he did not write angry letters to Nantucket football coach Vito Capizzo, holding back on the wrath that had been visited upon Wellington Mara, he found other targets for his venting.

Such as the game officials. One particular episode stands out: In the late stages of a 1972 game between Nantucket and Provincetown, with Matt's grandson Peter Dooley quarterbacking the Whalers, the old man was so enraged by a call that he stepped out onto the field to argue with the referee. It was a showdown of local legends: Matt Jaeckle, the greatest Nantucket High football fan who ever lived, and Manny Pena, who, in addition to refereeing high school football games throughout Cape Cod, was also well known as a top high school basketball official and baseball umpire. For more than forty years, Pena was involved as a player, manager, and umpire in the acclaimed Cape Cod Baseball League, a summertime proving ground for college players that has sent hundreds of its graduates on to the big leagues. When he was made a posthumous selection to the Cape Cod League Hall of Fame in 2005, one of the co-inductees was former Brewster Whitecaps outfielder Bobby Kielty, whose home run in Game 4 of the 2007 World Series helped bring victory to the Red Sox.

As Coach Capizzo remembered the 1972 episode between Pena and Jaeckle, "We had Gary Santos back for a punt, and he called for a fair catch, but three Provincetown players plowed into him. And Manny stood there and did nothing. I was out there on the field myself. That's when Matt came running out."

Matt was seventy-one years old at the time. The standoff ended when two Nantucket players got on either side of the old man, each hoisting him up by the elbow and carrying him to the sideline, his little legs kicking all the way. After the game, Manny Pena needed a police escort to get off the island. And it is an event that nearly forty years later still gets people riled up. Jake Pena, Manny's son, said, "I know my father had a few incidents like that, and it upsets me that someone would go on the field and argue with him. He was a fine official." To which Matt's grandson Peter Dooley said, "Too bad. You have to be willing to take some shit if you're going to make bad calls."

Matthew Laurence Jaeckle was not a native-born Nantucketer, and he had no blood ties to the island's glorious whaling past. For all his

Nantucket values and love of the quiet, rural life, he came into the world in about as urban an environment as possible—New York City's Hell's Kitchen in 1901, the son of German immigrants. He was what his daughters called "a change-of-life baby" and grew up at a time when his parents, Andrew and Christine Jaeckle, were aging and short of money.

When he was twelve, Matt was sent to stay with an older sister who was living on Nantucket, a move that changed the course of the boy's life.

The 1920 U.S. census for Nantucket shows him living on the Somerset Dairy Farm, which at the time was owned by an Alfred Starbuck. Working on the farm agreed with Matt; he was a smart kid and had a lot of modern ideas about how to run a farm. It was this drive and intelligence that landed him at the Stockbridge School of Agriculture at the Massachusetts Agricultural College, located in Amherst, Massachusetts.* School records reveal that he was a solid B student and that he earned an A in Poultry. He was a member of the Alpha Tau Gamma fraternity, and he participated on the club boxing team.

When he returned to Nantucket in 1922, college degree in hand, he was a strikingly handsome young man, small, energetic, with long arms and deep, Hollywood eyes. In possession of the know-how required to run a farm, in little more than a decade he owned one: Nantucket Historical Association files show the Somerset being willed to him in 1933 by an Elizabeth Maroney "Lizzie" Starbuck, Alfred's widow.

He was married by then, having fallen in love with a Canadian gal named Vera Milton who had come to the island for employment as a nanny. They raised their three daughters on the farm, each of them learning football as they learned to walk.

At some point during the 1950s, Matt suffered a heart attack. He eventually sold the farm and took a job as superintendent of streets; in his later years, after retiring, he worked part-time as a clerk at Haley's Liquor Store.

In September 1977, with Vera already in declining health, Matt suf-

---

* The Massachusetts Agricultural College is now known as the University of Massachusetts. The Stockbridge School of Agriculture remains a part of the school.

fered a stroke. He was taken to Nantucket Hospital, where Joan, Jeanne, and Jane sat by his side. Later in the day, Jane volunteered to go home and look in on their mother.

As Matt lay there in the hospital bed, taking his last breaths, Joan and Jeanne could hear a skein of geese flying overhead. They looked out the window at the geese, soaring over the island that had been home to Matt Jaeckle since being liberated from Hell's Kitchen more than a half-century earlier.

And then Joan and Jeanne looked back at their father. Old Matt Jaeckle was dead.

Thirty years and two Super Bowl championships later, the 2007 New York Giants held off the Tampa Bay Buccaneers in their wild-card playoff opener, claiming a 24–14 victory at Raymond James Stadium in Tampa. A week later, they shocked everyone with a 21–17 victory over the Dallas Cowboys, who were 13–3 during the regular season, including two victories over the Giants. The 'Boys were threatening in the game's final seconds, but quarterback Tony Romo's would-be game-winning touchdown on fourth-and-11 from the New York 23 was intercepted in the end zone by cornerback R. W. McQuarters with sixteen seconds remaining. The Giants were going to the NFC championship game.

After enjoying a first-round bye, the Patriots took out the Jacksonville Jaguars a week later as Tom Brady completed twenty-six of twenty-eight passes for 263 yards and three touchdowns. It was the Pats' seventeenth consecutive victory, and of course, more individual records tumbled: this time it was unearthed that Brady's 92.9 pass completion rate was the highest in NFL history for a regular-season or playoff game.

The Patriots were continuing to add new wrinkles to their offense. There was, for instance, a variation on a play in which center Dan Koppen snapped the ball directly to fullback Kevin Faulk rather than Brady, who was in shotgun formation. Brady's job was to leap as though the ball had been snapped over his head, the hope being that the defense wouldn't know that Faulk had the ball. But here's what happened when the Pats ran the play against Jacksonville: Brady leaped into the air according to the script, and Faulk raced by as though he had the ball. Only he did not. The ball had been snapped directly to Brady after all. In a play the Pats called "Double Pop," Brady got the ball, turned, and then acted like a quarterback who doesn't have the ball but wants everyone to think he has the ball. And everyone bought it, assuming he was an empty-handed quarterback just going through the motions. Under no pressure, he threw a six-yard touchdown pass to Wes Welker.

During the postgame press conference, a producer from a Japanese television network brought some levity to the chaos when he told the quarterback, "It looks very Zen of you."

"I'm all Zen," replied Brady.[3]

So now the Patriots had that going for them too.

The NFL's two conference championship games, which would determine the participants in Super Bowl XLII, were played on Sunday, January 20. The Patriots were up first, hosting their old/new rivals, the San Diego Chargers—old in that the two teams were original entries in the American Football League, new in that their recent showdowns had become gridiron soap operas, what with accusations about team logos being defaced and the Chargers' LaDainian Tomlinson adding to the Spygate discussion with his if-you're-not-cheating-you're-not-trying comment.

Despite Tomlinson spending most of the day on the sideline with a banged-up knee . . . and quarterback Philip Rivers plugging along with knee woes of his own . . . and tight end Antonio Gates playing with a dislocated toe . . . the Chargers made a game of it. Trailing 14–9 in the third quarter, their offense limited to three Nate Kaeding field goals, the Chargers got the ball back when cornerback Drayton Florence intercepted a Brady pass intended for Donte Stallworth for a first down at the New England 49.

Rivers threw passes of seventeen, fifteen, and six yards to help get the Chargers down to the New England 7, and a three-yard gain by backup running back Michael Turner put them at third-and-1 at the 4.

Enter Junior Seau, the onetime Chargers great who would still have been chillin' in retirement back home in San Diego—and riding the waves with Donald Takayama—had he not decided to give it another go with the Patriots. The Chargers gave the ball to Turner, whose plan to follow left tackle Marcus McNeil was foiled when Seau broke through and dropped him for a two-yard loss. The Chargers had to settle for yet another field goal by Kaeding.

Brady provided some insurance in the fourth quarter, finding Welker for a six-yard touchdown, and soon Gillette Stadium was celebrating the Patriots' 21–12 victory—and their fourth trip to the Super Bowl in the Belichick era.

It had not been a good day for Brady. Nor was it a good day for Randy Moss, held to just one catch for eighteen yards. And it had not been a good week: a Florida woman had taken out a restraining order against Moss, accusing him of battery and not allowing her to seek medical attention after he visited her at her Fort Lauderdale home. Speaking with the *Herald*'s Karen Guregian, Moss, who admitted visiting the woman, said, "I know what took place. I know what happened," and, "Me physically hit a woman? No. Never."[4] The woman eventually withdrew the restraining order, and the case was closed; for now, though, it was easy to speculate that Moss's off-the-field problems had contributed to a bad game.

But the Pats were in. And they were 18–0, one victory better than the 17–0 Dolphins of 1972. The difference, of course, being that the Dolphins, playing in the days of the fourteen-game schedule, ended their season with a Super Bowl victory.

That one final victory still awaited the Patriots. But first, there was the question of which team would be providing the competition for the newly crowned AFC champs. So they all went home and settled in, Matt Jaeckle–style, and watched the Giants and Green Bay Packers battle to overtime in the NFC championship game. The Giants escaped with a 23–20 overtime victory.

The Giants could have won it in regulation, but kicker Lawrence Tynes missed a thirty-six-yard field goal attempt with four seconds remaining, sending the game into overtime. Brett Favre, the Packers' thirty-eight-year-old quarterback, was then intercepted by Corey Webster to set up another Giants drive, and Tynes, having already missed two field goal attempts, got himself back in the good graces of good New

Yorkers everywhere with a game-winning forty-seven-yard kick.

The regular season had ended with the Patriots and Giants meeting in a thriller in the Meadowlands. Now the postseason would end with these same two teams meeting in Super Bowl XLII in Glendale, Arizona. The Giants were confident that they could continue their Cinderella ride, and the Patriots were confident that they'd come out of it as the greatest team in football history.

Outside Gillette Stadium, a collection of buses that would transport the Patriots to Logan Airport, where the team would board its Phoenix-bound charter, sat idling. But before leaving the stadium, Belichick gathered his players around the locker of Marquise Hill, the young Patriots defensive lineman who had died in a jet ski accident earlier in the year. The players had kept Hill's locker as a shrine, some of its contents still in place.

"When we left, it was going to be our last time in that locker room this year," Belichick said a couple of days later at a Super Bowl Week press conference. "I just wanted to remind everyone, and I'm sure they know. I don't even know if I needed to say it."[5]

For one Patriot player in particular, the visits to Hill's locker had been a daily occurrence throughout the season. Like Marquise Hill, defensive lineman Jarvis Green grew up in New Orleans. They both played at Louisiana State University and later became teammates on the Patriots. One of Green's ways of remembering Hill was to occasionally wear his old friend's shoulder pads out to the field during games. As the Pats left for Phoenix, for the Super Bowl, Green made sure that Hill's pads were with him; he hoped one day to give them to Hill's son, Ma'Shy, two years old at the time.

"It was a quick, private moment," Hill said a year later, recalling the team visit at Hill's locker. "I think I wore the pads eight or nine times. We should have been playing in the Super Bowl together. The least I could do was bring his shoulder pads with me."

19

THE CATCH

The Westin Kierland Resort and Spa, in Scottsdale, Arizona, was built in 2002 on a patch of undeveloped desert next to an existing golf course. Designed to capture the history and culture of Arizona, its three-tiered lobby pays homage to the Grand Canyon, with the upper level representing the peaks, the middle level the plateaus, and the lower level the valleys.

The main attraction on the middle level is the Ali Shonak Library, a richly appointed lobby bar featuring floor-to-ceiling bookcases, leather chairs, and elegantly upholstered couches. It is an inviting place to kick back and talk with friends, close a business deal, or perhaps nurse a snifter of brandy while meandering through a classic tome borrowed from the bookcase.

For Andre Tippett, seated on a butterscotch-colored couch on a sunny but chilly Saturday afternoon in February 2008, the Ali Shonak Library had been appropriated as a waiting room. But the man everyone calls Tipp, once a crushing linebacker who played his entire National Football League career with the New England Patriots, wasn't looking so ferocious on the afternoon before the undefeated Patriots would meet the New York Giants in Super Bowl XLII at University of Phoenix Stadium. Sitting nervously on the couch, fidgeting from side to side, Tipp, forty-eight years old, his eleven football seasons a collection of long-ago yesterdays, was holding his cell phone with both hands, occasionally looking down on its face, as if pleading with the damned thing to go off.

Born in Alabama, raised in New Jersey, Andre Tippett had taken a circuitous route to the NFL. After attending Ellsworth Community College in Iowa Falls, Iowa, for a year, he moved on to the University of Iowa and enhanced his pro prospects when he was named an All-America selection his senior year. The Patriots picked him in the second round of the 1982 draft; during the 1984 and '85 seasons, he recorded thirty-five sacks, which remains the highest two-season total by a linebacker in NFL history. He was a five-time Pro Bowl selection and a member of the first Patriots team to make it to the Super Bowl—the upstart Pats who got trounced by the Chicago Bears on January 26, 1986, at the Louisiana Superdome. He would later be named to the league's all-decade team for the '80s.

As great football players go, he was the goods. Yet one year earlier, nearly to the day, Tippett had waited for a phone call that never came. Though he had been among the Hall of Fame selection committee's ten finalists for enshrinement at Canton, the afternoon came and went, and he was not among the six inductees for the class of 2007.

Now, with the entire professional football community converged on greater Phoenix for the Super Bowl, Tipp, in his capacity as executive director of community affairs for the Patriots, was camped out with the rest of the New England delegation at the Westin Kierland.

Meanwhile, at the Convention Center in downtown Phoenix, hundreds of media representatives were assembled to await the football equivalent of white smoke billowing from the Vatican chimney. The NFL Network was providing live coverage of the Pro Football Hall of Fame's selection announcements, and Tipp, not wanting to idle in his hotel room, chose to plant himself on that couch in the Ali Shonak Library, joined by a collection of friends, family members, and Patriots employees. The flat screen was tuned to the NFL Network.

As Tipp and his friends watched and listened, Rich Eisen of the NFL Network was explaining the process by which the Pro Football Hall of Fame makes its selections. It took only a few minutes for Eisen to lay out all the whys and wherefores, but for Tippett it seemed like hours.

And then, finally, Stephen A. Perry, the president and executive director of the Pro Football Hall of Fame, stepped to the podium to announce the class of 2008.

Fred Dean . . . Darrell Green . . . Art Monk . . . Emmitt Thomas . . .
I don't think I'm going to make it, Tipp said to himself.

Finally, Perry uttered the name "Andre Tippett." *Andre Tippett.* For
only the second time in the history of the New England franchise, a
player who had spent his entire career with the Patriots was headed for
the Hall of Fame, the other being offensive lineman John Hannah.

Tippett is still in the neighborhood of 240 pounds, his playing weight.
And possessing perfect posture and authoritative, thrown-back shoulders, the man has an I-can-still-play-this-game look about him. But now
the big man in the Patriots T-shirt, tan slacks, and sneakers broke down
and cried, right there in the Ali Shonak Library, right there in front of
everybody.

"I'm emotional," Tipp said that day. "I played emotionally. I'm emotional. It's something that I believe in. This is special. That's the only
way you can sum it up. It's a special day for me, and a special day to the
organization and my family. It's a dream come true."

It should have been one of the happiest days in the history of the
franchise, and a nice appetizer leading into Sunday's Super Bowl. It was
not. Though owner Robert Kraft immediately placed a call to Tipp's cell
phone and offered congratulations, after which the owner's son, team
president Jonathan Kraft, came down to the lobby and planted a big hug
on the big man, the Patriots were dealing with a crisis. That morning,
the *Boston Herald* had served up a pre–Super Bowl bombshell: citing
an unnamed source, the paper claimed that six years earlier, when the
Pats registered one of the most stunning upsets in sports history with
their 20–17 victory over the St. Louis Rams in Super Bowl XXXVI, they
had done so after a team employee secretly videotaped the Rams' walkthrough the day before the game.

Both teams had held walkthroughs at the Louisiana Superdome on
the Saturday in question, with the Patriots holding their session first.
"After completing the walkthrough," the *Herald* reported, "[the Patriots]
had their team picture taken and the Rams then took the field. According to the source, a member of the team's video staff stayed behind after
attending the team's walkthrough and filmed St. Louis' walkthrough. At
no point was he asked to identify himself or produce a press pass, the
source said. The cameraman rode the media shuttle back to the hotel

with news photographers when the Rams walkthrough was completed, the source said."[1]

The article noted that "it's not known what the cameraman did with the tape from there. It's also not known if he made the recording on his own initiative or if he was instructed to make the recording by someone with the Patriots or anyone else."[2]

Spygate II was under way.

The scene for this controversy had been set two days earlier when U.S. Senator Arlen Specter, a Republican from Pennsylvania, told the *New York Times* that he planned to order NFL commissioner Roger Goodell to appear before the Senate Judiciary Committee to explain why the league had destroyed the tapes it obtained from the Patriots during its investigation into the team's taping of the Jets' defensive signals. Specter, who also spoke ominously of looking into the NFL's antitrust exemption, told the newspaper he had twice written to Goodell and had yet to receive a response.[3]

The *Times* article also brought up the name of one Matt Walsh, a former Patriots employee who at one time handed out postgame notes in the Foxboro Stadium press box before moving on to bigger and better things: he landed a gig in the team's video department. And here he now was, asking the *Times*, in reference to the videotaping incident, "Was it a surprise that they were doing it or a surprise that they got caught?"[4]

On the day the *Times* article ran, Goodell was scheduled to appear at the Phoenix Convention Center to deliver the league's state-of-the-game address, an exercise that over the years has become a Super Bowl Week tradition: the commissioner extols the virtues of the great game of football and ladles out some statistical and anecdotal information about how the NFL is moving ever upward, a reliably self-congratulatory speech that is followed by a question-and-answer session. This year's address took on added significance because of the presence of the Patriots in the Super Bowl—and now a threat from a U.S. senator that the commissioner was going to be dragged before Congress. That Specter was an avid fan of the Philadelphia Eagles and known for dialing into the Philly talk shows after a big game (Arlen on the car phone?) brought some additional sizzle to the controversy: would the distinguished senator from Pennsylvania be looking into the possibility that the Patriots cheated their way to victory over his "Eggles" four years earlier in Super Bowl XXXIX? Inquiring minds wanted to know.

And there was this: it had been widely reported that Specter received contributions from Philadelphia-based Comcast, which had been in a major catfight with the NFL after the cable giant planned to place the NFL Network on a premium programming package. Goodell, in his state-of-the-game address, said he'd be happy to meet with Specter; as for his decision to have the Spygate tapes destroyed, their contents, he explained, "were totally consistent with what the team told me. There was no purpose for them."

Later that night, as Robert Kraft and Jonathan Kraft were riding in a limo to attend a function hosted by the commissioner, Jonathan received a call from Stacey James, the team's vice president of media relations. As Jonathan Kraft looked directly at his father, the cell phone pressed to his ear, he listened as James told him he had just gotten off the phone with the *Herald*'s John Tomase, who was seeking comment for his story on the Rams' walkthrough.

Jonathan Kraft, forty-three at the time, grew up a fan of the team he now runs, attending games at the old stadium in Foxborough with his parents and brothers back when Robert's only connection to the Patriots was that he had season tickets. One of Jonathan's earliest football memories is of him and his brothers sneaking in rolls of toilet paper under their jackets and then throwing them down to the field when the Patriots scored a touchdown—behavior, he is quick to admit, that would get a fan ejected from modern-day Gillette Stadium. Now, with the Pats one victory away from taking their rightful place as the greatest team in NFL history, he was standing outside the commissioner's party on an unseasonably cold Phoenix night, talking with lawyers on his cell phone.

The next morning, prior to a scheduled team meeting with his players at the team's hotel, Belichick asked his captains—quarterback Tom Brady, running back Kevin Faulk, defensive lineman Ty Warren, and linebackers Larry Izzo, Junior Seau, Mike Vrabel, and Tedy Bruschi—to step out to the hallway.

Bruschi's recollection of the meeting is that Belichick told his captains about the *Herald* story and said, "This is a bunch of bullshit. None of this ever happened. But what I'm asking you is, do you think I should address this with the team right now?"

"No," said Bruschi, "we don't need to address this. It's all about the game now."

As he walked into the meeting, Bruschi thought: *Here we go again.*

Belichick did not bring up the *Herald* story at the team meeting.

T hirty years from now . . . forty years from now . . . fifty years from now . . . for as long as they are alive, Eli Manning and David Tyree will be asked to talk about the Catch. And for as long as they are physically able to do so, the aging onetime quarterback and the aging onetime wide receiver will be asked—come on, please, one more time—to reenact the Catch. Just as an eighty-two-year-old Charlie Chaplin was handed a bowler hat and bamboo cane, for old times' sake, when he ended years of self-imposed exile in the Swiss Alps to appear at the 1972 Academy Awards, there will always be somebody handing a football to David Tyree and asking him to press it against his head . . . for old times' sake.

While the pass that Manning completed to Tyree with under two minutes remaining in Super Bowl XLII was not the game-winning play in the Giants' 17–14 upset of the Patriots, it is the play that everybody will remember. It is the reason Manning-to-Tyree will always have special meaning to football fans in general and Giants fans in particular, and it is the reason the Patriots and their fans will forever regard the 2007 season as no more than a glorious might-have-been.

The Patriots, clinging to a 14–10 lead, were seventy-five seconds away from winning the Super Bowl. The Giants were on third-and-5 at their own 44-yard line, and Manning was in huge trouble: as he dropped back and looked for the open man, he was swarmed by Patriots. Defensive linemen Richard Seymour and Jarvis Green each got a hand on the Giants quarterback, with Green, wearing Marquise Hill's shoulder pads, remembering that "my hand actually went under Manning's shirt. I could feel *his* shoulder pad."

Had Manning gone down, the Giants would have been looking at a fourth-and-long at around their own 37-yard line. Somehow, Manning broke loose from the vicelike grip Green had on him; somehow, with yet more Patriots now converging on him, a fast-charging Mike Vrabel dead ahead, he reared back and threw the ball into the air, a desperation attempt for a game-saving first down.

Half of the greatest play in football history had just taken place.

David Tyree, in his fifth season with the Giants as a wide receiver and special teams player, was hovering around the 25-yard line, right where a multicolored Super Bowl logo was painted into the turf. Manning had made his desperation pass, and now Tyree leaped as high as he could, his arms extended, hoping to finish the play with a desperation catch. Joining Tyree in his pursuit of the ball was the Patriots' Rodney Harrison, who, looking like a volleyball player about to spike the ball, extended his right arm in *his* leap into the air. Just as Tyree wrapped his hands around the ball, he was bludgeoned by Harrison; as they both came back down to earth, the Giants wideout fell into a backward jack-knife as he landed on top of the New England safety. Tyree pressed the ball into the top of his helmet with his right hand as he was beginning his descent, and then, just as his left foot hit the ground, he applied his left hand to the ball. When the two players landed, Harrison moved on top of Tyree to jar loose the ball. But Tyree refused to let go, just as Manning refused to go down.

"All year, watching film of him, people would touch him and he'd just lay down," recalled Green of Manning. "And I thought he was going to be doing the same thing. But you've got to remember, it's competitive sports, it's the Super Bowl, it's the biggest game in the world. And in that game, Eli came out of it like a warrior."

At the precise moment it appeared Green and/or Seymour was about to sack Manning, newly elected Hall of Famer Andre Tippett, sitting in the stands with his family, turned to his nine-year-old son Coby and said, "Do you know how cool it's going to be to have another Super Bowl ring?"

Recalling the game more than a year later, Tippett said, "And then that sucker threw that ball, and I slumped back in my chair and said, 'You gotta be shitting me.' That's exactly what I was saying."

In a luxury suite in another section of the stadium, Giants owner

John Mara—son of Wellington Mara, to whom old Matt Jaeckle had written his angry letter some forty years earlier—had a different reaction to the Catch.

"How can we not win this now?" he said.[5]

And so it would be.

On first-and-10 at the New England 24, Manning was dropped for a one-yard loss by Adalius Thomas. On second-and-11, he looked to his left and attempted a short pass to Tyree. Incomplete. Now he looked to his right, and he hit Steve Smith for a twelve-yard completion, giving the Giants a first down at the 13 with thirty-nine seconds remaining.

Manning did not need those thirty-nine seconds.

Wide receiver Plaxico Burress, lining up to Manning's left, did a little fake as he moved toward the end zone, and Patriots cornerback Ellis Hobbs bought it wholesale.

"I gave him a slant move and he stopped his feet," Burress said after the game. "Once he stopped his feet, I knew I had him."[6]

Alone in the end zone, Burress caught the nice, easy pass lofted to him by Manning.

With thirty-five seconds remaining in the game, the Patriots trailed 17–14.

When the Giants kicked off, Laurence Maroney returned the ball seventeen yards to the New England 26. And in a classic illustration of how one football game has the power to alter the loyalties of players and ex-players alike, consider that one of the special teams performers who tackled Maroney was Zak DeOssie—the onetime Brown University player whose dad, Steve DeOssie, was close friends with Belichick from their days together on the Giants. A few years earlier, Belichick had taken his sons down to Providence to watch Zak DeOssie play for Brown; now that same player, a first-year member of the Giants, was doing everything in his power to destroy Belichick's dream season.

The Patriots had a first down at their own 26, with twenty-six seconds remaining in the game. They would have to move the ball some forty yards, and do it quickly, in order for Stephen Gostkowski to have a realistic shot at a game-tying field goal and to set the stage for the first Super Bowl in history to go into overtime.

Though slowed by an ailing right ankle, and having a terrible day,

Brady had come up big on his previous drive, a twelve-play march down the sideline ended with a six-yard touchdown pass to Moss with 2:24 remaining, giving New England a 14–10 lead.

If Manning had crumbled under the weight of Seymour and Green . . . if he had not been able to elude the charging Vrabel . . . if Tyree had not outleaped Harrison . . . if he had not held on to the ball as the two men were crashing to the turf . . . if Hobbs had not been faked out by Burress with thirty-nine seconds remaining in the game . . .

If.

If any one of those plays had turned out differently, the Super Bowl probably would have ended with a Brady-to-Moss touchdown having provided the winning margin. But Manning *did* elude Seymour and Green . . . Tyree *did* jump a little higher than Harrison . . . he *did* press the ball against his helmet . . . Hobbs *was* faked out by Plaxico Burress.

Young Zak DeOssie *did* help bring down Maroney.

And the Patriots *did* lose.

After failing to connect with Gaffney on his first pass attempt of the drive, Brady was sacked for a ten-yard loss, the fifth time in the game he had been dropped by the ferocious New York defense. With only nineteen seconds remaining, and trapped way back at his own 16, Brady had but one course of action: go deep to Randy Moss. He did, twice, and both passes were incomplete.

The Giants got the ball back with one second remaining. Before Eli Manning could even drop to one knee to knock that last second off the clock, Belichick was already across the field to shake hands with Giants coach Tom Coughlin. To Belichick, the game was over.

The coach drew criticism for leaving the field before the game had officially ended. And for the first time since he started coaching the Patriots to Super Bowl victories, he was widely criticized for some of the in-game decisions he made. Given that Brady clearly was struggling, the football intelligentsia wanted to know why Belichick didn't consider having Maroney run the ball more often. The coach also made a disastrous decision in the third quarter to go for a first down on fourth-and-13 from the New York 31 rather than have Gostkowski attempt a field goal of about forty-eight yards. Instead, Brady's pass attempt to Gaffney was incomplete. The football season over, it was now open season on Bill Belichick.

Did Belichick go for the first down because he had lost confidence in Gostkowski after the rookie shanked a second-quarter kickoff out of bounds following the Patriots' first touchdown? Rather than supply answers during his postgame presser, Belichick delivered collections of words, slowly, and with pauses, some of them barely audible. Why didn't he have Gostkowski make the third-quarter field goal attempt? "Fifty-yard field goal," he said. "Lots of field position. So. . . ."[7]

Wrote Rich Cimini in the *New York Daily News*, "Forty minutes after the worst loss of his career, Belichick sat in the first row of the Patriots' bus, Bus No. 5642, staring solemnly at the stat sheet. He looked like a wax figure. The spy finally got his."[8]

The coach was even mocked for the red hooded sweatshirt he wore on the field during the game. He would later be parodied on the irreverent cartoon series *South Park*. On an episode of *Jeopardy*, one of the clues was, "One second from defeat in the 2008 Super Bowl, this losing head coach threw a hissy fit and stalked off the field." To which the contestant confidently answered, "Who is Bill Belichick?"

Spygate II came to a screeching halt three months later when Matt Walsh, after signing an indemnity agreement with the NFL, finally met with the commissioner and, later, Senator Arlen Specter. Though it was made clear that Walsh had attended the Rams' walkthrough, presumably to set up video equipment for the next day's Super Bowl, he produced no damaging tapes. The *Herald* retracted its story and issued an apology "to its readers and to the New England Patriots' owners, players, employees and fans for our error."[9]

Belichick has yet to respond specifically to any of the biting criticisms that were aimed at him, including the litany of ranting, panting, good-versus-evil pieces that came and went. When asked about those stories in an interview for this book, he said, "You mean, when it's personal? Then it's unprofessional. When it's personal, if that's the level they want to take it to, that's their choice. But that's a bad reflection on them.

"I know that there's, on a daily basis, some positive things and some negative things. I certainly don't see all of either side of it. And if I focused on that, I don't think I'd be able to do a very good job with what I'm trying to do.

"There are some things I'm aware of. But there's plenty of it that I'm not."

The Nantucket Gals were in attendance for Super Bowl XLII, the first time they had ever seen the Patriots play outside of Foxborough. As one of the perks for having been named "Fans of the Year" by the Patriots in 2005, they were in a position to purchase tickets for the Pats' next visit to the Big Game, and they had agreed they wouldn't miss this for anything.

But they knew the ghost of old Matt Jaeckle was also going along for the ride. Of that there was no doubt. Before they left, Jeanne Dooley was getting up an island Super Bowl pool and taking bets, and she was surprised when Mary Haley, who works over at the Nantucket Bank, placed a wager on the Giants—in memory of Matt Jaeckle, who years earlier had worked part-time at the liquor store Mary's father owned.

After checking in at a motel in Scottsdale, Arizona, the Gals took great pains to set up their room for the celebration they were certain would cap their day. They arranged a table with snacks, drinks, and the mixings for Jane's toddies, and they decorated the walls with GO PATS!! signs that Joan's granddaughter Christy Bassett made just for the occasion.

When the game ended, they didn't have much interest in analysis, dissection, and finger-pointing, other than to make one point: old Matt Jaeckle had played a role in all this. "He's haunting us," Joan said, and Jeanne and Jane agreed. They returned to the room and ripped down the signs Christy had made.

The plane ride home was miserable. Because of the haste with which the trip was arranged, they were seated in three different sections of the plane; Joan and Jeanne immediately went to sleep, but Jane commiserated with a fellow Patriots fan while nursing a couple of toddies.

When they arrived back on Nantucket and retreated to their homes, Jane entered through the back door, as she and her husband Ralph usually do. She went through the kitchen and into the living room and, looking straight ahead, could see the top of the mantelpiece, on which were displayed two bobble-head dolls. One of them was Tom Brady. The other was the Sam Huff figurine that years ago sat atop old Matt Jaeckle's TV set.

Jane walked over to the mantelpiece and turned the Sam Huff figurine so that its face looked at the wall. It remains in that position to this day.

20
THE ONLY SHOW IN TOWN

The beauty of having so many teams playing so well at one time is that there is always another exciting new ride at the carnival. And now everyone was hopping on the Celtics bandwagon. Folks had been converging on the Garden all season, every game a sellout, but David Tyree's catch changed everything. Just like that, the Patriots were yesterday. This was today; today was the Celtics.

Following a 96–90 victory over the Dallas Mavericks at the Garden on January 31, with Ray Allen and Paul Pierce each scoring twenty-six points and Rajon Rondo collecting a game-high twelve rebounds, the Celtics were going to have four days off before a February 5 rematch against the Cavaliers in Cleveland. The timing for the time off was perfect: Kevin Garnett had missed his third consecutive game because of an abdominal strain, and nobody knew for sure when he'd be returning. That was the bad news. The good news was that, at 36–8, the Celtics were not exactly stumbling through the winter.

Garnett had been everything the Celtics hoped for, and so much more. Fiercely competitive and possessing an astounding work ethic, he was the embodiment of what the old-timers liked to call Celtic Pride.

And just what, exactly, was Celtic Pride?

"Hard work . . . focus . . . attention to detail . . . putting team defense above all else," said Bob Cousy, the great Celtics point guard who played on six championship teams during his storied NBA career.

"We had things so under control that that one proverbial bad apple would have no effect on the barrel," he said, referring to his teams in the '50s and early '60s. "We wouldn't allow anything or anyone, no matter how heralded or whatever their reputation was, to interfere in any way other than a positive way."

Cousy could just as easily have been talking about ubuntu, could he not?

"I read a number of times about ubuntu, and how the team bought into it," he said. "It created the kind of sustained intensity that we used to have. There is, I think, a link between Celtic Pride and ubuntu."

Call it ubuntu. Call it Celtic Pride. Whatever it was, Kevin Garnett ate it up. Doc Rivers remembers a scene from early in the season when the Celtics were about to play the Lakers to wrap up their four-game western swing. He had found a quote somewhere attributed to Lakers coach Phil Jackson about how the Celtics had yet to play the Lakers in Los Angeles, and Rivers planned to deploy the comment to fire up his team.

"I search the media for things I can use to engage my players," he said. "[Jackson] was asked a question, and he said something like, 'Well, we'll see, they haven't played out west, and they end up with us and we're going to beat 'em up a bit,' or something like that. But that's Phil. I know that. And the question kind of led him there, and it sounded a lot worse than he intended it. But I was going to use it anyway. But before I get a chance to use it, Kevin stands up in front of everyone and yells, 'And don't forget what Phil said!'"

After the Celtics cruised to a 110–91 victory over the Lakers on December 30 at the Staples Center, Jackson told reporters, "Well, that was a rather long, laborious night for us."[1]

The Celtics returned to the Garden and began the New Year with victories over Houston and Memphis. They were now 16–1 at home, their lone setback at the Garden the December 19 affair with Detroit in which Chauncey Billups pump-faked Tony Allen into a key foul. And as the home victories piled up and the JumboTron routinely came alive with the *American Bandstand* video featuring the bearded young man in the Gino T-shirt—he was now being referred to as Gino even though the picture on his T-shirt was of Gino Vannelli, a Canadian pop singer who debuted in the early '70s—fans began to notice the effect it had on Garnett. When "Gino" appeared, Garnett would thrust a fist up to the JumboTron as though paying homage to some basketball god.

With Garnett's help, Gino T-shirts were becoming popular items. And then, late in the season, the *Wall Street Journal* came up with one of the most interesting Celtics-related stories of the season: reporter Amol Sharma had solved the mystery of Gino. The young man in the Gino Vannelli T-shirt was identified as Joe Massoni; the newspaper also reported the sad news that he was only thirty-four years old when, in 1990, he died of pneumonia.

As the Gino craze was growing, some fans theorized that identifying the young man in the video would somehow ruin the magic, but this superstition could not have been further from the truth. The Celtics continued to win, and Kevin Garnett continued his late-night salute to the bearded young man in the brown bell-bottoms and Gino Vannelli T-shirt.

Garnett also had a positive effect on those around him. Pierce was no longer burdened with being a lone star on an otherwise lackluster team; the quality of his game was elevated, sure, but so were his spirits. You could see it on his face.

Center Kendrick Perkins, who turned twenty-four midway through the season but was already in his fifth NBA campaign, having been drafted out of high school, was clearly benefiting from Garnett's presence. He started seventy-eight games, and his game averages of 6.9 points, 6.1 rebounds, 1.44 blocks, and 24.5 minutes were all career highs. Best of all, his 61.3 field goal percentage was the highest in franchise history . . . sort of. Cedric Maxwell's mark of 60.9 percent in 1979–80 was in the books as the franchise record—and it remained the franchise record because Perkins didn't take enough shots to qualify for the league lead. But in the Celtics' world of ubuntu, it did not matter.

"I didn't even know about it until after the season," Perkins recalled. "My friends were asking me, 'How come you didn't get that record?' I said, 'We won, man.' And I also told them it's fair. I said, 'What if some guy took only four shots all season and made them? Should that guy get the record?'"

Asked who informed him that he was giving the record a run for its money, Perkins said, "Cedric Maxwell told me."

Garnett's abdominal injury kept him out for nine games, during which the Celtics went 7–2. To look at Garnett's absence from a glass-half-full perspective, the Celtics now had an opportunity to see if there were players on the bench with the right stuff to step in and play a heightened role. In a 117–87 victory at Miami on January 29, second-year forward Leon Powe had the game of his life, scoring twenty-five points and collecting eleven rebounds. Powe, a native of Oakland, California, whose football career at Golden Gate Elementary School ended when his first and only career punt landed *behind* him, made a name for himself in basketball at Cal/Berkeley; the Celtics landed him in the second round of the 2006 draft after trading a 2007 pick to the Denver Nuggets. It was not the first time Danny Ainge had acquired a player who could help with a second-round pick, and it would not be the last time.

Ryan Gomes, a second-round pick in the 2005 draft, was one of the players the Celtics gave up to make the Garnett trade. In 2007 Big Baby Davis and Gabe Pruitt were both second-round picks. As Jeff Howe of the *Boston Metro* later observed, "The fearless attitude Danny Ainge brought to the court every night in the 1980s made his opponents hate him. Now, in the Celtics' front office, that same mentality Ainge displays throughout the NBA draft process has him envied . . . [he] has been one of the league's most active and successful general managers on draft night, particularly in the all-too-wasted second round."[2]

But while he had engineered two historic trades to bring Ray Allen and Kevin Garnett to Boston and built a roster that included *three* second-round picks in Powe, Pruitt, and Big Baby, Ainge knew he'd have to make some midseason changes to strengthen the team for the playoffs.

The first move was announced on February 27, and the fact that the 2007–2008 NBA All-Star Game had been played in New Orleans a couple of weeks earlier played a role. P. J. Brown, a tough center/forward who had logged fourteen seasons in the NBA with the Nets, Heat, Hornets, and Bulls, was living in semi-retirement in Louisiana since the end of the 2006–2007 season after turning down comeback offers from several teams, including the Celtics. But the offers were being delivered by front-office suits; now, with the All-Star Game being played in New Orleans, Brown, who was in attendance, found himself being lobbied by Paul Pierce and Ray Allen, who had each made the Eastern Conference squad.*

"They just pulled me over and said, 'Man, we'd really love to have you on the team,'" Brown told the *Globe*. "With our experience, we think you can help our young guys and add some stability to our team. . . . That made a huge difference in this whole deal. If that doesn't happen, you probably don't see me here today."[3]

After Ainge completed the Brown acquisition, his next move was to add depth to the backcourt. And it arrived on March 4 in the person of Sam Cassell, a well-traveled fifteen-year veteran willing to come aboard as a role player for a championship-caliber team.

The Celtics would be going into the postseason with Rondo, in his second NBA season and with no playoff experience, as their point guard. Cassell, who played on two NBA championship teams with the Houston Rockets at the beginning of his career, was to be the insurance policy.

The talk shows were alive with a new level of excitement. True, the Celtics already had their new Big Three, and they had the promising young Rondo, but what they lacked was the kind of depth that only veterans can provide. And everybody knew it. When Brown made his Celtic debut, in the third quarter of a 116–93 victory over the Bulls on March 7, the packed Garden crowd greeted him with a long ovation. Cassell made his Garden debut a week later and was similarly embraced by the fans when he logged fourteen minutes in a 111–82 pasting of Seattle.

Cassell's job was to provide some insurance for Rajon Rondo. But while Rondo may have needed seasoning, he didn't need anyone to tell him how to be a tough NBA player. On March 18, the Celtics entered Houston's Toyota Center to take on the Rockets, who were riding a twenty-two-game winning streak, the second-longest in league history. The two teams had been on the court for barely a second when Rondo locked up with veteran Rockets point guard Rafer Alston, both players

---

* Kevin Garnett led all players in fan balloting conducted by the NBA, with 2,399,148 votes, but missed the game because of his abdominal injury.

earning technical fouls. Though no punches were thrown, the death stare that Rondo fixed on Alston was its own statement: *Don't think for a minute that I'm some kid.*

"They had won twenty-two in a row; they felt like they were the bad guys," Rondo recalled. "We felt like we were the team to beat, period. We felt like *we* were the bad guys. I guess we bumped into each other, and actually the opening tap went out of bounds. We said a couple of words, and we started pushing each other."

And the death stare?

"I was letting him know I didn't want to lose," Rondo said. "That's how I am. I love to bring it. I love competing. Whether it's a rebound, a jump ball, whatever I have to do to win, I want to win."

This was precisely the kind of channeled anger Danny Ainge was hoping Rondo could bring to the Celtics. Here was a player who, as he entered his second season, was still reading that he was a weak link on the rebuilt Celtics, and that, in the end, his poor shooting would stand out on a team with three All-Stars. Consider, for example, this rather damning assessment of his shooting touch in *ESPN: The Magazine*'s preview of the 2007–2008 season: "Would-be college senior shoots worse than some real high school seniors."

"Everyone's entitled to their opinion," Rondo would later say, when shown the article. "I'm a smart player. I know what I have to work on. The majority of people who are talking about me have never played the game, and I know they haven't played at the level I have.

"I heard it all. 'He can't shoot.' 'He can't lead the team.' 'He's not a winner.' 'He won't know how to handle three All-Stars.' 'He's going to get lost in the game.' 'He's a small point guard.' My attitude was, show 'em they're wrong."

On the night of the Rondo-Alston mixer, the Celtics rolled to a 94–74 victory. The team was in the midst of a stretch of five road games in eight nights, including three games in four nights in the so-called Texas Triangle: San Antonio, Houston, Dallas. They began their Triangle adventure by escaping San Antonio with a 93–91 victory, with Cassell stepping in with seventeen points, including a three-pointer with forty-six seconds remaining to put the Celtics ahead for good—this on a night when Ray Allen sat out with a jammed left ankle. Next, they stopped the Rockets' winning streak, with some help from the Rajon Rondo death stare.

Dallas was next. Understand that the Texas Triangle was deemed sufficiently formidable as to merit its own set of statistics, which is to say the Celtics were aware that no team had won consecutive games in the three cities since the Sacramento Kings in 2001. And the Celtics had not done so since the 1986–87 season—which happened to be the last season in which they'd reached the NBA Finals.

Ray Allen's left ankle had healed enough to allow him back into the lineup for the March 20 matchup in Dallas, and with thirty-one seconds remaining, he nailed a three-pointer to put the Celtics ahead to stay in what would be a 94–90 victory.

"No one in this locker room has done this," Garnett said after the game. "What's good about it is we've done it together and we've done it the way we said we wanted to do things from Day One."[4]

The hoo-ha over the Texas Triangle aside, what was important to the Celtics was that their Big Three was back on the floor, Garnett having overcome his abdominal strain and Allen the ankle injury. Danny Ainge had provided depth with the acquisitions of Brown and Cassell; the next challenge, with the playoffs just three weeks away, was to make sure everybody remained healthy.

On April 5, the Celtics went into Charlotte and posted an easy 101–78 victory over the Bobcats. The Big Three didn't even play, with Garnett and Allen sitting on the bench and Pierce back in Boston to be on hand for the birth of his daughter, leaving it to Leon Powe (twenty-two points, nine rebounds) and James Posey (nineteen points) to lead a makeshift lineup. The win was hugely significant on two levels:

> From a historical perspective, it was Boston's sixty-first victory, which established an NBA record for the biggest single-season turnaround. The maladroit 2006–2007 Celtics, remember, won just twenty-four games.

> From a strategic perspective, the victory clinched home-court advantage throughout the playoffs, which would prove to be a significant edge.

The only remaining question was the identity of the Celtics' first-round playoff opponent. The answer arrived on April 15, when the Atlanta Hawks clinched the eighth and final Eastern Conference post-season berth. Their April 20 playoff opener would be the Hawks' first playoff appearance in nine years, and everyone was in agreement that they didn't have a chance against the Celtics.

Everyone was wrong.

Until this point in the story, hockey played next to no role in Boston's Wicked Good Year. Like the pre–new Big Three Celtics, the Boston Bruins were perennially looking to turn back the clock and make some semblance of a return to their glory years—the early '70s, when Bobby Orr and the Big Bad Bruins won two Stanley Cups.

The Bruins remained highly competitive—and indeed, highly entertaining—for many years after Bobby Orr, Gerry Cheevers, Johnny Bucyk, Johnny "Pie" McKenzie, Kenny Hodge, and the ever-flamboyant Derek Sanderson retired from hockey and moved on with their lives. With players ranging from Rick Middleton and Terry O'Reilly to Cam Neely and a gifted young defenseman named Raymond Bourque, the Bruins were always good enough to be considered among the preseason favorites to compete for a Stanley Cup.

And as was the case with Boston's other pro sports teams, Bruins players knew how to tip their caps to those who came before them. When Bourque joined the Bruins in the fall of 1979, management made the outrageous decision to give him uniform number 7, which had been worn by Phil Esposito during his time in Boston. During the 1968–69 season, Esposito became the first NHL player to amass one hundred points in a season, and two years later he submitted one of the greatest campaigns in league history, with seventy-six goals and seventy-six assists—152 points in all. During his seven full seasons in Boston, he led the NHL in goals six times and in total points five times. A memorable (and, to some, inappropriate) bumper sticker of the era told it all: JESUS SAVES. ESPOSITO SCORES ON THE REBOUND.

When the Bruins traded Esposito to the New York Rangers early in the 1975–76 season, they should have retired his number then and there. They did not do so. Four years later, they assigned it to Bourque.

But in creating one of the greatest nongame moments in Boston sports history, Bourque literally gave Esposito the shirt off his back. In 1987 the Bruins came to their senses and invited the now-retired Esposito to the old Boston Garden to retire his number 7, the understanding being that Bourque would continue to wear it until his own career ended. As the ceremony was coming to an end, Bourque skated up to Esposito, pulled off his sweater, and handed it to the guest of honor. In doing so, Bourque revealed a second sweater he had been wearing under the first one, and it sported a new number: 77. The Garden erupted. Bourque wore number 77 for the remainder of his career, including his end-of-the-line stint with the Colorado Avalanche. (It's fascinating how these things work: when a Colorado native named Josh Bard joined the Red Sox in 2006, the catcher chose number 77 in honor of Denver Broncos linebacker Karl Mecklenburg . . . and Ray Bourque.)

However, the Bruins were unable to bring such drama to their on-ice endeavors, especially in the years following the 1990–91 Wales Conference Finals, which they lost to Pittsburgh in six games. Nearly two decades of postseason frustration followed; from the 1999–2000 season through the 2006–2007 season, they missed the playoffs entirely four times. Confidence in the team was at an all-time low. Bruins owner Jeremy Jacobs was routinely blasted by fans and media. When the owner's son, Charlie Jacobs, took a more prominent role in the running of the franchise when he was named executive vice president in 2002, the masses were not convinced that good times were ahead.

But new people were running the team's hockey operations. After easing longtime club executive Harry Sinden into retirement, the Bruins held a press conference on May 26, 2006, to announce that Ottawa Senators assistant general manager Peter Chiarelli was coming on board as the team's new general manager. Two months later, Chiarelli named former Bruins defenseman Don Sweeney director of hockey operations. Both were Harvard graduates. In September 2007, the great Cam Neely, who led the Bruins in scoring in seven of his ten seasons in Boston, signed on as a vice president. Chiarelli tried and failed with his first coaching hire, Dave Lewis, who lasted for only the 2006–2007 season, but hardscrabble Claude Julien, who'd had some success with the Montreal Canadiens and New Jersey Devils after years of riding the buses through the American Hockey League, was a comfortable fit as head coach.

And the Bruins had players. Zdeno Chara, the six-foot-nine defenseman with the hardest shot in the world, signed with the Bruins on July 1, 2006; on October 3, three days before he played his first regular-season game in a Boston uniform, he was named team captain. Left winger Marc Savard, another free-agent acquisition, was an established player who collected ninety-seven points in his first season as a Bruin in 2006–2007. Center Phil Kessel, the fifth overall pick in the 2006 draft, was seen as a rising young star. Goaltender Tim Thomas, who'd kicked around for years in the East Coast Hockey League, the American Hockey League, the International Hockey League, and leagues in Finland and Sweden, was proving, as he neared his thirty-fourth birthday, to be a top-flight NHL goaltender.

Bruins fans remained suspicious. They'd seen too many good teams go belly up in the first round of the playoffs. As recently as 2003–2004, the Bruins were 41–19–15 during the regular season and then jumped out to a three-games-to-one lead in their conference quarterfinal playoff series against Montreal . . . only to lose three straight games and get bounced in the first round.

First-round elimination had become the Bruin Way. The message from the fan base was clear: win a playoff round and *then* come talk to us.

The Bruins qualified for the 2007–2008 Stanley Cup playoffs as the eighth seed from the Wales Conference and would meet the Canadiens in the first round. There was some talk that center Patrice Bergeron, still recovering from the horrific concussion he'd suffered back in October, might make a comeback if the Bruins advanced past Montreal.

But everyone's dire forecast about the B's chances of advancing had been correct. The Canadiens went to the next round of the Stanley Cup playoffs; the Bruins went back to the drawing board. But rather than being blown off the ice by a superior Canadiens team, as had been the expectation, the Bruins took the series to seven games.

Where so many talented and powerful Bruins teams had failed to deliver the postseason goods, here now was a young, feisty Bruins team that had fought the good fight. Trailing 3–1 in the series, the Bruins roared back with two straight victories, beginning with a Game 5 shocker at the Bell Centre in which they scored four third-period goals en route to a 5–1 victory. They evened the series with a 5–4 victory in Game 6 at the Garden, left winger Marco Sturm scoring the game-winner at 17:23 of the third period.

Even after the Bruins were overwhelmed by the Canadiens in the deciding Game 7, losing 5–0 at the Bell Centre, New England hockey fans believed that this team, so recently a laughingstock, had a future. It did not go unnoticed, for instance, that coach Julien had benched Kessel for Games 2, 3, and 4 for reasons that had nothing to do with the young player's health. The coach just didn't like the way the kid was playing, and if this caused Kessel no small measure of embarrassment, then, well, that was just too bad. When he was given his skates back for Game 5, he scored the first of Boston's five goals. And then he scored two goals in Game 6, prompting Julien to remark, "If he wants to keep proving me wrong, I can take it."[5]

For the first time in recent memory, Bruins fans came out of a playoff series loss actually looking forward to next season.

And the Bruins were not the only feel-good hockey story of the spring. On April 12, at the Pepsi Center in Denver, a five-foot-five left winger named Nathan Gerbe scored two second-period goals to power Boston College to a 4–1 victory over Notre Dame and capture the 2008 NCAA Division I hockey championship.

The BC Eagles didn't get a rolling rally for their efforts. But when they returned home from Denver with their championship trophy in tow, they were whisked over to Fenway Park to meet the defending World Series champion Red Sox. Coach Jerry York and his players threw out a collective first pitch prior to the Red Sox' 8–5 victory over the Yankees.

* * *

The Celtics easily won the first two games of their opening-round
playoff series against the Atlanta Hawks, played at TD Banknorth
Garden. There wasn't much drama beyond Hawks point guard Mike
Bibby looking back on Game 1 and dismissing Celtics fans as "bandwagon jumpers," explaining that, a year earlier, "I remember them having
bags on their heads."[6] Bibby, brother-in-law of the Celtics' Eddie House,
was of course booed mercilessly in Game 2, the added bonus for Boston
fans being the fine play of *their* point guard, Rondo, who amassed twelve
points, eight assists, and six rebounds.

But then the series shifted to Atlanta's Philips Arena, where, to the
surprise of everyone except the plucky, upstart Hawks, the home team
posted a 102–93 victory—despite Garnett leading all scorers with thirty-
two points.

The upset also introduced a bit of controversy, this one with more
substance than Bibby's harmless cage-rattling with Celtics fans. When
the Hawks' Al Horford yelled something at Pierce after connecting on
a jump shot, the Celtics captain responded with a hand gesture that, at
the time, didn't seem to be a big deal. In the postgame analysis and dissection, it was barely mentioned. What *was* a big deal was that two days
later, in Game 4, the Hawks tied the series with a 97–92 victory.

With the series returning to Boston for Game 5, the NBA announced
that it was fining Pierce $25,000 for what it termed "a menacing ges-
ture." What Pierce had done was form a circle with his thumb and fore-
finger and hold the three remaining fingers up, which in the league's
view constituted a gang sign. The Celtics released a statement before the
game, quoting Pierce as saying, "I one hundred percent do not in any
way promote gang violence or anything close to it." As for the gesture, he
said, "I am sorry if that was misinterpreted in Saturday's game."

Judging from the cheers directed at Pierce as the Celtics rolled to a
110–85 Game 2 victory over the Hawks, Boston fans were unbothered
by the "menacing gesture" or the fine that followed it. The *Globe* did find
a concerned community activist who said, "Even if it wasn't a gang sign,
it gave the appearance that it was,"[7] but the *Herald* dug up a photo from
2005 showing Boston mayor Thomas Menino making almost the exact
same three-finger salute while posing with the hip-hop group Special

Teamz. The "menacing gesture" controversy faded away after a couple of days.

The Celtics were now one victory away from eliminating the pesky Hawks, but the Gino home-court advantage was turning out to be a much bigger factor than anyone anticipated: in a series that was supposed to be a sweep, the Celtics were winning at the Garden and losing on the road. And so it went in Game 6, the Hawks coming away with a 103–100 victory. The Hawks were just 37–45 during the regular season. They had barely made the playoffs. The franchise hadn't even *been* to the playoffs in nine seasons. And here they were, playing the team with the NBA's best record. The team with the new Big Three. The team with Celtic Pride, the team with ubuntu.

Is it possible there was some history at play here? Though the *Atlanta* Hawks had never won a playoff series against the Celtics, the franchise once did business as the *St. Louis* Hawks. And after losing a grueling seven-game series to the Celtics in the 1957 NBA Finals, the last game going to two overtimes, the *St. Louis* Hawks came back the next year and ousted the Celts in the Finals. And if one extends the history to before the era of the *St. Louis* Hawks, the franchise was known as the Tri-Cities Blackhawks. And their coach was . . . Red Auerbach.

Had the modern-day Atlanta Hawks handed the Celtics a shocking first-round elimination, perhaps somebody would have dredged up a Ghost of Red Auerbach angle, suggesting that, in the interest of a good story line, Red was feeling a tad nostalgic about the Tri-Cities Blackhawks and wanted to give their descendants some help in the playoffs. Maybe Wyc Grousbeck was wrong: maybe Red really *was* angry about the cheerleaders.

In the end, though, Red's ghost remained faithful to the team he made famous. The Celtics rolled to a 99–65 victory. Before the game was even over, Garden public-address announcer Eddie Palladino was letting fans know that tickets were on sale for the Celtics' upcoming playoff series against LeBron James and the Cleveland Cavaliers.

It had been a tough, emotional series for the Celtics, tougher than anyone anticipated. Looking back, though, Doc Rivers couldn't help but feel that the Hawks made the Celtics a better playoff team.

"I told our coaches after Game 4, 'If we get through this, it's going to be very good for us,'" he recalled. "If we didn't have that Game 5 and that Game 7 against Atlanta, I don't think the Cleveland series would have turned out the way it did.

"All season, we had been on every magazine cover and featured on every pregame show," he said. "There was the Three Amigos thing on ESPN. Even *I* was getting sick of it. But my biggest concern going into the playoffs was that we hadn't been tested. That's what Atlanta did for us."

21
PLAYING THE PALACE

T he spirit of Red Auerbach may not have been a presence during the Celtics' opening-round playoff series against the Atlanta Hawks, but Paul Pierce could practically smell Red's cigar smoke as Boston was closing out the Cleveland Cavaliers in an epic Game 7 of the Eastern Conference semifinals.

With 7.9 seconds remaining, the Celtics ahead by three points, the Garden roaring, the masses knowing they were witnessing one of those scrapbook moments that get passed down through the generations, Pierce was fouled by the Cavs' Sasha Pavlovic. He stepped to the line, poised to clinch the Celtics' trip to the Eastern Conference finals. His first shot was an adventure, clanging off the rim . . . bouncing into the air . . . and then finally, improbably, clumsily, plopping through the basket.

The next shot was clean. The Celtics won, 97–92. Bring on the Detroit Pistons, everyone hollered.

"The ghost of Red was looking over us," Pierce said, explaining a bad shot that somehow became a good shot. "I wish he was here today with us, but I just think that's him looking over us that guided the ball in."[1]

It was a game in which two great basketball players, Pierce for the home team, LeBron James for the Cavaliers, submitted performances worthy of a Ken Burns documentary. King James scored forty-five points, nearly half his team's total offensive output. It was the fourth-highest individual point total for a Game 7 in NBA history. Pierce scored forty-one points, including nine of Boston's first fourteen points as the Celtics jumped out to a 16–4 lead. He had twenty-six points by halftime.

"He just willed his team to victory," applauded King James after the game.[2]

Before the game was even finished, anyone with an ounce of interest in basketball history was thinking that, wait a minute, they'd seen this game before. Or one very close to it. Soon everyone was saying out loud what everyone had been thinking: the pace and the drama of this game, with two great players submitting performances for the ages, was not unlike the playoff showdown between the Celtics and Atlanta Hawks in Game 7 of the 1988 Eastern Conference semifinals. Larry Bird and the Hawks' Dominique Wilkins combined for eighty-one points, with Wilkins leading all scorers with forty-seven. Bird scored thirty-four points—twenty of them during a furious, frenzied fourth quarter—leading the Celtics to a 118–116 victory.

"I'm very aware of that game," Pierce said. "They don't ever let you forget it when you look up at the JumboTron. Neither one of us wanted our team to lose. . . . Just to be part of something like this, it's just a great feeling, man."[3]

The victory put things into perspective for young and old Celtics fans alike. With the team headed for a showdown with Detroit in the Eastern Conference finals, the Big Three and their teammates were offering the first real postseason connection to those great Celtics teams of the past. It was one thing for the game operations staff to throw a lot of old Larry Bird, Bill Russell, and John Havlicek clips onto the JumboTron to fire up the masses and offer a reminder about what was at stake, but now it was the playoffs and *these* Celtics were playing like *those* Celtics.

Doc Rivers was able to see the comparison from a unique perspective: in Game 7, 1988, Bird versus Wilkins, Rivers played for the losing Hawks.

"It didn't hit me until the end," Rivers said, connecting 2008 with 1988. "This one I appreciated more, because it was *our* guy making the big plays down the stretch."[4]

Danny Ainge, too, played in that long-ago classic. When it was over, the future general manager of the Celtics told reporters, "It will be a game to pull out the tapes in the future, and watch them and say, 'That was quite a game.'"[5]

Sure enough, folks *were* pulling out tapes of that game.

But before the Celtics and Cavaliers could get to their modern-day classic in Game 7, they waged a hard-fought series that once again came down to home-court advantage: each team won the games played in its home building.

James had an awful performance in Game 1, shooting just 2-for-18 and coming out of it with twelve points. He was getting his shots but missing them. Layups were rolling around the basket and not falling in. The Celtics, even with their 76–72 victory, weren't much better: though Kevin Garnett led all scorers with twenty-eight points, the other members of Boston's Big Three *combined* for four points—all of them by Pierce on 2-for-14 shooting. Allen had *zero* points, his first scoreless performance since 1997.

In Game 2, an 89–73 Boston victory, Pierce (nineteen points) and Allen (sixteen points) found some semblance of their scoring touches. James managed twenty-one points, but on just 6-for-24 shooting. He also committed seven turnovers. In the two losses at Boston, he was a combined 8-for-42 from the field and 0-for-10 on three-point attempts.

Using the media to send a message to his teammates, James said, "I've got to let them know that I'm not frustrated and I'm not getting down on this series. Being down 0–2, that's a tough hole to dig yourself out of, but we're going to have to do it if we want to move on."[6]

James's woes continued when the series shifted to Cleveland's Quicken Loans Arena for Game 3, but his teammates had apparently read the quote from their leader in the newspapers, including twenty-four-year-old guard Delonte West, the onetime Celtic who, along with Wally Szczerbiak and first-round pick Jeff Green, had been sent to the Seattle Sonics the previous June to bring Ray Allen to Boston. Late in the 2007–2008 season, the Cavaliers obtained West and Szczerbiak as part of a three-team trade with the Sonics and Chicago Bulls that also landed them center Ben Wallace, a four-time NBA Defensive Player of the Year, and guard Joe Smith.

And now West was playing a role in the Celtics' championship quest, but in a different uniform. While James and West each scored twenty-one points in Cleveland's easy 108–84 victory in Game 3, the Cavs outscoring the visitors 32–13 in the first quarter, West did his work on 7-for-11 shooting. James was just 5-for-16. Part of it was Boston's tenacious defense; part of it was that James was playing horribly. Put it together and his shooting total for the three games was now 13-for-48.

As for West, he admitted that being a former Celtic was helping him in this series.

"There's no doubt about it," he told reporters. "I remember their sets and basic philosophy, and at times I'm able to see what they're trying to do and communicate it to our coaching staff."[7]

Game 3 was the Celtics' most one-sided defeat of the season. Doc Rivers lost his temper on a foul call against Garnett and landed a technical. Rajon Rondo did not have an assist in twenty-four minutes on the floor. The veteran Cassell was even worse, shooting 0-for-6 and garnering just one point in eighteen minutes of action. And however much one wished to credit the Cleveland defense for shutting down Ray Allen, it was beyond debate that the veteran shooting guard was simply having an awful postseason: he scored just ten points in the Celtics' 108–84 Game 3 loss, hitting only four of twelve shots to go along with a couple of free throws. The Celts had posted the best road record in the NBA during the regular season—31–10—but now they were 0–4 on the road in the postseason.

Without "Gino," they couldn't seem to win a game. And the malaise continued in Game 4: Cavaliers 88, Celtics 77.

James had a garden-variety twenty-one points, but where he excelled was in finding wide-open teammates. He wound up with thirteen assists; during a particularly backbreaking stretch for the Celtics in the fourth quarter, he connected on a three-pointer, got an assist on Daniel Gibson's three-pointer, and then slammed home a one-handed dunk to give the Cavs a nine-point lead with 1:45 remaining. Pierce, locking up with James all night, managed just thirteen points—though he did bring about some discord in the King James court when he wrapped his mitts around the Cleveland star under the basket and spun him into the stands. Up jumped James's mother, Gloria, to cry foul, prompting her son to yell, "Sit your [expletive] down."[8]

And so it went. The teams returned to Boston for Game 5, Pierce scoring twenty-nine points to lead the Celtics to a 96–89 victory. And back they went to Cleveland, with James stepping up with thirty-two points, nineteen of them in the second half, as the Cavs tied the series with a 74–69 victory. The Celtics were now 0–6 on the road during the postseason, the worst record by a number-one seed in the era of playoff seeding, which began in 1984.

Game 7 differed in that Pierce and James were hot at the same time, shades of Bird versus Wilkins in 1988. But one aspect of the script remained unchanged: the home team was the winning team.

Now that his own season was over, LeBron James issued a warning to the Celtics and their fans: "Detroit is a very, very good road team," he said. "They take a lot of pride in playing on the road. I think they do even more than they do at home."[9]

Within four days, the King would prove to be a prophet.

As the Celtics moved on to the Eastern Conference finals against the Detroit Pistons, there was yet another comparison that could be made with the great Larry Bird–Dominique Wilkins showdown from the 1988 playoffs: as was the case twenty years earlier, expectations had to be revised after each team posted victories in the other team's building.

In the spring of '88, the Hawks emerged with a 112–104 victory in Game 5 at the old Boston Garden to put the Celtics on the brink of elimination. The Celts then set the stage for Game 7 by claiming a 102–100 victory in Game 6 at the Omni, Ainge lighting it up in the third quarter with nine points in an 11–4 Boston run. Said the 1988 Doc Rivers of the 1988 Danny Ainge, "The shots Danny made tonight were incredible."[10]

In the 2008 Eastern Conference finals, it was the Pistons who marched into a hostile environment and came away with a victory, just as LeBron James had warned might very well happen.

The Celtics did win Game 1 at the Garden, with Garnett scoring twenty-seven points and Rajon Rondo coming up big in the fourth quarter, scoring seven of his eleven points. But the Pistons roared back with a 103–97 victory in Game 2, the first time the Celtics had lost a home game since March 24, when the Philadelphia 76ers went on a 19–0 fourth-quarter run and came away with a stunning 95–90 victory.

Now, with the Celtics having lost a home game, everything changed. Winless in six road games in the playoffs, the Celtics would now have to win a game away from the Garden if they were going to advance to the NBA Finals. Celtics fans could surely take solace in knowing that Ray Allen had found his touch in Game 2: he scored twenty-five points while being limited to just twenty-nine minutes because of foul trouble. But as he put it after the game, "I would much rather be sitting here saying, 'I can't make a shot, but we won the game.' This is a test for us. We've talked about it the first two rounds. Now we're in a situation where we can't go on if we don't win on the road."[11]

More than merely going on "the road" for the next two games of the Eastern Conference finals, the Celtics were heading to the Palace at Auburn Hills, where the Pistons had drawn 905,116 fans during the season, tops in the NBA. In a world of professional sports sameness, especially in the modern-day NBA, where every building offers lots of smoke and mirrors, noise, leggy, smiling cheerleaders, and daring, acrobatic mascots, the Detroit basketball experience is somehow different. Part of it is that the Pistons' in-game presentation includes public-address announcer John Mason—just "Mason" when on the clock—who has a style, a cadence, and a delivery that is truly his own. When fans hear the words, "DEEEEEEE-troit BASKET-ball!!!" they know they are at the Palace.

But there is more to it than that. If there are cranky old-timers back in Boston who whine about the Pink Hats invading their beloved Fenway Park, there is no such hysteria in Detroit over the Pistons. The Palace is a place for basketball connoisseurs; you can feel it as soon as you walk in the door. It no doubt helps that the Pistons do not share a facility with Detroit's National Hockey League team, the Red Wings. While the Wings conduct their affairs at Joe Louis Arena in downtown Detroit, the Pistons have their Palace in the suburbs.

The difference is that the Pistons' championship tradition is a relatively recent phenomenon. Whereas the Celtics can trace their championship roots all the way back to 1957, when they beat the old St. Louis Hawks in the NBA Finals, the Pistons didn't win their first championship until 1989. They repeated in 1990 and brought a third title to

Detroit in 2004, with former Celtic Chauncey Billups named MVP of their five-game dismissal of the Los Angeles Lakers.

The Celtics' playoff history with the Pistons, while not as expansive as with the Lakers and 76ers, was still impressive as the two teams matched up in the spring of 2008. During the era of the original Big Three, the C's beat the Pistons in the playoffs in 1985 and 1987 and lost to them in '88, '89, and '91. Aging Celtics fans still get fired up when they talk about Pistons tough guy Bill Laimbeer, whose fight with Larry Bird in Game 3 of the '87 Eastern Conference semifinals culminated with Bird reaching over a crowd of players and firing a basketball at Laimbeer. Both players were ejected. Game 5 of the series ended with Bird making a never-to-be-forgotten steal of an Isiah Thomas inbounds pass to Laimbeer and moving the ball to Dennis Johnson, who rolled in the game-winning layup with one second remaining. In the heat of all this, the rivalry included the ever-faithful Johnny Most, the legendarily one-sided Celtics play-by-play announcer. At one juncture he leaned into his microphone and said of the Pistons, "They have been called a dirty ball club, and I can see why," followed by his disgust with "the yellow, gutless way they do things here." The quote is de rigueur at every Johnny Most Sound Alike Contest and is as good a reason as any to explain why YouTube was invented.

So, yes, Pistons fans old and young were rather familiar with the Celtics and all the history they carry with them when Game 3 was played at the Palace. But the Celtics took to heart all that talk about how they now had to win on the road: they claimed a 94–80 victory, with a fired-up Garnett contributing twenty-two points and thirteen rebounds to the cause. But when Garnett and Ray Allen each picked up two fouls in the first quarter, both of Allen's coming within four seconds, and both against guard/forward Richard Hamilton, it was a time for Boston's bench to shine. By the time the game was over, P. J. Brown and James Posey had each logged more than twenty minutes, with Posey scoring twelve points.

Now the teams traded home victories. Detroit rolled to a 94–75 victory in Game 4, Antonio McDyess leading the Motowners with twenty-one points and sixteen rebounds; the Celtics came out of Game 5 at the

Garden with a 106–102 victory as Kevin Garnett led everyone with thirty-three points and a fired-up Ray Allen added twenty-nine points, connecting on five of six three-point attempts.

Even before Game 6 unfolded at the Palace, both teams had established that home-court advantage, at least in this series, was of less significance than it had been ten days earlier. The Celtics, after all, had won Game 3 on the Pistons' home court, and they arrived for Game 6 knowing that, at the worst, they'd still have Game 7 at the Garden.

The Pistons enjoyed a ten-point fourth-quarter lead, and this was when all things Palace should have come together and inspired the worn-down Celtics to ponder a rosy outlook for Game 7; instead, the Celtics went on a 19–4 run and in so doing turned down the volume inside one of the NBA's loudest arenas.

When it was over—Celtics 89, Pistons 81—Boston players could be heard mocking Mason as they exited the court, muttering, "DEEEEEEE-troit BASKET-ball!!!" It wasn't nearly as demonstrative as what the New England Patriots were accused of doing a year earlier on the Chargers' logo at Qualcomm Stadium, and there was no Piston to play the role of LaDainian Tomlinson and decry the injustice of it all, but the point was made: having won two games of this series on the opposing team's court, the Celtics were feeling invincible.

The individual parts that make up the Big Three were working beautifully. Pierce had twenty-seven points in Game 6. Allen had seventeen points. Garnett had sixteen.

They were ready for what lay ahead: a series that everyone, from kids to codgers, could easily embrace. And would, for the rest of their lives.

22

A WICKED GOOD NIGHT

After it was over, after the Duck Boats returned to port, after the last piece of confetti was scooped up, after forward Leon Powe and center/forward P. J. Brown collected their championship bonuses and moved on to new teams, and after both the victorious Celtics and the vanquished Lakers began the process of reloading for a new season, Larry Bird put it out there that the 2008 NBA Finals had been too much about history and not enough about the here and now.

Indeed, this latest installment in the greatest rivalry in basketball had been a celebration of every second of every game ever played between the Boston Celtics and the Minneapolis/Los Angeles Lakers, with a glittering array of yesterday's legends being asked to take a bow and tell us what it was like Back Then. Look into one corner and there's Bill Russell posing for a picture with Kevin Garnett. Look into another corner and there's Lakers forward Luke Walton talking about living in this really cool house on Avon Hill Street in Cambridge, back when the old man, Bill Walton, was helping the Celtics to the 1986 NBA championship. Tommy Heinsohn, a Celtics legend who broke into the NBA in 1956, watched the home games from deep inside the TD Banknorth Garden at Legends, the high-end bar/restaurant for high-rollers, while holding hands with his wife, Helen, who by now was too sick to take a seat in the arena. When the series shifted to Los Angeles for Games 3, 4, and 5, look again and, yes, that was Lakers legend Jerry West disembarking the plane holding the Larry O'Brien Trophy, which would go to the winner.

And there was Larry Bird. Lots and lots of Larry Bird. And Magic Johnson. Lots and lots of Magic Johnson. It was as though the late, great Broadway impresario David Merrick, who brought *Gypsy*, *Hello Dolly*, and *42nd Street* to the stage, had come back from the beyond to produce the 2008 NBA Finals, turning the affair into:

LARRY BIRD
&
MAGIC JOHNSON
Starring
In
THE 2008 NBA FINALS
With
*Kevin Garnett * Kobe Bryant * Paul Pierce*
*Lamar Odom * Ray Allen * Derek Fisher*

"When I was watching the Finals, I thought they had too much of me and Magic going on," Bird recalled. "We had our time, and now it's all about Kobe and Kevin and Paul and Ray. It's their time now."

What Larry Bird and Magic Johnson shared, beyond their enormous athletic talent and off-the-charts competitiveness, was a respect for the heroes of their own yesterdays—and not just in basketball. Late in Bird's career, it was unearthed that the Celtics superstar sought pregame inspiration during the playing of the national anthem by gazing up at the retired uniform number of *Bruins* superstar Bobby Orr. But Magic was not above mixing in a little Barnum with his basketball; he was delighted that the 2008 NBA Finals became a circus of nostalgia and that he was in the center ring.

"I thought it was a natural part of the rivalry, just like, when we first played against each other [in the NBA], it was natural to bring up Jerry West, Wilt Chamberlain, and Elgin Baylor, and Bill Russell and John Havlicek and those guys," he recalled.

"The history is what makes the rivalry so great, and I think it's also great for all the new fans to understand it. Their parents are telling them about the players who made it a great rivalry, and now it's a great stage for the great players today—Kevin Garnett and Paul Pierce and Ray Allen and Kobe Bryant and on and on and on."

And what a history it was. Beginning with the 1958–59 season, when the franchise was still based in Minneapolis, and extending through the 1968–69 season, the Lakers met the Celtics in the NBA Finals on seven occasions. The Lakers lost every time, culminating with an aging collection of Celtics going into the Los Angeles Forum for Game 7 of the '69 NBA Finals and emerging with a 108–106 victory. Now, that was a long time ago, and not many fans are up on the game details, or know that Jerry West became the only player ever from the losing team to be named Most Valuable Player of the NBA Finals. But everyone seems to know that the Lakers planned to release thousands of balloons from the Forum ceiling after they won the championship and that player/coach Bill Russell, hearing of the plan, famously told West, "Those balloons are staying up!"

The rivalry was wonderfully renewed in the 1980s, only now it was Magic Johnson leading the Lakers against the Celtics' vaunted Big Three of Bird, McHale, and Parish. The Celtics continued their forever mastery of the Lakers in a thrilling seven-game NBA Finals in 1984, with McHale taking down the Lakers' Kurt Rambis with a memorable Game 4 clotheslining that emptied both benches. Like Bird tangling with Laimbeer and Johnny Most spewing his unique brand of venom on all things Pistons, the McHale-Rambis episode has a lofty and lasting perch on YouTube.

But the Lakers finally toppled Boston in the Finals in 1985, and again in '87. And thus was the decade of the '80s remembered in basketball circles as the era of Bird versus Magic. And here they were again, older, heavier, very much involved in new pursuits but very, very much a part of the 2008 NBA Finals.

And once again the spirit of Red Auerbach paid a visit. Though he had played a role in every one of the Celtics' sixteen championships, he was on the floor as head coach for nine of them. So, too, had the Lakers' Phil Jackson won nine championships as a head coach—six of them with the Chicago Bulls during the Michael Jordan era and three of them with the Lakers. The fact that Jackson had jumped from the aging

Bulls to the up-and-coming Lakers bothered Auerbach; holding court with reporters at the Garden before the Celtics' 2005 season opener, the aging and frail patriarch of Boston's NBA franchise said, "Phil obviously is a good coach. You don't win that many games without being a damn good coach. But remember one thing—he's been very fortunate. He picks his spots. That's all I care to say."[1]

A delicious subplot had been slipped neatly into place for Celtics fans: no way was Phil Jackson going to pass the sainted Red Auerbach on *their* watch.

Game 1 was played on June 5 at TD Banknorth Garden, and midway through the third quarter yet another subplot involving Phil Jackson was introduced. With 6:49 remaining in the period, just as Lakers superstar Kobe Bryant made a running jumper to give the Lakers a four-point lead, Kendrick Perkins inadvertently slammed into Paul Pierce; the Celtic captain crashed to the paint and began writhing in agony as he clutched his right knee. Celtics fans immediately feared the season was over. As Doc Rivers would say later, "Honestly, I thought the worst."[2]

Helped off the court by teammates Brian Scalabrine and Tony Allen, Pierce was dropped into a wheelchair under the seating bowl and rushed to the locker room, the whole dramatic scene captured by an embedded behind-the-scenes ABC camera and watched by millions of television viewers.

What happened next was either one of the great miracles in modern sports history or one of the best acting jobs in modern theatrical history. Everyone would have an opinion over the next couple of days—including Coach Phil, transforming himself into Dr. Phil just for the occasion.

Just one minute and forty-five seconds of elapsed playing time later, Pierce came bounding back out to the court, his damaged knee wrapped in black, *Rocky* music blaring from the Garden public-address system. He was immediately fouled by Bryant and made one of two free throws, but it was what followed that cemented Pierce as the next in an ever-growing cast of Celtic postseason heroes. He drained two three-pointers within a span of twenty-two seconds, the first putting the Celtics ahead by a point, the next putting them up 75–71. He finished the quarter with fifteen points, having shot 5-for-5, and 3-for-3 from three-point land. The Celtics captured Game 1, 98–88.

Pierce's comeback was instantly dubbed a "Willis Reed moment." The New York Knicks legend had suffered a thigh injury in Game 5 of the 1970 NBA Finals against the Lakers, missed all of Game 6, and then hobbled out to the Madison Square Garden court and delivered the first two baskets of Game 7, thus inspiring his team to victory. It is considered the greatest moment in Madison Square Garden history.

Phil Jackson seemed mildly skeptical of the seriousness of Pierce's injury during his postgame remarks to the media, but now, on an off day before Game 2, the Willis Reed comparison got him all worked up. Jackson, it should be noted, played his entire twelve-year NBA career in a Knicks uniform; though he missed the 1969–70 season because of an injury, those were still *his* Knicks, and the guy who hobbled out to the court in Game 7 was *his* teammate.

"Well, if I'm not mistaken, I think Willis Reed missed a whole half and three-quarters almost of a game and literally had to have a shot, a horse shot, three or four of them in his thigh to come back out and play," Jackson told the media. "Paul got carried off and was back on his feet in a minute. I don't know if the angels visited him at halftime . . . but he didn't even limp when he came back out on the floor. I don't know what was going on there. Was Oral Roberts back there in their locker room?"

Both Pierce and Perkins (he came out of Game 1 after the collision with a sprained left ankle) spent a good portion of the off day between Games 1 and 2 receiving medical treatment and riding stationary bikes. Pierce held a session with the media, but it was as much about being on the trainer's table as on the court. He talked about everything from ice and rubdowns to MRIs and even laser treatments; when asked what bothered him most about the ailing knee, he said, "I think mostly my range of motion, just being able to squat all the way down. I can't quite do that yet. My walk is pretty good actually, but when I go down into a squat position, that's when I feel it the most, when I bend it. Like if you look at the knee, if you bend it all the way, there's some pain there."

But not enough pain to keep Pierce from decimating the Lakers in

Game 2 the next night. He responded with twenty-eight points, and reserve Leon Powe came off the bench and scored twenty-one points in fifteen minutes as the Celtics escaped with a 108–102 victory— "escaped" being the proper word here, given that Boston nearly gave the game away. Leading by as many as twenty-four points in the fourth quarter, the Celtics saw their lead shrink to just two points with thirty-eight seconds remaining. But Boston's finely tuned defense did the job, with Pierce blocking a Sasha Vujacic three-point attempt with twelve seconds remaining, and James Posey clinching it with a pair of free throws.

As the teams headed to Los Angeles for Games 3, 4, and 5, fans and media alike were naturally offering all kinds of commentary, dissection, and analysis about what the Lakers needed to do to get back into the series. But one comment seemed to stand out, and it was submitted by none other than Red Sox pitcher Curt Schilling, a hero of World Series championships in 2004 and 2007. Schilling had signed a one-year, $8 million contract to return to the Sox for 2008 but was idled by a shoulder injury that would keep him out for the entire season. In the meantime, he kept busy in a variety of pursuits, one of which was his personal blog at 38 Pitches.com.

While an impressive cast of Red Sox and Patriots players had been in attendance for Game 2 at the Garden, including David Ortiz, Jon Lester, Richard Seymour, and Vince Wilfork, Schilling had scored a courtside seat next to the Lakers bench. The next day, Schilling uploaded on his blog a post about his up-close-and-personal experience, including some observations on Kobe Bryant, who had scored thirty points for the Lakers, twenty-one of them in the second half.

"From the first tip until about four minutes left in the game I saw and heard this guy bitch at his teammates," Schilling wrote.

Every TO he came to the bench pissed, and a few of them he went to other guys and yelled about something they weren't doing, or something they did wrong. No dialog about "hey let's go, let's get after it" or whatever. He spent the better part of 3.5 quarters pissed off and ranting at the non-execution or lack of, of his team. Then when they made what almost was a historic run in the 4th, during a TO, he got down on the floor and

basically said "Let's f'ing go, right now, right here" or something to that
affect. I am not making this observation in a good or bad way, I have no
idea how the guys in the NBA play or do things like this, but I thought
it was a fascinating bit of insight for me to watch someone in another
sport who is in the position of a team leader and how he interacted with
his team and teammates. Watching the other 11 guys, every time out
it was high fives and "Hey nice work, let's get after it" or something to
that affect. He walked off the floor, obligatory skin contact on the high
five, and sat on the bench stone faced or pissed off, the whole game. Just
weird to see another sport and how it all works. I would assume that's his
style and how he plays and what works for him because when I saw the
leader board for scoring in the post season his name sat up top at 31+ a
game, can't argue with that. But as a fan I was watching the whole thing,
Kobe, his teammates and then the after effects of conversations. He'd
yell at someone, make a point, or send a message, turn and walk away,
and more than once the person on the other end would roll eyes or give
a "whatever dude" look.[3]

Schilling's blog, and the guessing over how or if Bryant would react
to it, emerged as yet another subplot going into Game 3 at the Staples
Center. Die-hard Lakers fan Jack Nicholson was in attendance, as were
Sylvester Stallone, Steven Spielberg, Adam Sandler, Dyan Cannon,
Dustin Hoffman, Penny Marshall, Spike Lee, and, of course, the bad
boy from Dorchester, Donnie Wahlberg. But the biggest star of them all
was the "stone faced and pissed off" Kobe Bryant, who scored thirty-six
points to power the Lakers to an 87–81 victory.

When asked about Schilling's blog, Bryant delivered one of the best
lines of the postseason.

"Go Yankees," he deadpanned.

Pierce struggled in Game 3, scoring just six points and missing twelve
shots. Here was a polished NBA star who had grown up in Inglewood,
just a few miles from the Staples Center, and it was only natural that
fans and media would speculate about the added anxiety and pressure
Pierce faced, what with coming back home, making the obligatory social
calls, and then trying to wow everybody on the hometown hardwood.

Not so, said Pierce, who let it be known that he'd have "plenty of time to visit with my friends and family in the summer. So I'm just approaching these games the same way I would as if I were playing anywhere else."

But Pierce did have a lot of friends in the stands, and he absolutely impressed them in Game 4. So, too, did Kevin Garnett . . . Ray Allen . . . James Posey . . . Eddie House . . .

Home-court advantage being what it is in the NBA, the Lakers should have defeated the Celtics in Game 4, thus evening the series. Instead, it turned out to be a shocking, improbable, and—there's that word again—*historic* 97–91 victory by the visitors from Boston. Consider, first, that the Lakers pushed the Celtics all over the court in the first quarter, taking a 35–14 lead. The history books delivered some sobering news to the Celtics: since the 1970–71 season, when the numbers crunchers from the Elias Sports Bureau burst on the scene and began keeping track of such things, no team had ever come back to win a game in the NBA Finals after trailing by twenty-four points.

At halftime the Celtics trailed 58–40. That's when Pierce approached Doc Rivers with an idea.

"Paul came to me at halftime and said, 'I want to guard Kobe,'" Rivers said. "'Let me guard him. I'm foul-less. I can commit some fouls, be physical with him. It would take him off the post.' So we went with it, and it was terrific."

Bryant missed only four shots in the first half. In the third quarter, he made only two of seven shots. And the Celtics began to light it up, going on a 19–3 run to end the quarter, including a slam dunk by P. J. Brown with one second remaining. The Lakers now led only 73–71.

The Celtics tied the game three times in the fourth quarter, sucking the hometown energy out of the Staples Center. The Celtics finally took the lead—for good—when Eddie House connected on an eighteen-foot jumper with 4:07 remaining. But the clincher took place with just under sixteen seconds remaining, when Ray Allen drove past Sasha Vujacic for an easy layup.

Sometimes an image from the losing team is what everyone remembers. In the sixth inning of Game 6 of the 1947 World Series, the Brooklyn Dodgers' diminutive Al Gionfriddo raced to the outer reaches of

Yankee Stadium, some 415 feet from home plate, and reached over the fence to rob the great Joe DiMaggio of what would have been a three-run homer, yet the image that gets played again and again is of a disgruntled Joltin' Joe kicking dirt as he slows up at second base. On September 20, 1964, the Pittsburgh Steelers held on for a 27–24 victory over the New York Giants at Pitt Stadium, but the photograph of that game that hangs in the Pro Football Hall of Fame shows the battered Giants quarterback Y. A. Tittle slumped on his knees in the end zone, his hands in his lap, his helmet nowhere to be seen, blood trickling down over his left eye. To some, the enduring image of Game 4 of the 2008 NBA Finals will be of Laker Sasha Vujacic sitting on the bench during a time-out following Allen's basket, angrily swiping away the arm of a teammate who tries to console him. It got as much play as anything the victorious Celtics did that night.

Boston's 97–91 victory was what proud coaches like to call a team effort. Posey contributed eighteen points, including two three-pointers in the fourth quarter, and House, in the words of *Herald* sportswriter Mark Murphy, "added 11 points, four rebounds and a lot of energy."[4]

They were one victory away from their seventeenth NBA championship.

The next day the coaches of both teams appeared at press conferences held at a recreational facility in nearby El Segundo. Rivers had ready answers to a variety of questions—offering a diplomatic comparison between Kobe Bryant and Chicago Bulls legend Michael Jordan, explaining what Ray Allen had meant to the Celtics during the season, and offering his opinion as to why an overwhelming number of hoop pundits had picked the Lakers to win the series. He was even asked about the preseason Duck Boats adventure—when Charlie Perry, aka Admiral Amnesia, took Rivers and the newly assembled Big Three for a ride through Boston on *Haymarket Hannah*.

And then Rivers was stopped, numbed, by a question from Yahoo! Sports columnist Adrian Wojnarowski.

With Game 5 slated for Sunday—Father's Day—Wojnarowski wanted to know what it would have meant for Doc Rivers had his own father lived to see the Celtics win a championship.

Rivers paused for a good long while and began tapping a finger on the side of his head.

"We can come back to that if you want to," Wojnarowski said.

"That's just a tough one for me to talk about," said Rivers.

Someone followed with a question about Red Auerbach. The coach responded, and then returned to his late father, Grady Alexander Rivers.

"He's just very important in my life," he said. "It's still very difficult for me to talk about because I haven't had a lot of time, really, to reflect on it. . . . It's very, very difficult. But I do think about it. I think about it a lot."

Some Internet posters grumbled that an inappropriate question had been posed by Wojnarowski, a passionate writer whose book on legendary high school basketball coach Bob Hurley, *The Miracle of St. Anthony,* is one of the first great sports tomes of the twenty-first century. What went unsaid, until now, was that Rivers went online the next day and found the Father's Day column Wojnarowski had filed. The coach liked it and sent the writer an e-mail to tell him so.

"It wasn't a bad question to ask, not at all," Rivers would later say. "I could tell I made him feel bad, and I didn't mean to do that. It was so tough for me, and some people will never get that. People who have lost their father or their mom will."

"I thought about [my father] a ton during that period, but I hadn't talked about [him] of late. I hadn't even heard my dad's name lately. So it really caught me off guard. I was trying to collect myself."

The Celtics did not win the NBA championship on Father's Day. They were without center Kendrick Perkins, who had suffered a shoulder strain late in Game 4, and the Lakers again ran the Celtics off the court in the first quarter, jumping out to a 39–22 lead. But as in Game 4, the Celtics staged another stunning comeback. They pulled even in the fourth quarter and were back within two points when Pierce sank two free throws with 1:14 remaining.

But Bryant saved the night and, for the time being, the Lakers' season. As Pierce moved toward the basket in an attempt to tie the game, Bryant reached in and knocked the ball to Lamar Odom, who then got the ball back to Bryant on the other end. His slam-dunk provided some breathing room for the Lakers, who escaped with a 103–98 victory.

As Donnie Wahlberg was leaving the Staples Center, he ran into pop star Justin Timberlake, who wanted to know, in light of the game's outcome, why Wahlberg wasn't wearing a Celtics jersey.

"I don't even know why you're here," Wahlberg remembers barking back at Timberlake. "Aren't you from Orlando?"

And the question must be asked: was Wahlberg being serious?

"It was good-natured, but there was definitely a little edge," Wahlberg said. "There's always a little edge when you're from Dorchester."

Sean Grande, a New York native who was introduced to the New England sports scene as a Boston University undergraduate in the early '90s, was in his seventh season as the radio voice of the Celtics—the successor, four times removed, of Johnny Most. All good announcers bring a measure of uniqueness to their job, Most's being bombast, irascibility, and an off-the-charts brand of homerism; Grande, among other things, does it with a carefully prepared, erudite monologue that he delivers at the beginning of the pregame show he does with former Celtic Cedric Maxwell.

On Tuesday, June 17, 2008, one hour before Game 6 of the 2008 NBA Finals at TD Banknorth Garden, Grande used his monologue to make note of the fact that it was twenty-two years to the day since the Celtics drafted University of Maryland star Len Bias, who within thirty-six hours would die of a drug overdose.

"It's been a long twenty-two years," Grande told his listeners. "Too few celebrations. And far too many funerals."

Nothing would ever bring back Len Bias. Or Reggie Lewis, a rising star who dropped dead in 1993, leading to speculation that he, too, had been involved with drugs. And for Celtics fans to analyze the deaths of Bias and Lewis strictly in basketball terms had always been an awkward exercise, and one deemed by some to be inappropriate. Yet like it or not, and on many different levels, the Celtics had yet to recover.

On this night, using the entire 2007–2008 season as a preamble to Game 6, Sean Grande said what was on everyone's minds:

"The Celtics earned many things during their spectacular winter of content. Respectability. Credibility. And enough wins to earn them the last word. The chance to end the NBA season where they began it. At home. So tonight, at the Garden, on Causeway Street, on the parquet floor, the Celtics can complete that twenty-two-year star-crossed odyssey and return the franchise to its rightful place atop the basketball world. . . . And it will be worth the wait. Because there's no journey too long, no journey you can't complete, when the destination is home."

Just five and a half years removed from the day newly installed Celtics owner Wyc Grousbeck was told by a soon-to-be-dismissed club executive that "this is a Red Sox town," Game 6 of the NBA Finals proved to be the coolest, hippest event on the planet. Donnie Wahlberg and Mike Rotondi and Marty Joyce were at their courtside seats, of course, but they were wedged into a glitzy crowd that included Leonardo DiCaprio, Steven Tyler, and the filmmaking Farrelly brothers, Bobby and Peter, who four years earlier had to reshoot the ending of their Red Sox–themed romantic comedy *Fever Pitch* because the Sox wrecked the script by winning their first World Series in eighty-six years. The owners of the Sox, Patriots, and Bruins were in the house. So, too, was Patriots coach Bill Belichick, who received a rousing ovation each time he was shown on the JumboTron. Pats players included Larry Izzo, Adalius Thomas, Wes Welker, Vince Wilfork, and backup quarterback Matt Cassel. Celtics legends in attendance included Bill Russell, John Havlicek, and JoJo White. And Tommy Heinsohn, sitting inside Legends with Helen.

Everything seemed to go wrong for the Celtics in the run-up to Game 6. Ray Allen learned after Game 5 that his seventeen-month-old son had diabetes, the diagnosis having been delivered in Los Angeles. He remained on the West Coast an extra day and then traveled back to Boston with his family on a red-eye. As for the rest of the team, the Celtics were late getting out of Los Angeles following Game 5 because of a mechanical issue with their aircraft. Perkins, having missed Game 5 because of shoulder strain, was still iffy for Game 6. Rajon Rondo had a sore ankle.

But just as quickly as their luck had turned, suddenly all was right in the Celtics' world. Allen learned that the reports on his baby boy were encouraging. The players felt rested and ready. Perkins was in the starting lineup. Rondo too.

And then, at 9:00 PM, the game began.

Years from now, it will likely be forgotten that the Lakers took the early lead, just as it is forgotten that the New England Patriots took a 3–0 lead over the Chicago Bears in Super Bowl XX, a game that ended with the Pats suffering a humiliating 46–10 defeat. On this night, the Lakers scored the first four points of the game . . . they went up 13–12 on a three-pointer by Bryant . . . and 18–16 when onetime Cambridge schoolboy Luke Walton hit on a pair of free throws with 3:31 remaining in the first quarter.

At the end of the quarter, the Celtics held a modest 24–20 lead. And then they delivered a knockout punch of epic proportions. The run— stampede might be a better word—began with 6:58 remaining in the second quarter, the Celtics ahead 32–29, when Posey took a feed from House and drilled a three-pointer. Posey then stole a Vujacic pass, after which House put in a three-pointer. The Celtics' lead had just swelled to nine points. Phil Jackson called a time-out. Whatever he said, it did not work.

The Celtics outscored the Lakers 34–15 in the second quarter, taking a 58–35 halftime lead back to their locker room. There would be no buzzer-beating, game-winning basket on this night, no dramatic, Celtics-patented, last-second, game-saving steal. Instead, the entire second half was an ever-escalating victory celebration, a twenty-four-minute victory lap, all cheers, high-fives, and hugs.

With 4:01 remaining, Doc Rivers made the move everyone had been waiting for most of the fourth quarter: he removed Kevin Garnett, Ray Allen, and his captain, the long-suffering Paul Pierce, from the game.

With thirty seconds remaining, Pierce led the charge to steal a bit of symbolism from the NFL playbook: he and his teammates hoisted a Gatorade bucket, spilling its reddish liquid all over Doc Rivers. The coach's stained shirt would later be auctioned off for charity by sports radio WEEI, with an anonymous donor submitting a high bid of $35,000. The Gatorade people kicked in an added $20,000, the result being that $55,000 was directed to the Shamrock Foundation, the philanthropic wing of the Celtics.

The Celtics' 131–92 pasting of the Lakers was the largest margin of victory in a title-clinching game in NBA history. When it ended, Garnett dropped to the parquet and kissed the leprechaun that's painted on center court, and then yesterday and today were brought under one stunning spotlight as Bill Russell found Garnett and hugged him. The spirit of Red Auerbach made yet another appearance: fire laws be damned, everyone lit up cigars.

Wyc Grousbeck, harkening back to his Princeton rowing days, thought about how cool it would have been to take the Lakers' shirts.

Seven months and twenty days after the Red Sox took out the Colorado Rockies in the World Series, and four months and fourteen days after the Patriots suffered a 17–14 loss to the New York Giants in the greatest Super Bowl ever played, the Boston Celtics were champions of the NBA.

And there were no outcries from reporters asking Doc Rivers about his father after the game.

"My first thought," he said, "was what would my dad say, and honestly I started laughing because I thought he would probably say, if you knew my dad, 'It's about time. What have you been waiting for?'"

T he city of Boston hosted another rolling rally on Thursday, June 19, two days after Game 6, but it did not include Charlie Perry, aka Admiral Amnesia, the man who nine months earlier had the power to make Doc Rivers and the new Big Three say, "Quack, quack, quack."

His absence was the result of a scheduling issue. The tourist season was already in full bloom by mid-June, a busy time of the year for Boston Duck Tours, so the drivers already slated to work that day were deployed for the rolling rally. It happened to be Perry's day off, and anyway, said manager Cindy Brown, it seemed only fair to let some of the other drivers in on the fun.

"I was a little upset," Charlie Perry said. "The Celtics had just won a championship, and I kind of felt connected to it."

He stayed at home that day, playing ball with his seven-year-old son, Samuel.

D onnie Wahlberg's brash prediction on ESPN in July 2007 that the Red Sox, Patriots, and Celtics would all win championships had come within one phenomenal, improbable catch by the Giants' David

Tyree of actually happening. But he had been right about the Red Sox, and, damn it, right about the Celtics.

But there was no time to celebrate or gloat. He went right back to work, finishing a television pilot called *Bunker Hill*, shot on location a couple of miles from the Garden in Charlestown. And then Wahlberg and the rest of the New Kids on the Block hit the road for a reunion tour that was phenomenally successful; just as the Celtics had returned to past glory, so, too, had NKOTB.

Several months later, while the reunited New Kids were touring in Europe, Wahlberg was approached at an airport in Scotland by a throng of worshipful, grown-up fans who were following the group from city to city. As Wahlberg made polite talk with the fans, one of them asked if he thought it strange that these people, who had never lost their teenage passion for the New Kids on the Block, would trek through Europe to be with their idols.

The question was a revelation for Wahlberg, who took out his Black-berry and began showing the fans pictures of *his* idols, the Boston Celtics.

"Maybe it explains why I'm so patient with you," he told them as he showed picture after picture of Pierce, Allen, Garnett, and the rest. "I'm the same way. I'm the fan of a basketball team. If I have two days off, I'll fly to Phoenix to see the Celtics play the Suns. And I don't find anything strange about it.

"We're all just looking for a good time."

EPILOGUE
WHAT IT ALL MEANS

For Boston sports fans, the twenty-first century was off to a smashing start. The Patriots won three Super Bowls and came within one history-making catch by the New York Giants' David Tyree from winning a fourth. The Red Sox won their first World Series in eight-six years, and added another two years later. Now the Celtics were champions of the National Basketball Association. But to fully appreciate it all—and in particular, what took place during those seven months and twenty days between October 28, 2007, and June 17, 2008—it is helpful to examine what had been going on in other North American sports hotbeds over the years.

Let's start with Cleveland. Go back to December 27, 1964. When Frank Ryan threw three touchdown passes to Gary Collins to lead the hometown Browns to a 27–0 victory over the Baltimore Colts in the NFL championship game at Cleveland Municipal Stadium, nobody had any way of knowing it would be a long, long time before sports fans on the shores of Lake Erie would again call themselves number one—in anything. The Cleveland Indians have made two trips to the World Series since then, losing both times. The Cleveland Cavaliers, who entered the NBA as an expansion team in 1970, have yet to win a championship. The city had a couple of flings with major league hockey in the 1970s—the Crusaders of the World Hockey Association and a National Hockey League team called the Barons, the name appropriated from the hugely popular minor league team that had played in the city for years. But neither the Crusaders nor Barons ever won anything, and, anyway, neither team stayed around very long.

As for the Browns, they never made it back to the NFL championship game or to its better-marketed descendent, the Super Bowl. Browns owner Art Modell eventually moved the team to Baltimore and renamed it the Ravens, after which the NFL did a makeup call by using expansion to give Cleveland a new edition of the Browns. And they haven't made the Super Bowl, either.

Philadelphia: Until the Phillies won the World Series in 2008, the city had been without a championship since 1983, when the 76ers, led by future Hall of Famers Moses Malone and Julius Erving, swept the Lakers in the NBA Finals. Philly's championship drought inspired writer Lee Jenkins, for an October 2008 piece in *Sports Illustrated*, to do the math and determine that the collective misfortunes of the Phillies, 76ers, Eagles, and Flyers added up to a hundred losing seasons over twenty-five years. "Historically, We Suck," was the spot-on headline for the article, which noted that, of the nation's thirteen metropolitan areas with teams in all four major leagues, only Philly, poor, poor, Philly, had gone at least seventeen years without a parade.

Seattle has the honor of having won two league championships by teams that no longer exist. The Seattle Metropolitans of the Pacific Coast Hockey Association won the Stanley Cup in 1917, topping the Montreal Canadiens. The Seattle SuperSonics won the NBA championship in 1979, the high point in the history of the franchise before it was relocated to Oklahoma City in 2008 and renamed the Thunder. That leaves the baseball Mariners and the football Seahawks as Seattle's lone big league sports franchises—and neither team has ever won a championship, though the Seahawks made it to Super Bowl XL, losing to the Pittsburgh Steelers.

San Diego often gets dismissed as never having won a championship, which is being disrespectful to the late, great American Football League. The Chargers, an original AFL club in 1960 and based in Los Angeles, relocated to San Diego in 1961, and in 1963 rolled to a 51–10 victory over the then Boston Patriots in the AFL championship game. Yet the point is made: it remains the only pro sports championship in San Diego history. The Chargers lost their only Super Bowl appearance; the Padres are 0-for-2 in the World Series; and the NBA Clippers weren't much to look at during the six years they were based in San Diego. The city also had a fling with major league hockey, with the San Diego Mariners doing business in the World Hockey Association in the mid-seventies. Though the Mariners played respectable hockey for three seasons, qualifying for the Avco Cup playoffs each time, no championship parades were held in their honor.

And then there is Boston, with all those newly won championships. Indeed, the mantelpiece was getting crowded with trophies. While fans in Cleveland, San Diego, and elsewhere were dialing into the local talk shows and making do with the annual wait-til-next-year routine, fans in Boston simply sat back and watched the Red Sox, Patriots, and Celtics make history.

This level of good fortune is rare. While there have been many cases in which a local team strings together a collection of championships, forging what the sportswriters like to call a "dynasty," these good times often come during a stretch when the other teams in town fail to win the big one. Or "just plain suck," to use a modern term. The Dallas/Ft. Worth area is a good example: while the Dallas Cowboys were winning three Super Bowls in four years during the '90s, the region's big league baseball team, the Texas Rangers, was continuing their streak of never having been to the World Series—a run of futility that began in 1961, when the Rangers were hatched as the expansion Washington Senators. The Dallas Mavericks, who entered the NBA in 1980, didn't even make the playoffs from 1991 to 2000.

The National Hockey League arrived in Dallas in 1993 when the Minnesota North Stars were reborn as the Dallas Stars. In 1999, they beat the Buffalo Sabres in six games to win their first Stanley Cup. But the Cowboys, while still competitive, had by then stopped making Super Bowl appearances. The Mavericks were still mediocre, and the Rangers, while making it to the playoffs in 1996, 1998, and 1999, were sent home in the first round by the Yankees on each occasion.

Sometimes, though, everyone gets hot at once.

Baltimore sports fans had plenty to cheer about in 1971, beginning with Super Bowl V on January 17 at Miami's Orange Bowl. The showdown between the Baltimore Colts and Dallas Cowboys is best remembered as one of sloppy play and missed opportunities—writer Tom Callahan, in *Johnny U: The Life & Times of John Unitas*, graciously refers to it as a "hard-hitting but homely game"[1]—but in the end the Colts prevailed, 16–13, Jim O'Brien's thirty-two-yard field goal with five seconds remaining in regulation breaking the tie.

The Colts were the only team to bring a championship to Baltimore in 1971, but the basketball Bullets and the baseball Orioles fought the good fight. In April, the Bullets were swept four straight by the Milwaukee Bucks in the NBA Finals; in October, the Pittsburgh Pirates took down the Orioles in the World Series, Steve Blass going the distance on October 17, 1971, for a 2–1 victory in Game 7.

Still, it had been a good year for Baltimore: from Super Bowl V to Game 7 of the World Series, three teams had played for championships in exactly nine months.

When documentarian Ken Burns produced his epic nine-part documentary on the history of baseball for PBS, he devoted an entire chapter, or inning, to what he called "The Capital of Baseball." He was referring to New York, and specifically a ten-year period from 1949 through 1958 when at least one of the city's big-league ball clubs—the Yankees, Giants, or Brooklyn Dodgers—played in the World Series. In five of those seasons, the World Series was an all–New York affair.

New York's other professional sport teams fought the good fight during this decade of baseball supremacy, but only the 1956 New York football Giants delivered a championship, defeating the Chicago Bears, 47–7, on December 30, 1956, at Yankee Stadium, two months and twenty days after the Yankees defeated the Brooklyn Dodgers in the World Series. The Rangers made it to the Stanley Cup Finals in the spring of 1950, losing to the Detroit Red Wings in seven games, and the Knicks made it to the NBA Finals three straight years, losing to the Rochester Royals in 1951, and to the Minneapolis Lakers in '52 and '53.

New York sports fans had plenty to celebrate in 1969. On January 12, 1969, quarterback Joe Namath backed up his bravado when he led the New York Jets to a 16–7 victory over the Baltimore Colts in Super Bowl III. Nine months later, the Amazin' Mets defeated the heavily favored Baltimore Orioles for their first World Series championship. And seven months after Tom Seaver, Tommy Agee, Cleon Jones, and the rest of the Amazin's rode through the Canyon of Heroes, the Knicks topped the Los Angeles Lakers for the 1969–70 NBA championship.

Cleveland, too, had its run as the epicenter of championship showdowns—especially if one chooses to toss in a minor league team to help make the argument work. In the spring of 1948, Cleveland's longtime entrée in the American Hockey League, the beloved Barons, swept the Buffalo Bisons to win the Calder Cup. That fall, the Cleveland Indians won what to date remains their last World Series championship, defeating the Boston Braves in six games—the decisive game taking place at Braves Field, part of which exists today as Nickerson Field on the campus of Boston University. And the year ended with the Cleveland Browns of the old All-America Football Conference rolling to a 49–7 victory over the Buffalo Bills in the league championship game.

"I remember Cleveland calling itself 'The City of Champions' that year," said Russ Schneider, who for more than forty years covered sports for the *Cleveland Plain Dealer* and the *Cleveland Press*. But even when letting the minor league Barons sneak under the fence to add spice to the debate, it is important to understand that sports fans back in the day didn't embrace every championship game with the fervor and passion of the modern-day fan. While it's true that 2,620,627 fans turned out at Cleveland Municipal Stadium to root for the pennant-winning 1948 Indians, the locals were less supportive of their fledgling football team, the Browns. When they defeated Buffalo that year to secure the All-America Football Conference championship, only 22,981 fans turned out for the game, which was played in the same stadium that had been filled with Indians fans during baseball season.

When the Red Sox, Patriots, and Celtics all played for championships during those seven months and twenty days from October 2007 to June 2008, they were coming off seasons in which every game was a sellout: the Red Sox sold out all eighty-one regular-season games at Fenway Park; the Celtics had a sellout crowd of 18,624 for every one of their home games; and the Patriots, with a waiting list for season tickets said to be in the thousands, banged out Gillette Stadium from start to finish.

"In those days in Cleveland," said Schneider, "football was more or less a curiosity. I went to some games that year just to see what it was all about. But people weren't going crazy over the Browns."

Where fans did go crazy—and over every sport in town—was in Philadelphia during a stretch of eight months and nine days between May 16, 1980, and January 25, 1981. For years, sportswriters have borrowed from Dickens in writing about the "best of times, the worst of times," but never were those words more appropriate: the 76ers, Flyers, Phillies, and Eagles all played for championships during those eight months and nine days . . . with only the Phillies coming out of it with the champagne.

The 76ers were first up. After taking out the Celtics in the Eastern Conference Finals, they faced the Lakers in the NBA Finals, with the Western Conference champions moving Magic Johnson to center in place of an injured Kareem Abdul-Jabbar in Game 6 at the Philadelphia Spectrum. Johnson scored 42 points as the Lakers won the game, 123–107, to secure the NBA championship.

Just eight days later, in Game 6 of the Stanley Cup Finals, the New York Islanders captured the first of what would be four consecutive championships with a 5–4 victory over the Flyers, Bob Nystrom's goal in overtime adding fresh wounds to the still-mending hearts of Philly fans.

In October, the Phillies clinched the World Series with a 4–1 Game 6 victory over the Kansas City Royals, as veteran left-hander Steve Carlton allowed just one run in seven innings. Considering the Phillies had never won a championship in their history—"The Phillies use Lifebuoy and they still stink," went the joke, referencing the soap manufacturer's billboard at the old Baker Bowl—it was enough to help Philly fans get over what had happened with the 76ers and Flyers back in the spring.

The cycle came to an end on January 25, 1981, with the Eagles meeting the Oakland Raiders in Super Bowl XV. They were out of it early. Quarterback Ron Jaworski's first pass of the game was intercepted, setting up the first of three touchdown passes by Raiders quarterback Jim Plunkett, the onetime Heisman Trophy winner and Patriots first-round draft pick who, at thirty-three, had resurrected his career in Oakland.

In 1986, Boston had a chance to place all four of its teams in championship games. Three of them got there. The Bruins, alas, were swept in the first round of the Stanley Cup playoffs by the Montreal Canadiens. But what a year for Boston fans, beginning with another of those best-of-times/worst-of-times scenarios: the 1985 New England Patriots, with eight players winding up as Pro Bowl selections, shocked the football world by winning nine of their last eleven regular-season games to make the playoffs as a wild-card entry. They further shocked the football world by winning three playoff games, all on the road, earning them their first-ever trip to the Super Bowl.

In Super Bowl XX, played on January 26, 1986, at the Lousiana Superdome, the Patriots suffered one of the most humiliating defeats in the history of the franchise, a 48–10 loss to Mike Ditka's Chicago Bears. The game was so lopsided that by the end of the day William "The Refrigerator" Perry, the Bears' wide-body defensive lineman, was getting a chance to throw a pass on a halfback option. He was sacked, but plunged into the end zone for a touchdown on the next play.

However Boston sports fans felt about what the Patriots had done—great regular season, historic march to the Super Bowl, embarrassing loss to the Bears—it was all tempered by the fact that (1) the Red Sox got off to a great start when the 1986 baseball season began, and (2) the Celtics were closing out perhaps the greatest season in the history of the franchise. The Big Three of Larry Bird, Kevin McHale, and Robert Parish was now buoyed by the presence of veteran Bill Walton, a onetime star now retooled as a valuable sixth man, and the Celtics were virtually unbeatable.

Having lost just fifteen games during the regular season and then breezing past Chicago, Atlanta, and Milwaukee in the first three rounds of the playoffs, losing just one game, they met the Houston Rockets in the NBA Finals. It took six games, with the Celtics claiming their 16th NBA championship with a 114–97 victory at Boston Garden on June 8, 1986.

The Red Sox came close to chasing away their own personal demons in the 1986 World Series, but then Bill Buckner committed one of the most talked-about errors in sports history when Mookie Wilson's grounder went between the legs of the aging, hobbling first baseman in the 10th inning of Game 6, allowing the New York Mets to claim victory. Two days later, on October 27, 1986, the Mets emerged with an 8–5 victory over the Red Sox in Game 7 to capture the World Series.

Boston sports fans seeking a silver lining to the Red Sox's stunning loss to the Mets in the World Series needed only to look at the big picture: from January 26, 1986, to October 27, 1986—a span of ten months and one day—three of Boston's teams played for championships.

It was a great run.

But that's all ancient history. Perhaps the best way to illustrate Boston's extraordinary run of athletic good fortune from October 2007 to June 2008 is to simply point out what happened *after* the Red Sox, Patriots, and Celtics played for championships.

The 2008 Red Sox found themselves in another fight for first place in the American League East, only this time the competition was with the surprising Tampa Bay Rays, who, after years of last-place anonymity, were ready for their close-up.

But the Red Sox had other problems besides the plucky, upstart Rays. Once again, they had a Manny Ramirez crisis. In fact, several of them. The talented left fielder got into a heated exchange with teammate Kevin Youkilis during a June 5 game against the Rays, and in early July, before an interleague game against the Houston Astros at Minute Maid Park, he shoved Red Sox traveling secretary Jack McCormick to the ground after the former Boston cop had been unable to handle the outfielder's request for sixteen tickets to that day's game. Ramirez was fined by the Red Sox.

And then there was the matter of getting Ramirez into the lineup. He was complaining of pain in his right knee. The Red Sox ordered MRIs on both knees, this after Ramirez had pulled himself out of the starting lineup before a game against the Yankees. The tests came back negative.

Finally, on July 31, the Red Sox made a three-team trade with the Los Angeles Dodgers and Pittsburgh Pirates that landed Ramirez in Los Angeles and brought talented outfielder Jason Bay to Boston. His knees miraculously cured, Ramirez hit .396 with 17 home runs and 53 RBI in

53 games for the Dodgers, who lost to the Philadelphia Phillies in the National League Championship Series.

Meanwhile, Bay played well for the Red Sox, hitting .293 with 9 home runs and 37 RBI in 49 games. There were inevitable Bay vs. Ramirez statistical comparisons running in the daily papers, but they missed the point: had Ramirez remained with the Red Sox, it's unlikely he would have put up his Dodger-like numbers the second half of the season.

Tampa Bay won the American League East, with the Red Sox qualifying for the playoffs as the wild card. The two teams met in the American League Championship Series, but the Red Sox were never really able to set up their starting pitching as they would have wanted, as ace right-hander Josh Beckett had been suffering from an oblique strain. The team was also without 2007 World Series MVP Mike Lowell, who was suffering from a torn right hip labrum that would require off-season surgery.

The Rays won the series in seven games.

The Patriots went into the 2008 season as the overwhelming favorite to return to the Super Bowl, but in the first quarter of their September 7 opener against the Kansas City Chiefs at Gillette Stadium, Tom Brady limped off the field after being tackled by the Chiefs' Bernard Pollard. He underwent surgery to his left knee and missed the remainder of the season.

Brady's replacement was Matt Cassel, a career backup both at the University of Southern California and for the Patriots until, in the second week of the 2008 season, he started his first game at quarterback since his days at Chatsworth High School outside of Los Angeles. Despite criticism during training camp that the Pats had no suitable replacement should Brady get hurt—during a preseason game against Tampa Bay, television analysts Marshall Faulk and Sterling Sharpe were especially tough on Cassel—the unproven, thrown-into-the-fire quarterback guided the Patriots to an 11–5 record.

Alas, it was not good enough to get the Patriots into the playoffs.

The 2008–2009 Bruins emerged as the top team in the Eastern Conference, with 116 points. Here was a chance, finally, for the Bruins to teach a new generation of Boston sports fans that hockey once ruled this town. The exciting, rebuilt 2008–2009 Bruins wound up with all the major individual honors: Claude Julien won the Jack Adams Award as coach of the year; Zdeno Chara won the James Norris Memorial Trophy, given to the league's top defenseman; and the stellar play of Tim Thomas helped the Bruins land the Vezina Trophy, emblematic of goaltending superiority.

Boston roared through the first round of the Stanley Cup playoffs, sweeping the hated Montreal Canadiens in four straight games. But the Bruins faced stiffer-than-expected competition from the Carolina Hurricanes in the second round, with the 'Canes coming into TD Banknorth Garden on May 14 for a game and emerging with a 3–2 victory in overtime. There would be no rolling rally for the Bruins.

The Celtics cruised through much of the 2008–2009 season, including a franchise-record nineteen-game winning streak, and were looked upon as the smart pick to win a second consecutive championship. But it soon became obvious that something was wrong with Kevin Garnett. Hobbled by a right knee strain for much of the second half of the season, Garnett rested for several games, briefly returned to the action, and then went back to the bench.

He missed the entire postseason. So, too, did forward Leon Powe, who underwent surgery to repair a torn anterior cruciate ligament and meniscus in his left knee.

The Celtics were eliminated in the second round of the playoffs by the Orlando Magic, who rolled to a 101–82 Game 7 victory on May 17 at the Garden.

On July 30, 2009, shortly before the Red Sox were to host the Oakland Athletics in a Thursday afternoon matinee at Fenway Park, the *New York Times* published a story on its website charging that David Ortiz and Manny Ramirez, key players on Boston's World Series–winning teams in 2004 and 2007, were among the 104 big league players who tested positive for performance-enhancing drugs in 2003. Ramirez had only recently returned to the Dodgers' lineup after serving a fifty-game suspension for violating Major League Baseball's drug policies, but this marked the first time Ortiz had been dragged into baseball's ever-widening doping scandal.

That Ortiz and Ramirez might have been juicing in 2004 and 2007 inspired many fans outside of New England to submit that Boston's World Series championships were now "tarnished" or "tainted," as if every other team that won the Fall Classic over the past fifteen years had done so with players who simply did a lot of push-ups and finished all their milk. *New York Times* columnist George Vecsey understood the speciousness of the tainted/tarnished argument, weighing in on August 1, 2009 with words that got right to the point: "They count. For all the instant disillusionment and partisan morality, the Red Sox' championships in 2004 and 2007 still stand."[2] To help make his case, Vecsey pointed out that Yankees fans "will conveniently omit the fact that Alex Rodriguez, Roger Clemens, Jason Giambi, and even good old Andy Pettitte have been connected to illegal stuff in recent years."

But logic often has no place in a good, old-fashioned, down-and-dirty sports argument, and perhaps that's just as well. As such, Boston fans would have to fight this battle on their own. In the end, though, they had a choice: raise their shields to defend their sports history, or simply sit back and know that present-day reexamination lacks the power to wipe away the events that took place during those seventh months and twenty days between October 2007 and June 2008.

It really was a wicked good year, even if, a bit further down the road, things got a little messy.

ACKNOWLEDGMENTS

When I set out to write *Wicked Good Year,* my goal was to tell some of the narrative through the eyes of Boston's ever obsessive sports fans. But what I wanted, needed, were fans who not only possessed interesting and compelling stories from their own lives, but who would be willing to share those stories with me—and, thus, *you.*

With these ground rules in place, I went looking. Before long, the cast had been assembled: Andrew J. Urban II, a fine, decent man who inspires us to reexamine whatever stereotypes we may have formed about autograph collectors; Mike Rotondi, easily the most down-to-earth Rich Guy I have ever met; Marty Joyce, the bombastic stalker of the Celtics sideline who reminds us that, in the end, sporting events exist to offer a measure of escapism from our daily toil; and Donnie Wahlberg, whose fame and artistry are quickly put aside when he talks about being a kid from Dorchester trying to sneak into the old Garden.

And the Nantucket Gals: Joan Fisher, Jane Hardy, Jeanne Dooley. At first, it was tough to inspire these ladies to kick back and . . . *talk.* It wasn't until I took the ferry to Nantucket and met them on their own beloved turf that the curtains were pulled away and—presto!—the stories began to flow. The turning point came during a guided automobile tour of the island, when they pointed out the actual door at the Pacific National Bank that Joan slammed on the day she stepped unhappily into retirement.

"Now *that's* what I'm looking for!" I exclaimed. To which Jane replied, "Well, why didn't you say so?"

Donnie Wahlberg being the obvious exception, the fans who were asked to participate in this project are unaccustomed to having the contents of their lives spilled on the table for examination. I thank them for their time, their candor, and their patience—especially when I called them, sometimes late at night, with the latest question that needed to be answered *right now.*

As for the athletes, coaches, and front-office folks who were interviewed for this book, they know the drill. Still, it's never a given that they will be willing to step away from garden-variety X's and O's and expand on a conga line of behind-the-scenes topics. On the Celtics, Coach Doc Rivers gave me two hours of his precious time following a morning practice session and spoke with such raw unfiltered emotion that at one point the tape recorder was turned off as we discussed our common angst over having lost a parent. Here's hoping that in a world of mega-salaried athletes and meddlesome, behind-the-scenes handlers, Doc never loses his old-time values and coaching philosophies.

My interview with Danny Ainge proved that the spirit of Red Auerbach is alive and well in the Celtics' offices, even if Ainge admitted that he doesn't agree with some of the decisions Red made in his last years running the club. Thanks also to Celtics owners Wyc Grousbeck and Steve Pagliuca, and to Paul Pierce, Kevin Garnett, Ray Allen, Rajon Rondo, Kendrick Perkins, Glen Davis, Gabe Pruitt, and other Celtics players who spent time with me. I will always cherish the chats I had with Helen Heinsohn in the pressroom before Celtics home games. And thanks to you, too, Tommy Heinsohn, for taking the time to talk about Helen, your beloved Redhead from Needham.

One of the things I admire about Red Sox manager Terry Francona is that he has chosen to make his year-round home in the Boston area. Living in the shadow of Fenway Park has given him a keen understanding of what Red Sox Nation is all about; with the exception of Joe Morgan, who happens to be a Massachusetts native, no Red Sox manager in my thirty-plus years as a sportswriter *gets it* the way Francona does.

Thanks, too, to Red Sox closer Jonathan Papelbon, for telling me about that night at the Ale House, and to second baseman Dustin Pedroia, for admitting that he wasn't as cocky and confident during those first anxious weeks of the 2007 season as we were led to believe. Also: David Ortiz, Tim Wakefield, Manny Delcarmen, and the never-short-of-words Curt Schilling. In baseball operations, I am indebted to Theo Epstein, Jason McLeod, Jed Hoyer, and Amiel Sawdaye.

Veteran Patriots linebacker Tedy Bruschi also met with me during his off-season, and he provided some insights into his comeback from a stroke that had not been previously reported. Bruschi teaches us that physical talent alone does not make the athlete; that other qualities, which cannot be measured statistically, are just as important.

A special thanks to quarterback Tom Brady, who in agreeing to speak with me for this book departed from his self-imposed ban on doing interviews while he was recovering from the knee injury that ruined his 2008 season. Thanks, too, to Patriots owners Robert Kraft and Jonathan Kraft and to Coach Bill Belichick, and to the team's newest Hall of Famer, Andre Tippett.

Countless other players, too numerable to name, were involved in the process through my daily reporting for the *Boston Herald*. Thanks to all of them for what they did, on and off the field, for making this a wicked good year indeed.

Ahh, yes, the *Herald*. What a joy it has been to write a column for a newspaper that values sports the way the *Herald* does. It has been said that newspapers will soon go the way of high-button shoes and the butter churn, but this information has not been relayed to sports editor Hank Hyrniewicz and assistant sports editors Mark Murphy and Joe Thomas, who continue to put out one of the nation's liveliest and newsiest sections. Our night staff has saved me from more mistakes than I care to admit to, and our writers make the *Herald* a must-read for the serious Boston fan. It scares me to think how much would fall between the cracks were it not for Sean McAdam, Michael Silverman, John Tomase, Karen Guregian, Ron Borges, Gerry Callahan, Steve Bulpett, Mark Murphy, Steve Conroy, Steve Harris, Dan Ventura, Rich Thompson, Jocko Connolly, and so many others. The *Herald's* Matt West is one of the finest sports photographers anywhere, and I was thrilled when he agreed to provide the images you see in these pages.

I made frequent use of stories written by reporters at many other newspapers, especially the *Boston Globe, Providence Journal, Hartford Courant, Worcester Telegram,* the *Metro West Daily News,* and the *Patriot Ledger* of Quincy, Massachusetts. I value New England's many fine sportswriters for their talent, their hustle, and, especially, for the passion and camaraderie they bring to the press box.

Dozens of books have been written on Boston sports over the years, and I consulted several of them to help me see the Big Picture. The best of them all is *Red Sox Century,* by Dick Johnson and Glenn Stout. Every Red Sox fan should have a copy. Among the other books I consulted were *Top of the World,* by Peter May; *The Blueprint,* by Christopher Price; *Deep Drive,* by Mike Lowell and Rob Bradford; *Dynasty,* by my old *Herald* pal Tony Massarotti; *The Big Bam,* by Leigh Montville; *At Fenway,* by Dan Shaughnessy; and two books by Michael Holley, *Never Give Up* cowritten with Tedy Bruschi and *Red Sox Rule.*

The manuscript went through several drafts and was read and sometimes reread by Michael Holley, Mark-John Isola, Sean Grande, Karen Guregian, Sean McAdam, Paul Perillo, and the incomparable Sara Bejoian. They were asked to pull no punches. They did not. I am grateful.

The media relations people at Boston's professional sports teams were extremely helpful—not only with arranging countless interviews, but also providing a name here, an anecdote there, to help flesh out the narrative. I can comfortably say that the Celtics' Heather Walker went above and beyond the call of duty, this because she was taking my calls right up to the day before she gave birth to her baby girl, Samantha Mae. Jeff Twiss of the Celtics (along with WEEI's Glenn Ordway and the *Globe*'s Bob Ryan) were go-to guys for questions about obscure facets of Celtics history. On the Red Sox, Pam Ganley helped set up several interviews at the same time she was stepping into her new role as the team's director of media relations. With everything that was going on, she could have ignored an e-mail or phone call or two. That never happened. The Patriots' Stacey James kept adding new requests to that legal pad he's always lugging around, and all of those requests were answered. Berj Najarian helped get me some time with Bill Belichick, and Casey O'Connell and Scott Barboza helped with other interviews. The Bruins' Matt Chmura gets the number-one star for helping with all my hockey questions.

A huge dept of gratitude to my many friends in television for helping me locate vitally needed video of games, interviews, and sportscasts. Those who went above and beyond the call of duty are Jason Romano of ESPN, Andy

Levine of Comcast Sports New England, and Mike Coppola of NESN. And a special thanks to Dave Cherubin of NECN for being a valuable sounding board and, more important, a trusted friend for many years.

Libby Oldham of the Nantucket Historical Association and the staff of the Stockbridge School of Agriculture did a lot of my work for me when I looked into the life of Matt Jaeckle, and Marilyn Beyer of the Perkins School for the Blind offered a tutorial on that wonderful school. Former Celtics executive Jan Volk provided insights as to how things work in an NBA front office. For my crash course in Ubuntu 101, I turned to no less an authority than Marquette University's Stephanie Russell, the same woman who taught it to Doc Rivers.

Also Cindy Brown and Charlie Perry of Boston Duck Tours; Dick Nottebart, who provided background on his late uncle, former major leaguer Don Nottebart; Bill Nowlin, yet another fine Red Sox historian; and Jake Pena, who relayed some great stories about his late father, referee extraordinaire Manny Pena.

Also Jay Wessel and Brian MacPherson, both of whom helped out when my computer crashed; Marten Vandervelde, who transcribed hours of taped interviews; J. C. Bejoian, who printed copies of the first manuscript. Thanks to Paige Arnof-Fenn, Rusty Sullivan, and the trustees of the Sports Museum, and to the board of directors of the Oldtime Baseball Game: J. C. Bejoian, Ben Weiss, Bill Novelline, Andrew Novelline, Marlinda Langone, Jesse Haley, and Dave and Sue Leibovitch, along with score table mavens Glenn Koocher and John and Karen Kosko. Both of these organizations serve as a daily reminder of just how special, and important, Boston's sports history is to all of us.

One of my routines while writing this book was to take a daily break for some mid-morning coffee and conversation. The coffee was provided by the hippest place on the planet, the Diesel Café in Davis Square in Somerville, Massachusetts. The conversation was provided by, among others, Christopher Castellani, (whose novel, *The Saint of Lost Things,* is a hugely entertaining read), Tim Fish, Lance Brisbois, Greg Ciaglo, Mark-John Isola, and crossword puzzle king Adam Leveille.

A big thanks to Jon Scher for being my sounding board on all matters baseball—all matters, period—beginning with our days at *Baseball America* in the early eighties.

Leslie Beale is my friend, my neighbor, and, like me, a lover of chocolate labs. At a time when we were both writing books, nothing cleared our heads better than loading up Zoe, Billie, and Roxy for a trip to Mystic Lake.

For those wondering about the title of this book, I need to tell you about the night my friends Dan Kopcso, Patrick Gigante, and Marten Vandervelde joined me for an evening of cigars and lies at a place called Stansa in Boston's North End. As we debated possible titles, Gigante, a twenty-six-year-old personal trainer whose Boston accent should make him a must-get for any Hollywood producer looking to capture the flavor of this town, put down his cigar and said, "I got it: Wicked Good Year."

Kopcso looked at me looking at Gigante and said, "Please tell me you're not considering this."

It wasn't that Dan didn't like the title. He did. What worried him was the possibility that Pat would never stop talking about it. And to my knowledge, he has not.

As for the *subject* of this book, the credit goes to my literary agent, Stacey Glick of Dystel & Goderich in New York. Not only did she have the original idea—*Hey, why not a book about the Red Sox, Patriots, and Celtics all playing for championships!*—she went out and sold the project. Which brings us to the folks at HarperCollins. A big thanks to Mauro DiPreta for green-lighting the project, and to Kate Hamill for her extraordinary skills as an editor, sure, but also for those many encouraging phone calls and e-mails. Thanks for not rubber-stamping a single word, Kate. To say that you made this a better book is a gross understatement.

I am blessed to tell you I personally witnessed most of the events covered in this book, including the 2007 World Series, Super Bowl XLII, and the 2008 NBA Finals. As the late, great Red Sox broadcaster Ken Coleman used to say, being there is twice the fun. But being there means being away from home, and that means time away from the people who matter most—my friends and family. You'll note that this book is dedicated to my late brother, Paul Buckley, who taught me how to be a Boston sports fan. When I attended my first Red Sox game in 1964—I was eight years old—I looked out at the array of confusing numbers on the left-field scoreboard and announced that I'd never be able to figure it out. "Don't worry, I'll teach you," said Paul, who was eleven.

And you did, Paul. Speaking for Susan, Danny, Ryan, Shaun, Billy, John, Joan, Kevin, and their families, and for all the nephews and nieces and *their* families, and for your beautiful granddaughter, Ella, you are indeed missed. And this is for you.

NOTES

Chapter 1 : Duck Boats

1. See "Ducks Win Celebrated Status in WWII," available at: http://wisconsinducktours.com/history.html.

Chapter 2: Escape from Loserville

1. Gerry Callahan, "Worst Yet to Come in Loserville," *Boston Herald*, October 18, 2000.
2. Steve Buckley, "As Pedro Goes, So Go Sox," *Boston Herald*, October 7, 1999.
3. Tony Massarotti, "Pedro Hurt, Sox Fall," *Boston Herald*, October 7, 1999.
4. Tony Massarotti, "Sox Finish Off Indians, Next Stop: New York," *Boston Herald*, October 12, 1999.
5. Michael Silverman, "Valentin Turns on It; Veteran Finds Swing in Time," *Boston Herald*, October 12, 1999.
6. Bud Shaw, "Be Glad Red Sox Put Indians Away Before Yanks Did," *Cleveland Plain Dealer*, October 12, 1999.
7. Peter Botte, "Boston Feasts on Red-Faced Clemens," *New York Daily News*, October 17, 1999.
8. David Lennon, "Shortcomings Are Apparent," *Newsday*, October 17, 1999.
9. Michael Silverman, "Jimy Not Incited by Georgie," *Boston Herald*, October 19, 1999.
10. Michael Felger, "Market Yields Gains; Belichick Happy with Weekend Shopping," *Boston Herald*, April 17, 2000.

11. Nick Cafardo, "Choice Picks by Patriots?" *Boston Globe*, April 17, 2000.

12. Joe Stein, "Grading the Draft," *San Diego Union-Tribune*, April 17, 2000.

13. Mark Murphy, "C's Far from Finished; Learn from Pats' Demise," *Boston Herald*, February 5, 2008.

Chapter 3: "A Scouting/Player Development Machine"

1. Tony Massarotti, "Big-Time Brushback; Minor Pitcher Makes a Major Sensation," *Boston Herald*, March 25, 2005.

2. Ibid.

3. Chris Snow, "Schilling Will Take the Mound vs. Twins Today," *Boston Globe*, March 25, 2005.

4. Steve Buckley, "Selling the Shirts Right Off Their Backs," *Boston Herald*, July 21, 2006.

5. Steve Buckley, "Ortiz Goes on Foxx Hunt," *Boston Herald*, August 2, 2006.

6. Steve Buckley, "Team Woes Weigh on Ortiz," *Boston Herald*, September 3, 2006.

7. Saul Wisnia, "The Jimmy Fund of Dana-Farber Cancer Institute," *Arcadia* (2002).

8. Tony Massarotti, "Lester Keeps the Faith," *Boston Herald*, September 7, 2006.

9. Gordon Edes and Liz Kowalczyk, "Lester Diagnosed with Cancer; Sox Pitcher Has Form of Lymphoma," *Boston Globe*, September 2, 2006.

10. Bob Hohler, "Francona Managed, Despite Physical Woes," *Boston Globe*, October 9, 2005.

11. Jeff Horrigan, "Papelbon Gets New Start," *Boston Herald*, September 16, 2006.

12. Steve Buckley, "Closing One Door Opens Many Others in Future," *Boston Herald*, September 16, 2006.

13. Sean McAdam, "Dawning of the Age of Epstein," *Providence Journal*, November 26, 2002.

14. Ian Browne, *Dice K: The First Season of the Red Sox $100 Million Man* (Lyons Press, 2008), p. 26.

15. Jerry Crasnick, *License to Deal: A Season on the Run with a Maverick Baseball Agent* (Rodale, 2005).
16. Browne, *Dice K*, p. 43.

Chapter 4: Urban Legend

1. Steve Buckley, "Fenway's First Batsman: Harvard's Wingate Made History When He Stepped to the Plate on April 9, 1912," *Boston Herald*, April 29, 2001.
2. Bill Nowlin, *Day by Day with the Boston Red Sox* (Rounder Books, 2006); and Craig Lammers, "Charles Pinkney," Baseball Biography Project of the Society of American Baseball Research, available at: Bioproj.SABR.org.
3. Dan Shaughnessy, *At Fenway: Dispatches from Red Sox Nation* (Crown, 1996), p. 48.
4. Glenn Stout and Richard L. Johnson, *Red Sox Century: One Hundred Years of Red Sox Baseball* (Houghton Mifflin, 2000), p. 147.
5. Dan Shaughnessy, *The Curse of the Bambino* (Penguin Books, 1991), p. 30.
6. David Halberstam, *Summer of '49* (Morrow, 1989), p. 24.
7. Leigh Montville, *The Big Bam: The Life and Times of Babe Ruth* (Doubleday, 2006), p. 102.
8. Ibid.

Chapter 5: Savior?

1. Steve Buckley, "He Fathered '67 Red Sox Family Album," *Boston Herald*, June 24, 2007.
2. Jonathan Eig, *Opening Day: The Story of Jackie Robinson's First Season* (Simon & Schuster, 2007), p. 136.
3. Don Zimmer, with Bill Madden, *The Zen of Zim: Baseballs, Beanballs, and Bosses* (St. Martin's Press, 2004), p. 170.
4. Tony Massarotti, "Hey Fake Fans: Make Like Damon and Leave," *Boston Herald*, June 2, 2006.

Chapter 6: Swinging Out of His Ass

1. Peter May, "Wife's Surgery Sends Cabrera on Home Run," *Boston Globe*, September 21, 2004.
2. Steven Krasner, "Red Sox Journal," *Providence Journal*, September 21, 2004.
3. Michael Silverman, "Red Sox Notebook," *Boston Herald*, September 21, 2004.
4. Ibid.
5. Amalie Benjamin, "Regained Edge, Sharper Play; Pedroia Soared Once He Got Back His Swagger," *Boston Globe*, October 2, 2007.
6. Steve Buckley, "Foytack Now Shares a Dubious Record," *Boston Herald*, April 23, 2007.
7. Steve Buckley, "New Villain for Rivalry; Right or Wrong, Lowell Fits Role," *Boston Herald*, June 3, 2007.

Chapter 7: There Once Were Three Fans from Nantucket

1. Jerry McDonald, "Moss: Make Me Happy, I'll Catch More Passes," *Oakland Tribune*, November 15, 2006.
2. Dave Del Grande, "Moss More Honest Than Davis," *Oakland Tribune*, November 16, 2006.
3. Bud Geracie, "In the Wake of the Year," *San Jose Mercury News*, December 30, 2006.
4. Mark Purdy, "Coach Art Shell Deserves a Better Shot," *San Jose Mercury News*, December 27, 2006.
5. Phil Barber, "Latest Raiders Refrain to Be 'Bye, Bye, Moss?'" *Santa Rosa Press Democrat*, December 13, 2006.
6. "Report: Moss Tested Positive for Marijuana Last Season," Associated Press, September 30, 2002.
7. Jim Cour, "Tough Week Takes Its Toll on Moss," Associated Press, September 30, 2002.
8. Rick Morrissey, "Moss Just Latest Star Athlete to Fall Off Pedestal," *Chicago Tribune*, September 29, 2002.

9. Sid Hartman, "Moss Says, 'I Play When I Want to Play,'" *Minneapolis Star-Tribune*, November 22, 2001.

10. John Tomase, "A Memory That Will Never Fade; Incident Had Real Effect on Moss' Public Persona," *Boston Herald*, May 4, 2007.

11. Ibid.

12. Ron Borges, "Those Who Know Enigmatic Moss Differ on What Patriots Can Expect," *Boston Globe*, May 13, 2007.

13. Bruce Newman, "The Race for Ralph," *Sports Illustrated*, April 2, 1983.

14. Mike Reiss, "They Get Talented but Troubled Receiver for Fourth-Round Pick," *Boston Globe*, April 30, 2007.

Chapter 8: Courtside

1. Dan Shaughnessy, "Celtics Have Become Masters of Misdirection," *Boston Globe*, May 21, 1995.

Chapter 9: Kid Stuff

1. Associated Press, "Yankees on Top in Payroll," April 3, 2007.

2. Rob Bradford, "Lester Has Fun Again," *Boston Herald*, July 23, 2007.

3. Jeff Horrigan, "Ortiz Reports Progress," *Boston Herald*, July 24, 2007.

4. Gordon Edes, "Red Sox Continue Fireworks; They Explode on Flammable Rays," *Boston Globe*, July 6, 2007.

Chapter 10: Terry's Cloth

1. Rob Bradford, "Gibbons Tucks It to MLB; Joins Tito in Shirt Flap," *Boston Herald*, September 6, 2007.

2. Steve Buckley, "'Fashion Police' Break Law; Do Tito a Disservice," *Boston Herald*, August 30, 2007.

3. George King, "Watson's Visit Irks Francona," *New York Post*, August 30, 2007.

4. Ibid.

5. "They Said It," as told to Ben Reiter, *Sports Illustrated*, December 24, 2007.

6. Jeff Goldberg, "It's Dress Down Day; Francona Furious with MLB Official," *Hartford Courant*, August 31, 2007.

7. Nick Canepa, "Take Five," *San Diego Union-Tribune*, September 2, 2007.

8. Jeff Gold, "Keep Your Shirt On, Skip Francona Loses Cool After MLB Check to See if He Wore Uniform Top," *Newsday*, August 31, 2007.

9. John Ryan, compiler, "Chatter Box," *San Jose Mercury News*, August 31, 2007.

10. Jerry Crasnick, "MLB Acknowledges In-Game Uniform Check Timed Poorly," ESPN.com, August 31, 2007.

11. Buckley, "'Fashion Police' Break Law."

Chapter 11: A New Big Three

1. Kevin McNamara, "It's a Lot Easier Being Green," *Providence Journal*, August 31, 2007.

2. Ibid.

3. S. L. Price, "The Truth Revealed," *Sports Illustrated*, December 8, 2008.

4. Desmond Conner, "It's Now or Never: Celtics Trade Their Future for Garnett," *Hartford Courant*, August 1, 2007.

Chapter 12: Spygate

1. Gerry Callahan, "With All Due Respect, Pats' Underdog Act Won't Work," *Boston Herald*, January 21, 2004.

2. Christopher L. Gasper, "NFL Suspends Harrison; League Says Patriots Safety Used a Performance-Enhancing Substance," *Boston Globe*, September 1, 2007.

3. Ibid.

4. Will McDonough, "Parcells to Leave: His Poor Relationship with Kraft Cited; Contract Controversy Looms," *Boston Globe*, January 20, 1997.

5. Kevin Mannix, "Football Tuna Out of Water," *Boston Herald*, February 1, 1997.

6. Bill Livingston, "Belichick's Hiring an Interim Sham," *Cleveland Plain Dealer*, February 5, 1997.

7. Leonard Shapiro, "Belichick Suddenly Quits Jets After 1 Day; Coach Cites Uncertainty of Ownership," *Washington Post*, January 5, 2000.

8. Gary Myers, "Jets Prez Says Coach in Chaos," *New York Daily News*, January 5, 2000.

9. Michael Felger, "Pats Get Their Man," *Boston Herald*, January 28, 2000.

10. Tony Grossi and Mary Kay Cabot, "The New Top Dog: Former Browns Ball Boy Eric Mangini Is Now the Coach," *Cleveland Plain Dealer*, January 8, 2009.

11. Michael Felger, "Mangini Chooses Pats; Replaces Crennel on 'D'," *Boston Herald*, February 13, 2005.

12. John Tomase, "Mangini: No Ugly Break-up," *Boston Herald*, January 18, 2006.

13. Michael Felger, "Patriots Insider," *Boston Herald*, September 10, 2007.

14. "Play of the Game," *Boston Herald*, September 10, 2007.

15. Ibid.

16. John Tomase, "Pats Caught on Tape; Face Punishment from Commish," *Boston Herald*, September 12, 2007.

17. Jason Wilde, "Packers: Patriots Games," *Wisconsin State Journal*, September 13, 2007.

18. Ibid.

19. Mike Reiss, "A Sorry State: Belichick Apologizes as Probe Continues," *Boston Globe*, September 13, 2007.

20. Dan Shaughnessy, "His Bill Comes Due Big Time," *Boston Globe*, September 14, 2007.

21. Gerry Callahan, "Bill's Success Still the Rule; Wins Prove Worth Price," *Boston Herald*, September 18, 2007.

22. Christopher L. Gasper, "Belichick Is Mum After Promising to Comment," *Boston Globe*, September 15, 2007.

23. Margery Eagan, "Cheaters Make Poor Sports: Belichick's Way Is a Lesson in Cowardice," *Boston Herald*, September 16, 2007.

24. Karen Guregian, "Sinking to a New Level," *Boston Herald*, January 15, 2007.
25. Nick Canepa, "Does Belichick's Patriot Act Rely on Covert Video-tape?" *San Diego Union-Tribune*, September 11, 2007.
26. Jackie MacMullan, "Players Hand It to Embattled Coach," *Boston Globe*, September 17, 2007.
27. John Tomase, "Patriots Beat," *Boston Herald*, September 17, 2007.
28. Michael Wilbon, "The Patriots' Game: No Mercy, They Rule," *Washington Post*, October 2, 2007.
29. John Tomase, "'72 Dolphins Dis Pats, Weiss," *Boston Herald*, October 7, 2007.

Chapter 13: Chemistry Class

1. Michael Lee, "In NBA, Wins Can Multiply the Power of Three," *Washington Post*, October 30, 2007.
2. Molefi Kete Asante and Ama Mazama, *Encyclopedia of African Religion* (Sage Publications, 2008), p. 143.
3. Steve Bulpett, "Celts See Light; Rivers' Move Speaks Volumes," *Boston Herald*, November 9, 2007.
4. Steve Bulpett, "Garnett Gives Rookies Some Treatment," *Boston Herald*, October 6, 2007.

Chapter 14: Return to October

1. Tony Massarotti, "Goners Without Gagne; Sox Need Reliever to Quickly Find His Role," *Boston Herald*, September 18, 2007.
2. Steve Buckley, "Lineup's Leadoff Shuffle a Good Sign for Sox," *Boston Herald*, June 13, 2007.
3. Steve Buckley, "No Excuses for Gagne," *Boston Herald*, August 11, 2007.
4. Tony Massarotti, "Return of Ramirez Is Power Boost to Lineup," *Boston Herald*, October 6, 2007.
5. Steve Buckley, "Dice-K's Not Hot," *Boston Herald*, October 16, 2007.
6. Alex Spicer, "Sox' Three Straight Homers Loses Its Clout," *Boston Herald*, October 17, 2007.

7. John Horton, "Just a Win Away: Raucous Fans Ready for Tribe to Seal the Deal at Home," *Cleveland Plain Dealer*, October 17, 2007.
8. Ibid.
9. Michael K. McIntyre, "Anthem Singer Was Special to Sox Pitcher," *Cleveland Plain Dealer*, October 18, 2007.
10. Michael Silverman, "Red Sox Notebook," *Boston Herald*, October 19, 2007.
11. Jeff Horrigan, "Red Sox 11, Indians 2," *Boston Herald*, October 22, 2007.

Chapter 15: A Fall Classic with a Classic Ending

1. Bob Nightengale, "Little Engine That Hit .327; Banty Pedroia Continues to Defy Doubters," *USA Today*, September 15, 2008.
2. Jeff Horrigan, "Sox a Win Away from Making More History," *Boston Herald*, October 28, 2007.
3. Steve Buckley, "Painful Decision by Wake," *Boston Herald*, October 24, 2007.
4. Jim Caple, "Sweeps, Blowouts, Insects . . . but Little Drama This Postseason," ESPN.com, October 27, 2007.
5. Mike Vaccaro, "Dynasty Next? Red Sox Make It Look Easy," *New York Post*, October 28, 2007.
6. Steve Buckley, "Red Sox 4, Rockies 3," *Boston Herald*, October 29, 2007.
7. Ibid.
8. John Powers, "Chance at Immortality Swings His Way," *Boston Globe*, October 29, 2007.
9. Buckley, "Red Sox 4, Rockies 3."

Chapter 16: Rematch in Indianapolis

1. Steve Buckley, "Struggling Bergeron Discusses Health; Injured Center Feels Better," *Boston Herald*, November 9, 2007.
2. Christopher L. Gasper, "Washington Slapped Here—Patriots Make 'Skins History in Latest Rout," *Boston Globe*, October 29, 2007.
3. Karen Guregian, "52 Pickup," *Boston Herald*, October 29, 2007.

4. Gregg Easterbrook, "Colts-Patriots Tilt Shaping Up as Battle of Good vs. Evil," ESPN.com, October 25, 2007.
5. Tedy Bruschi with Michael Holley, *Never Give Up: My Stroke, My Recovery, and My Return to the NFL* (John Wiley & Sons, 2007).
6. John Tomase, "Patriots Beat," *Boston Herald*, November 5, 2007.
7. Gregory Lee Jr., "Moss Had a Big Hand in Victory—Receiver's Spectacular Play Draws Accolades," *Boston Globe*, November 5, 2007.
8. Steve Buckley, "Rivals Don't Disappoint with Instant Classic," *Boston Herald*, November 5, 2007.
9. Gary Myers, "Spy Bowl Just Latest NFL Grudge Match," *New York Daily News*, December 16, 2007.
10. Steve Buckley, "Coaches Shake Things Up," *Boston Herald*, December 17, 2007.

Chapter 17: Pursuing Banner 17

1. Marc J. Spears, "Sense of Entitlement: With Winning Spirit in the Air, Hopeful Celtics Reward Fans," *Boston Globe*, November 3, 2007.
2. Steve Bulpett, "Celtics 2007 Grand Opening: Green Put Red Mark on Parquet Floor," *Boston Herald*, November 3, 2007.
3. Tony Massarotti, "Celts' Revival Begins with Impressive Win," *Boston Herald*, November 3, 2007.
4. Steve Bulpett, "Grieving Rivers Back for Win," *Boston Herald*, November 11, 2007.
5. Associated Press, "Magic Cast Bad Spell on Celtics," November 19, 2007.
6. Steve Bulpett, "Time to Mention Green in Same Breath as Elite," *Boston Herald*, November 24, 2007.
7. Mark Murphy, "Celts Bow to King, Cavs; Too Many Mistakes in Overtime Loss," *Boston Herald*, November 28, 2007.
8. Mike Fine, "Celtics' Garnett Ready for Test," *Patriot Ledger*, December 19, 2007.
9. Steve Bulpett, "C's Find They Measure Up; Learn from First Home Loss," *Boston Herald*, December 20, 2007.

10. Associated Press, "Davis Helps Celtics End Pistons' Winning Streak," January 6, 2008.
11. Mark Murphy, "A Happy New Year for Celts; Match 2006–07 Win Total," *Boston Herald*, December 28, 2007.

Chapter 18: 16–0 . . . and Beyond

1. Eric McHugh, "NFL Films Won't Drop the Ball on the Patriots' Quest for Perfection," *Patriot Ledger*, December 29, 2007.
2. Jim Donaldson, "Let's Not Lose Sight of the Goal," *Providence Journal*, December 29, 2007.
3. Steve Buckley, "Everything Zen for QB Brady," *Boston Herald*, January 13, 2008.
4. Karen Guregian, "Moss: I Did 'Nothing Wrong,'" *Boston Herald*, January 17, 2008.
5. Steve Buckley, "Green Shoulders the Load," *Boston Herald*, January 30, 2008.

Chapter 19: The Catch

1. John Tomase, "Source: Pats Employee Filmed Rams," *Boston Herald*, February 2, 2008.
2. Ibid.
3. Greg Bishop and Pete Thamel, "Evidence of Discontent," *New York Times*, February 1, 2008.
4. Ibid.
5. Mike Vaccaro, "Amazing March: Giants' 83-Yard Drive in Final 2:39 One for the Ages," *New York Post*, February 4, 2008.
6. Tony Massarotti, "Giants 17, Patriots 14," *Boston Herald*, February 4, 2008.
7. Rich Cimini, "Pats Cheated Out of Glory," *New York Daily News*, February 4, 2008.
8. Ibid.
9. *Boston Herald*, May 14, 2008.

Chapter 20: The Only Show in Town

1. Mike Bresnahan, "Success Is Short-Lived," *Los Angeles Times*, December 31, 2007.
2. Jeff Howe, "Ainge Works the Market," *Boston Metro*, November 26, 2008.
3. Marc J. Spears, "Brown in Town to Lend Depth; Free Agent Adds to the Front Court," *Boston Globe*, February 28, 2008.
4. Steve Bulpett, "Celtic Sweepstates; Winning Ticket in Texas After Besting Mavs," *Boston Herald*, March 21, 2008.
5. Steve Conroy, "Bruins Notebook," Boston Herald, April 20, 2008.
6. Sekou Smith, "Hawks: Light the Fire!" *Atlanta Journal-Constitution*, April 22, 2008.
7. Shira Spriner, "Pierce's Message Still Isn't Clear," *Boston Globe*, April 30, 2008.

Chapter 21: Playing the Palace

1. Marc J. Spears, "Double Clutch—Celtics Win Another Game 7 at Garden," *Boston Globe*, May 19, 2008.
2. Bob Ryan, "Pierce Stars in His Moment of Truth," *Boston Globe*, May 19, 2008.
3. Steve Buckley, Showdown for the Ages," *Boston Herald*, May 19, 2008.
4. Ibid.
5. Jeffrey Denberg, "A Heartbreaker for Hawks; Bird-Led Celtics Hang on 118–116 to Win Game 7," *Atlanta Journal-Constitution*, May 23, 1988.
6. Branson Wright, "Boston Stranglehold: Cavs Down, 2–0, as James' Woes Continue," *Cleveland Plain Dealer*, May 9, 2008.
7. Sam Amico, "Blast from Past," *Boston Herald*, May 11, 2008.
8. Mark Heisler, "They've Taken Off the Gloves in the East," *Los Angeles Times*, May 18, 2008.
9. Dan Ventura, "Despite Heroics, LeBron Reduced to Role of Spectator," *Boston Herald*, May 19, 2008.

10. Bob Ryan, "Celts Stay Alive, 102–100; Boston Digs in to Thwart Hawks' Rally, Force a Seventh Game," *Boston Globe*, May 21, 1988.

11. Tony Massarotti, "Light Finally on for Ray," *Boston Herald*, May 23, 2008.

Chapter 22: A Wicked Good Night

1. Mark Murphy, "Sorry, No Cigar (for Auerbach); Red's Forced to Kick Habit," *Boston Herald*, November 3, 2005.

2. Tony Massarotti, "Pain No Match for Paul," *Boston Herald*, June 6, 2008.

3. 38 Pitches.com, June 9, 2008.

4. Mark Murphy, "Gotta 'C' It to Believe It," *Boston Herald*, June 13, 2008.

Epilogue: What It All Means

1. Tom Callahan, *Johnny U: The Life & Times of John Unitas*, (Crown, 2006), p. 220.

2. George Vecsey, "Positive or Negative, There's No Changing History," *New Your Times*, August 1, 2009.

INDEX